# Credits

**Author**
Alex Büchner

**Reviewers**
Abhishek Bhardwaj
Anthony Borrow, S.J.
Brian A. Pool

**Acquisition Editors**
David Barnes
Sarah Cullington

**Development Editors**
Neha Mallik
Maitreya Bhakal

**Technical Editor**
Vrinda Amberkar

**Copy Editor**
Brandt D'Mello

**Project Coordinator**
Joel Goveya

**Proofreaders**
Lisa Brady
Elinor Perry-Smith
Lynda Sliwoski
Chris Smith

**Indexer**
Tejal Daruwale

**Graphics**
Valentina D'silva

**Production Coordinator**
Aparna Bhagat

**Cover Work**
Aparna Bhagat

# About the Author

**Alex Büchner** is the co-founder and technical lead of the leading Moodle, Totora, and Mahara partner, Synergy Learning. He has been involved in system and database administration for more than two decades and has been administering Virtual Learning Environments of all shapes and sizes since their advent on the educational landscape.

Alex holds a Ph.D. in Computer Science and an M.Sc. in Software Engineering. He has authored over 50 international publications, including two books, and is a frequent speaker on Moodle, Mahara, and related open source technologies. His first book on Moodle Administration by Packt Publishing has become the de facto standard on the topic.

The best learning experience in Moodle is provided when communication and collaboration is utilized. The same applies to writing this book, which would not have been possible without the support of the Packt Editorial team.

I would also like to thank the reviewers for their constructive feedback provided during the reviewing process, especially Anthony Borrow. This book would not be the same without your comments and suggestions.

Special thanks must go to all my colleagues at Synergy Learning. Your input to the book content has been invaluable.

I would like to thank all our customers. Without you, we wouldn't be aware of all the Moodle hitches and glitches that are out there. Keep them coming!

Last but not least, I would like to thank AB + ab for their patience while I have been hiding away writing this book. I will make up for it. Promise!

# About the Reviewers

**Abhishek Bhardwaj** is an 18 year old student of Computer Science who loves working with various web technologies, such as, HTML/CSS, PHP/MySQL, JavaScript, WordPress, Joomla!, Magento, and so on.

He also works with Java and Visual Basic.NET at times, when he's feeling ultra bored.

The quickest way to reach him is via Twitter: `http://twitter.com/abhishekwebin`

**Anthony Borrow, S.J.** is a Jesuit of the New Orleans Province, who has been active in the Moodle community for five years. Anthony has an M.A. in Counseling from Saint Louis University and a Masters of Divinity from the Jesuit School of Theology of Santa Clara University. Anthony has worked on the design and implementation of various database systems since 1992.

Anthony serves the Moodle community as its CONTRIB Coordinator. In that role, Anthony has presented at various MoodleMoots (conferences) across the United States and provided in-house training opportunities for institutions learning how to implement Moodle. Anthony has taught at Dallas Jesuit College Preparatory and provides technical advice to the Jesuit Secondary Education Association (`http://jsea.org`) and the Jesuit Virtual Learning Academy (`http://jvla.org/`). Anthony is currently serving the community at Cristo Rey Jesuit College Preparatory of Houston (`http://cristoreyjesuit.org`) in pastoral ministry, teaching, and counseling.

Anthony is the author of *Toward Greater Freedom*, a set of reflections based on the Spiritual Exercises of Saint Ignatius, available at `http://jesuitscholar.com/ SpiritualExercises/`, and co-author of the *Honduras* chapter of *Teen Gangs: A Global View*. He is the technical reviewer of various Packt books (*Moodle 1.9 Theme Design: Beginner's Guide, Moodle JavaScript Cookbook, Moodle as a Curriculum and Information Management System,* and *Moodle 1.9 Extension Development*).

I am grateful to the Moodle community for continually inspiring me to learn more about educational technologies and fostering an environment where every voice contributes to building that community.

**Brian Pool** is a graduate of Miami University in Systems Analysis and Salve Regina University in International Relations. He was an Air Force Lt. Col. and a pilot for 23 years, before switching to education. He is currently the Technology Coordinator at National Trail Local Schools in New Paris, Ohio. He has maintained Moodle servers and supported various Ohio schools' Moodle implementations for 6 years. In addition to that, he teaches A+ and Advanced technologies in the High School.

# www.PacktPub.com

This book is published by Packt Publishing. You might want to visit Packt's website at www.PacktPub.com and take advantage of the following features and offers:

## Discounts

Have you bought the print copy or Kindle version of this book? If so, you can get a massive 85% off the price of the eBook version, available in PDF, ePub, and MOBI.

Simply go to http://www.packtpub.com/moodle-2-administration-configuring-securing-customizing-extending/book, add it to your cart, and enter the following discount code:

**mooadebk**

## Free eBooks

If you sign up to an account on www.PacktPub.com, you will have access to nine free eBooks.

## Newsletters

Sign up for Packt's newsletters, which will keep you up to date with offers, discounts, books, and downloads.

You can set up your subscription at www.PacktPub.com/newsletters

## Code Downloads, Errata and Support

Packt supports all of its books with errata. While we work hard to eradicate errors from our books, some do creep in. Many Packt books also have accompanying snippets of code to download.

You can find errata and code downloads at www.PacktPub.com/support

PACKTLiB

# PacktLib.PacktPub.com

PacktLib offers instant solutions to your IT questions. It is Packt's fully searchable online digital book library, accessible from any device with a web browser.

- Contains every Packt book ever published. That's over 100,000 pages of content
- Fully searchable. Find an immediate solution to your problem
- Copy, paste, print, and bookmark content
- Available on demand via your web browser

If you have a Packt account, you might want to have a look at the nine free books which you can access now on PacktLib. Head to PacktLib.PacktPub.com and log in or register.

# Table of Contents

# Preface

Moodle has evolved from an academic project to the world's most popular Virtual Learning Environment (VLE). During this evolution, its complexity has risen dramatically and so have the skills that are required to administer the system.

Moodle 2 Administration is a complete, practical guide for administering Moodle sites. It covers setting up Moodle, configuration, and day-to-day admin task, as well as advanced options for customizing and extending Moodle.

The author, who has been at the cutting edge of Moodle administration since its advent, has adopted a problem-solution approach to bring the content in line with your day-to-day operations. The practical examples will help you to set up Moodle for large groups and small courses alike.

This is a one-stop reference for any task you will ever come across when administering a Moodle site of any shape or size.

A special theme has been designed for taking screenshots in this book. Your Moodle might look slightly different, but the content will be the same.

# What this book covers

Moodle has grown into a mature, sophisticated, and complex software system. As a result, Moodle administration covers a wide range of topics, which is the topic of this book. A fun way to demonstrate the various subjects is in the form of a tube/subway/metro/underground map (under Creative Commons license by Synergy Learning).

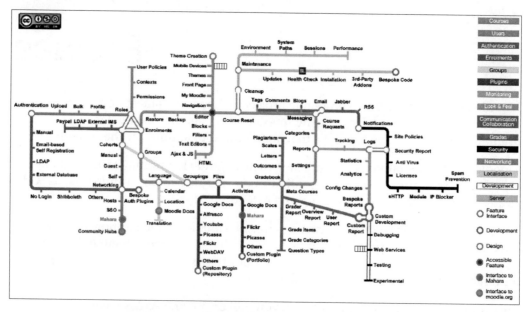

# Part I – Getting started

*Chapter 1, Moodle Installation,* tells you the most suitable Moodle setup for your organization, including software and hardware requirements. You will learn how to install Moodle in three environments, namely, LAMP/UNIX, Windows, and Mac OS, before manual and semi-automatic Moodle updates are covered in detail. Throughout, you will also learn how to perform some of the described operations using Moodle Command Line Interface (CLI).

*Chapter 2, The Moodle System,* covers the building blocks of the learning platform. First, we will cover the Moodle architecture, that is, the main Moodle components and where its data and code is stored. We then provide you with the skills to find your way around in Moodle via its intuitive user and administration interface. Finally, we deal with the management of files, which includes Moodle's standard file management, web host file management, and file management via the File system repository.

# Part II – Moodle configuration

*Chapter 3, Courses, Users, and Roles*, is an introductory chapter to give you an overview of Moodle courses, users, and roles. It covers the basics of these three key concepts and demonstrates how these three core elements are inherently intertwined.

*Chapter 4, Course Management*, tells you how to set up new courses and how to organize them in categories. The remainder of the chapter deals with an array of enrolment options, covering Moodle's internal enrolment (manual, self, and guest), cohort enrolment and synchronization, and database-driven enrolment; for instance, via LDAP, meta courses, and payment-driven enrolments.

*Chapter 5, User Management*, explains how to manage users on your system. We will first cover what user profiles look like and how they can be extended, before presenting (manual and bulk) standard user actions. We will then explain how to add users to Moodle manually (that is, one-by-one) and via batch upload. Then, you will learn about a plethora of authentication mechanisms Moodle equips us with. Finally, we will discuss best practices of user naming schemes.

*Chapter 6, Managing Permissions: Roles and Capabilities*, guides you through permission management. It applies roles and capabilities to users in different contexts. We will cover the assignment of roles, the modification of existing roles, and the creation of new roles before we deal with any administrative role-related settings.

*Chapter 7, Moodle Look and Feel*, tells you how to adapt your Moodle system to bring it in line with the corporate branding of your organization. We will cover the customization of the front page, the creation of Moodle themes, and support for mobile devices. You will also learn how to support users with accessibility requirements.

*Chapter 8, Moodle Plugins*, brings you up-to-date with the vast array of Moodle plugins. The areas that will be covered are activities, blocks and filters, repositories, portfolios, text editors, licenses, question types and behaviors, and plagiarism prevention.

*Chapter 9, Moodle Configuration*, deals with the pedagogical and technical configuration of your Moodle system. Pedagogical topics covered are collaboration, localization, grades and gradebook settings, and a number of miscellaneous parameters. Technical subjects dealt with include synchronous communication (instant messaging and video conferencing), asynchronous communication (messaging and RSS feeds), and a number of experimental settings.

# Part III – Moodle maintenance

*Chapter 10, Moodle Reporting,* will equip you with the tools you require to interpret and analyze the vast amounts of usage data Moodle is collecting. You will first learn about the monitoring facilities provided by Moodle that include activity reporting, user tracking, and some basic statistics. Then, we will take a look at third-party tools that cover report generation, web log analyzers, and live data trackers, such as Google Analytics.

*Chapter 11, Moodle Security and Privacy,* focuses on ensuring that the data in your Moodle system is protected from any misuse. You will learn about security notifications, user security, data and content security, and system security. We conclude the chapter with information on privacy and data protection concerns.

*Chapter 12, Moodle Performance and Optimization,* makes sure that your Moodle system runs to its full potential. We will cover configuring, monitoring, and fine-tuning your Virtual Learning Environment for maximum speed. You will learn how to optimize Moodle content before we focus on system parameters, namely, caching settings, session handling, memory management, module settings, and miscellaneous settings. We will also present some basic performance profiling and monitoring tools.

*Chapter 13, Backup and Restore,* focuses on ensuring that, in the event of a disaster, your data would not be lost. We will cover course backups, site backups, system backups, and restoring data from the taken data archives.

# Part IV – Enhancing Moodle

*Chapter 14, Installing Third-party Add-ons,* explains in detail how to extend your Moodle system via third-party add-ons. You will be able to distinguish between good add-ons and not-so-good add-ons before we cover extensions that are popular with other users. We will then cover how to install, configure, and uninstall third-party add-ons.

*Chapter 15, Moodle Integration via Web Services,* looks at ways to integrate Moodle with other systems via web services. We provide information about the basic concepts of Moodle web services, before you learn how to set up external systems and users controlling Moodle. This also covers the support for mobile apps.

*Chapter 16, Moodle Networking,* tells you how to connect disparate Moodle systems either in a peer-to-peer setup or via a Moodle hub. You will also be able to apply the learned networking techniques to connect the popular open source e-portfolio system Mahara to Moodle. We will also show you how to connect to the Moodle Community Hub and how to set up your own MOOCH.

# Part V – Appendix

The *Appendix, Configuration Settings*, provides you with a list of parameters that can be modified in Moodle's configuration file (`config.php`) and the impact each of the values will have. The areas covered are administration settings and system settings.

# What you need for this book

For Moodle, you must have the following components up and running on your server:

- **Database**: MySQL (version 5.0.25 or later, with InnoDB storage engine acvivated), PostgreSQL (version 8.3 or later), Microsoft SQL Server (version 2005 or later), or Oracle (version 10.2 or later)
- **Web server**: Apache is the preferred web server
- **PHP**: PHP 5.3.3 is required to run Moodle
- **PHP extensions**: Moodle makes use of a number of PHP extensions, most of which are compiled into PHP, by default

Depending on your specific setup, additional software and hardware might be required.

# Who this book is for

This book is written for technicians and systems administrators as well as academic staff, that is, basically for anyone who has to administer a Moodle system. Whether you are dealing with a small-scale local Moodle system or a large-scale multisite Virtual Learning Environment (VLE), this book will assist you with all kinds of administrative tasks. Some basic Moodle knowledge is helpful, but not essential.

# VLE job functions

A Moodle administrator is basically a VLE administrator who manages a Moodle system. A quick search through recruitment agencies specializing in the educational sector reveal a growing number of dedicated job titles that are closely related to VLE administration. A few examples are:

- VLE Administrator (or LMS Administrator or MLE Administrator)
- VLE Support Officer
- VLE Architect
- VLE Engineer
- VLE Coordinator

The list does not include functions that regularly act in an administrative capacity, such as IT support. It also does not include roles that are situated in the pedagogical field but often take on the work of a VLE administrator, such as, learning technologists or e-learning coordinators.

A VLE administrator usually works very closely with the staff who have responsibility for the administration of IT systems, databases, and networks. It has proven beneficial to have some basic skills in these areas. Additionally, links are likely in larger organizations where content management systems, student information management systems, and other related infrastructure is present.

Given this growing number of VLE administration-related roles, let us look at some key obligations of the job function and what skills are essential and desirable.

# Obligations and skill sets of a VLE administrator

The responsibilities of the VLE administrator differ from organization to organization. However, there are some obligations that are common across installations and setups:

- User management (learners, teachers, and others)
- Course management (prospectus mapping)
- Module management (functionality provided to users)
- Look and feel of the VLE (sometimes carried out by a web designer)
- Year-end maintenance (if applicable)
- Beginning-of-year setup (if applicable)
- Support teaching staff and learners

In addition to these VLE-specific features, you are required to make sure that the virtual learning environment is secure, stable, and performs well. Backups have to be in place, monitoring has to be set up, reports about usage have to be produced, and regular system maintenance has to be carried out.

If you host your own system, you will be responsible for all of the listed tasks and much more. If your VLE is hosted in a managed environment, some of the tasks closer to system level will be carried out by the hosting provider. So, it is important that they have a good understanding of Moodle. Either way, you will be the first person to be contacted by staff and learners if anything goes wrong, if they require new functionality, or if some administrative task has to be carried out.

With great power comes great responsibility!

While a range of e-learning-related activities are now taught as part of the course work for some academic and vocational qualifications (for instance, instructional design or e-moderation), VLE administration, per se, is not. Most VLE administrators have a technical background and often have some system or database administration knowledge. Again, it entirely depends on whether you host your VLE locally or it is hosted externally. The administration skills of a remotely-hosted system can be learned by anybody with some technical knowledge. However, for an internally-hosted system, you will require good working knowledge of the operating system on which the VLE is installed, the underlying database that is used, the network in which the VLE has to operate, and any further components that have to work with the learning system.

# Conventions

In this book, you will find a number of styles of text that distinguish between different kinds of information. Here are some examples of these styles, and an explanation of their meaning.

Code words in text are shown as follows:

If the `cron.php` script is invoked over HTTP (either using `wget` or `curl`), more memory is used than calling directly via the `php -f` command.

Any command-line input and output is written as follows:

```
mysqldump -u <user> -p <database> > backup.sql
```

**New terms** and **important words** are introduced in a bold-type font. Words that you see on the screen, in menus or dialog boxes for example, appear in our text like this:

Clicking on the **Enabled protocols** link in the **Overview** screen will guide you to the **Manage protocols** screen under **Plugins | Web services**.

 Warnings or important notes appear in a box like this.

 Tips and tricks appear like this.

# Reader feedback

Feedback from our readers is always welcome. Let us know what you think about this book, what you liked or may have disliked. Reader feedback is important for us to develop titles that you really get the most out of.

To send us general feedback, simply drop an e-mail to feedback@packtpub.com, making sure to mention the book title in the subject of your message.

If there is a book that you need and would like to see us publish, please send us a note in the **SUGGEST A TITLE** form on www.packtpub.com or e-mail suggest@packtpub.com.

If there is a topic that you have expertise in and you are interested in either writing or contributing to a book, see our author guide on www.packtpub.com/authors.

# Customer support

Now that you are the proud owner of a Packt book, we have a number of things to help you to get the most from your purchase.

# Errata

Although we have taken every care to ensure the accuracy of our contents, mistakes do happen. If you find a mistake in one of our books — maybe a mistake in text or code — we would be grateful if you would report this to us. By doing this you can save other readers from frustration, and help to improve subsequent versions of this book. If you find any errata, report them by visiting http://www.packtpub. com/support, selecting your book, clicking on the **let us know** link, and entering the details of your errata. Once your errata are verified, your submission will be accepted and the errata added to the list of existing errata. The existing errata can be viewed by selecting your title from http://www.packtpub.com/support.

# Piracy

Piracy of copyright material on the Internet is an ongoing problem across all media. At Packt, we take the protection of our copyright and licenses very seriously. If you come across any illegal copies of our works in any form on the Internet, please provide the location address or website name immediately so we can pursue a remedy.

Please contact us at `copyright@packtpub.com` with a link to the suspected pirated material.

We appreciate your help in protecting our authors, and in our ability to bring you valuable content.

# Questions

You can contact us at `questions@packtpub.com` if you are having a problem with some aspect of the book, and we will do our best to address it.

# 1
# Moodle Installation

Let's get started by installing Moodle.

After providing an overview that describes which setup is most suitable, software and hardware requirements will be outlined.

We will then cover the following:

- Installation of Moodle in a LAMP/Unix environment
- Installation of Moodle in a Windows environment
- Installation of Moodle in a Mac OS X environment
- Installation of Moodle via the Command Line Interface (CLI)
- Upgrading Moodle manually and via CLI, CVS, and GIT

You will only need to study the section(s) of the operating system(s) you are planning to use. Moodle can be scaled from a single instructor to an entire institution. We will only be able to cover the most "popular" installations and present solutions to some common problems. We assume that you are familiar with the basic system administration of the operating system on which you will be installing Moodle.

## Moodle installation—an overview

Before we start installing Moodle, you have to decide which setup is right for your organization. Once you have come to a conclusion, there are a number of prerequisites that you will need before we can get started.

# Choosing the best setup

There are a number of different environments in which you can set up Moodle. The three main criteria that should dictate the choice of the correct setup are:

- **Flexibility**: If you want to have full control over your system, be able to tweak system settings, and make frequent changes to the setup, then you are best off hosting your own server. However, if your preferred choice is to only administer your system while somebody else is looking after the operating system, the web server, and backups, then you are better off with a professionally-hosted setup, and particularly offerings provided by authorized Moodle Partners.

- **Scalability**: This is entirely driven by the number of concurrent users; that is, the number of active learners and teachers logged in to Moodle at the same time. A Moodle on a USB memory stick or on a single-processor desktop computer will not be able to cope with hundreds of simultaneously logged-in users. A load-balanced cluster, on the other hand, would be overkill for a small institution with a handful of learners. The following table provides some indicative setups for different types of educational organizations but is by no means complete:

| Organization | Likely setup |
|---|---|
| Single instructor | Desktop, laptop, memory stick |
| Small school/company | Shared server |
| Large school/company | Dedicated server |
| Medium–to-large college | Dedicated application and database servers |
| University/corporate | Load-balanced cluster |

Organizations require a server (either dedicated or shared) that is either hosted in-house or externally. If you decide to go down the hosted route, it is highly recommended to avoid a "cheap hosting" package, as their systems are not optimized for Moodle usage. This will have a significant impact on the performance of the system, especially with an increasing number of users.

- **Cost**: Budgetary constraints will certainly play an important role in your setup. Unless you already have the appropriate infrastructure in place, it is likely to be more cost-effective to host your Moodle system externally, as it saves you from having to purchase servers and provide a 24/7 data connection that caters to your learners' needs. Licensing cost is significantly higher if you use commercial operating systems, web servers, and database systems, instead of an open source solution. Either way, Moodle is designed to support a wide range of possible infrastructures suitable to your organization's IT policy needs.

In addition to these three key criteria that usually influence the decision about the underlying infrastructure, there are other factors that will have an impact on your decision, such as in-house expertise, compatibility with other systems, personal preference, and existing resources.

We will cover the three most popular operating systems for hosting Moodle—Linux, Windows, and Mac OS. For other setups such as on a memory stick, in a virtualized environment, or a larger multiserver cluster, please consult your local Moodle Partner (www.moodle.com). Some hosting companies offer quick one-click installations (often via the Fantastico installer, which usually doesn't contain the latest version). While the resulting Moodle system is sufficient for experimental sites, it is certainly unsuitable for production environments.

# Moodle prerequisites

There are a number of hardware and software requirements that must be installed before we can start installing Moodle.

## Hardware requirements

These requirements apply if you host Moodle yourself or if it is hosted on an external server (shared, virtual, dedicated, or clustered). On cheaper hosting packages, the hardware configuration is often insufficient to run Moodle efficiently.

- **Disk space**: Moodle takes up between 150 and 200 MB of disk space. However, this only provides you with an empty system and does not take into account the space you require for any learning resources. The faster the disks, the better. RAIDed disks are recommended, but are not essential on smaller installations.

- **Memory**: The (absolute) minimum requirement is 256 MB for a single-user instance, but more is necessary in a multiuser setup. A good rule of thumb is to have 1 GB of RAM for every 30-50 concurrent users. You have to double this calculation on Windows-based systems due to the higher overhead of the operating system.

 The more RAM the better. The faster the RAM the better.

- **Network**: While Moodle can run on a standalone machine, its full potential lies in a networked environment. A fast network card is essential, as is good upload and download speed if the VLE is accessed over the Internet.

## Software requirements

For Moodle 2, you must have the following components up and running on your server:

- **Database**: Moodle officially supports four database systems: MySQL (version 5.0.25 or later; the ACID-compliant InnoDB storage engine is highly recommended), PostgreSQL (version 8.3 or later), Microsoft SQL Server (version 2005 or later), and Oracle (version 10.2 or later).

- **Web server**: Apache is the preferred web server option, but Moodle works well with any other web server that supports PHP, such as Microsoft IIS.

- **PHP**: PHP 5.3.3 is required to run Moodle 2. There are a number of PHP settings which you might have to change in the php.ini or the .htaccess file (see http://docs.moodle.org/en/Installing_Moodle for more details).

- **PHP extensions**: Moodle makes use of a number of extensions, most of which are compiled into PHP by default. They are as follows:
  - ° **Compulsory extensions**: iconv, curl, ctype, zip, simplexml, spl, pcre, dom, xml, and json
  - ° **Recommended extensions**: intl, mbstring, openssl, tokenizer, xmlrpc, soap, and gd
  - ° **Conditional extensions**: mysql, pgsql, odbc (depending on database) and ldap, ntlm, and so on (depending on authentication mechanism used)

Depending on your specific setup, additional software and hardware might be required. It is assumed that the database, web server, PHP, and its extensions have been installed correctly, as this is not a VLE administrator task. Once this is the case, we are ready to go.

 Internet Explorer 6 is not supported by Moodle. A modern web browser (Internet Explorer 7+, Firefox 3+, Google Chrome, or Safari 3+) is required to access Moodle.

# Installation in a LAMP environment

Moodle is developed in Linux using Apache, MySQL, and PHP (known as the LAMP platform). If you have a choice, this is the preferred environment. There is ongoing debate whether PostgreSQL is the more suitable database option, but we will stick with MySQL as this is the system most administrators are most familiar with.

Also, some organizations are bound to using Microsoft SQL or Oracle. If this is the case, please refer to the respective installation guide as this is beyond the scope of this book.

# Downloading Moodle

Go to `download.moodle.org` to download Moodle. As you can see, there are quite a number of distributions to choose from.

There are four types of builds available on Moodle's download site:

- **Current stable builds**: For the current version of Moodle, there are two releases—the latest stable build and the latest official release. The *latest stable version* is created weekly (every Wednesday) and is the best choice for a new server. The *latest official release* contains the stable build as well as new fixes, but the version will not have gone through the weekly code review and might contain unresolved issues.

- **Older stable builds**: Older versions than the current version are maintained by the Moodle development team and bug fixes are back-ported. Sometimes, newly added functionality is back-ported. Currently, the oldest supported version is 1.9 and it is expected that this version will be supported until June 30, 2012.

- **Legacy versions**: For older versions, a stable build and the last release are made available. However, these are not maintained any further.

- **Upcoming release builds**: Moodle also offers you the option to download beta releases of the software (if available) and also the latest development release. These should only be downloaded for testing or development purposes, never in production environments!

Each version is made available in the two compressed formats: TGZ (use the tar command to uncompress) and ZIP (requires unzip). You can either download them by clicking on the respective link or, if you have (secure) shell access, retrieve the file directly by using the wget command (The file name is kept in sync with the current version number, which increases every 6 months; for example, moodle-latest-22, moodle-latest-24, and so on):

```
wget http://download.moodle.org/stable21/moodle-latest-21.zip
```

 The location where you install Moodle is referred to as dirroot.

Once you have moved the file to the location where you want to install it on your web server (dirroot), extract the file using the unzip command (or tar xvfz if you downloaded the TGZ version). In a hosted environment, you might have to use the uncompressing method provided by the web administration interface (cPanel, Plesk, or any bespoke system).

```
unzip moodle-latest-21.zip
tar xvfz moodle-latest-21.tgz
```

If you place the entire folder in your web server documents directory, the site will be located at www.yourwebserver.com/moodle. To access your site from www.yourwebserver.com, copy the contents directly into the main web server's documents directory.

 The URL via which Moodle is accessed is referred to as wwwroot.

Once this has been successfully done, you have to create the database that Moodle uses to store its data.

# Creating the Moodle database and the data directory

Moodle requires a database where it can store its information. While it is possible to share an existing database, it is highly recommended to create a separate database for Moodle. This can either be done via a web interface, as provided by hosted servers, or via the Unix command line.

## Using a hosted server

Most hosting providers provide a dedicated web interface to carry out basic database operations. Alternatively, you can use phpMyAdmin, an open source software that allows you to manage MySQL databases over the Web. It is part of most Linux distributions and also part of many control panels, such as cPanel or Plesk. (phpMyAdmin is often configured not to allow new databases to be created. If this is the case, you have to create the database from the database manager in your control panel.)

Once you have started phpMyAdmin, go to the **Databases** section and create a new database using the UTF collation. You don't need to create any tables; Moodle will be populating the database during the installation process.

While you can use the existing account of a database user, it is good practice to create a dedicated user for the Moodle database. This step is carried out in the **Privileges** section.

 Do not use the MySQL root account for your Moodle database!

phpMyAdmin allows you to perform both steps—creating a database and adding a new user—in a single action as shown in the following screenshot. We will create a user **book** and also check the **Create database with same name and grant all privileges** option.

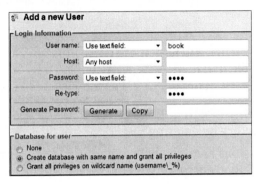

# Using the command line

If you don't have access to a web interface to create MySQL databases and user accounts or if you prefer to use a Linux shell, you can perform the steps via the command line:

1. Start the database command line tool by entering `mysql -u root -p` and enter the password at the prompt.

2. Create a database here (called `moodle`) by entering `CREATE DATABASE moodle;` (all MySQL commands have to be completed with a semicolon).

3. Set the default character set and collation order to UTF8 by entering `ALTER DATABASE moodle DEFAULT CHARACTER SET utf8 COLLATE utf8_unicode_ci;`.

4. Create a user and password (here `user` and `password`, respectively) and grant database access permissions by entering `GRANT SELECT, INSERT, UPDATE, DELETE, CREATE, CREATE TEMPORARY TABLES, DROP, INDEX, ALTER ON moodle.* TO user@localhost IDENTIFIED BY 'password';`

5. Exit the MySQL command tool by entering `QUIT`.

It is necessary to reload the grant tables using the following command line:

```
mysqladmin -u root -p reload
```

You have now completed the database setup. All we have to do now is to create Moodle's data directory before we are ready to start the installation of Moodle per se.

# Creating the Moodle data directory

Moodle stores most of its information in the database you have just created. However, any uploaded files such as assignments or pictures are stored in a separate directory. This data directory in Moodle is usually referred to as `moodledata`.

 The location which holds your Moodle data files is referred to as `dataroot`.

Later on, the Moodle installer will attempt to create this directory but, in some setups, this is not possible due to security restrictions. To be on the safe side, it is better to create `moodledata` manually or via a web-based file manager, as provided by some systems.

1. Create the directory by entering `mkdir moodledata`.

2. Change permissions recursively by entering `chmod -R 0770 moodledata` (if you use 0777 then everybody on the server will have access to the files).

3. Change the user of the directory to that of your web server (usually `apache` or `www-data`) by entering `chown -R apache moodledata`.

4. Change the group of the directory to that of your web server (usually `nobody` or `www-data`) by entering `chgrp -R nobody moodledata`.

 It is crucial to create `moodledata` on your server where it cannot be accessed publicly, that is, outside your web directory.

If you don't have permission to create the data directory in a secure location, create the `.htaccess` file in your home directory containing the following two lines:

```
order deny,allow
deny from all
```

This will prevent files from being accessed without the user having permissions to do so.

# Running the installer script

The installer script performs two main actions—populating the database and creating the configuration file `config.php`. The Moodle installer is initiated by entering the URL of `wwwroot` (the location where you copied Moodle) into your web browser; Moodle will recognize that it hasn't been installed yet and start the process automatically.

The Moodle installer has to set a session cookie. If your browser has been configured to trigger a warning, make sure you accept that cookie.

The first screen lets you choose the language to be used during installation. This is not the locale used for Moodle, only the language for the installation.

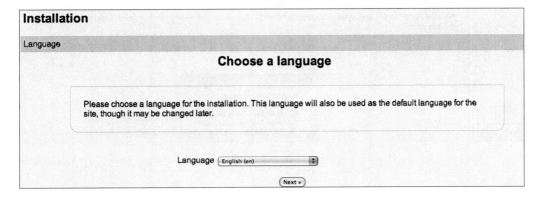

The following screen displays the expected values for the **Web address** of the site (wwwroot), the **Moodle directory** (dirroot)and the **Data directory** (dataroot). You might have to modify the data directory entry if the location of your moodledata differs.

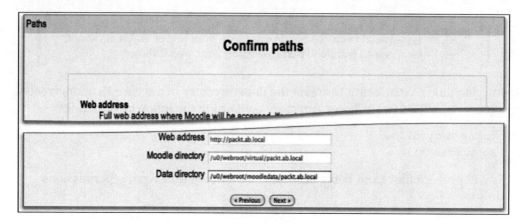

If dataroot cannot be located or does not have the correct permissions, an error message with details will be displayed. The same applies if dataroot is accessible directly via the Web and hence is not secure.

In the following screenshot, you have to select which database you wish to use. On my system, only the standard MySQL driver is installed. To use other database systems such as PostgreSQL, Oracle, or MS SQL Server, a driver has to be installed first.

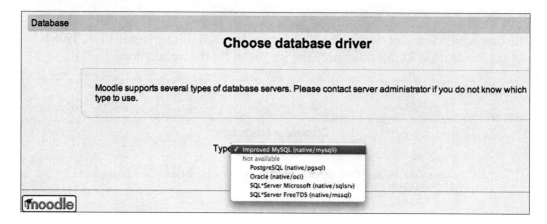

This interface is using the configuration details that have been previously established. This would look slightly different if you have chosen a different database driver to the native MySQL.

---

**Database settings**

**Improved MySQL (native/mysqli)**

Now you need to configure the database where most Moodle data will be stored. Database may be created if database user has needed permissions, username and password must already exist. Table prefix is optional.

| | |
|---|---|
| Database host | localhost |
| Database name | moodle |
| Database user | user |
| Database password | password |
| Tables prefix | mdl_ |
| Unix socket | ☐ |

( « Previous )  ( Next » )

---

| Setting | Description |
|---|---|
| Database host | The default is localhost (127.0.0.1), which is correct if the database is located on the same server as the web server. If it is located on a separate server, specify the IP address (preferably unresolved, to improve performance). |
| Database name<br>Database user<br>Database password | The database name, username, and password you enter when you run the `mysql` command. |
| Tables prefix | All tables that the Moodle installer is going to create will be prefixed with `mdl_`. This should only be changed if you run multiple Moodle installations using the same database. |
| Unix socket | If selected, the connection takes place through the filesystem as opposed to TCP/IP. A Unix socket file connection is marginally faster than TCP/IP, but can only be used when connecting to a server on the same computer. |

Once you see the following screen, you will know the Moodle configuration file config.php has been successfully created. If the creation of the configuration file fails (usually because of incorrect permissions) the installer will display the content of the configuration file. You will have to copy, the text from the screen and paste it to config.php in your dirroot.

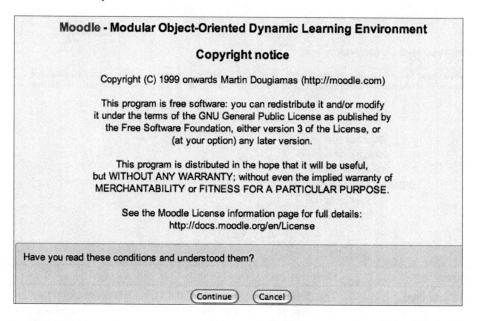

Before Moodle can proceed with the installation, you have to agree to the GPL license agreement. You can find the full license text at docs.moodle.org/en/License.

Once you have accepted the license agreement, the Moodle installer checks to see if certain components are installed. Not all modules are compulsory — see the *Moodle prerequisites* section in this chapter and notices on screen. The installer also verifies the key PHP settings. If any of the tests are not passed, it is important that you go back to the *Software requirements* section to resolve any problems and restart the installation process after the issues have been fixed. Otherwise, some features may not work or the installer will not continue, depending on the importance of the module.

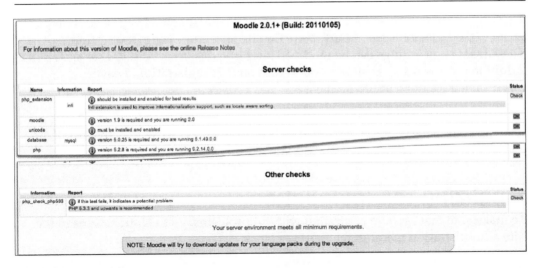

Once this screen has been confirmed, the Moodle installer will create all tables in the database. This process might take a few minutes.

Once the table creation and population have been concluded, you will see the screen to set up the administrator account. The default username is **admin**, which should be changed for security reasons. The self-explanatory fields you have to fill in are **New password**, **First name**, **Surname**, **Email address**, **City/town** and **Select a country**. All other fields are explained in great detail in *Chapter 5, User Management*.

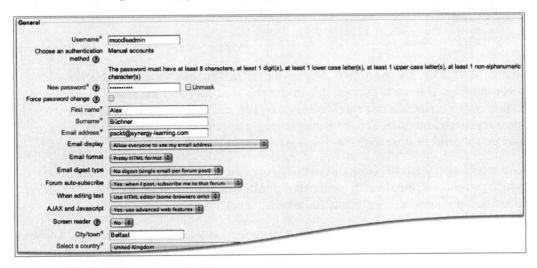

The last screen of the installation script asks you to enter some front page settings, namely, the **Full site name**, **Short name for site** and **Front page description**. These front page settings can be modified later (see *Chapter 7, Moodle Look and Feel*). Additionally, the installer allows you to turn on **Self registration**. Leave this disabled for now, until you have covered *Chapter 5, User Management*.

Once this information has been entered and the screen has been confirmed, you are ready to start using Moodle. However, it is recommended to finalize the installation and setting up the execution of the Moodle maintenance script.

# Finalizing the installation

To make sure that Moodle is running without problems, go to **Notifications** in the **Site administration** menu in the **Settings** block.

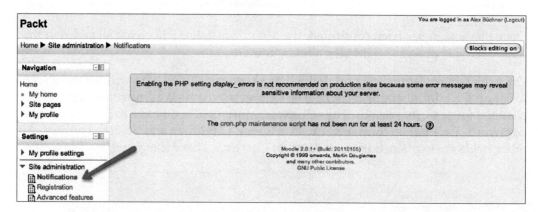

In my installation, there are two issues—a PHP setting has a value that is not recommended (I have to change this in the php.ini file) and the so-called cron maintenance script has not run for 24 hours. We will solve that mystery after we have registered our site. Other messages might appear in the **Notifications** area and you should resolve them in due course.

You might also want to check out http://<yoursite>/admin/health.php, which provides a mini health center that points out any additional issues. For each identified problem, a description, its severity level, and a solution are displayed.

Moodle provides some statistics about its usage on www.moodle.org/stats. To be included in these figures, you have to register your Moodle site. **Registration** (below the **Notification** link) with moodle.org (MOOCH) is optional and free, and you decide what information will be made public. Even if you opt out of providing any usage patterns for your site, it is still highly recommended to register, as you will get occasional notices from moodle.org. For example advanced security alerts.

After entering the details, you will have to confirm the submission and enter a **reCAPTCHA** (a slightly distorted image showing text). You also have the ability to unregister your site at any time.

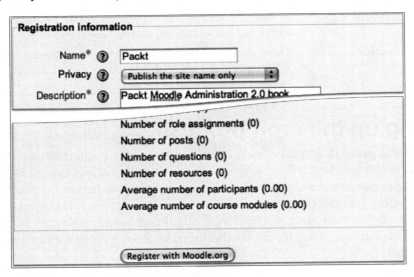

The settings for the registration screen are as follows:

| Field | Description |
| --- | --- |
| Name | The name of your site, as you just specified in the front page settings. |
| Privacy | You have the options:<br>• **Please do not publish this site (default)**<br>• **Publish the site name only**<br>• **Publish the site name with a link** |
| Description | A short narrative describing your site. |
| Site URL | The URL of your Moodle site. |
| Language | The language your site is published in. |
| Moodle version/release | Moodle version and build. |
| Postal address/Country | Enter your address and select the country in which your organization is located. |
| Geolocation | The latitude and longitude of your location. |
| Administrator | Your name. |
| Phone/Email address | Your contact phone number and e-mail address. |

| Field | Description |
|---|---|
| **Contact form** | By default, Moodle creates a form for other Moodle users to contact you—this can be turned off. |
| **Email notifications** | By default, Moodle e-mails you important information, such as upgrades and security issues. |
| **More information** | This is the data sent to `moodle.org` on a regular basis. This information will not be displayed to the public and will only be used for statistical purposes. |

# Setting up the cron process

Moodle has to perform a number of background tasks on a regular basis. The script that performs these tasks is known as a cron script and is executed by the so-called cron process. An entire page has been dedicated to this in the Moodle documentation; you can find it at `docs.moodle.org/en/Cron`. It is important that you set up the cron process. Otherwise, any timed Moodle features, such as scheduled backups, sending forum notifications, statistics processing, and so on, will not work.

The script `cron.php` is located in the `admin` directory and can be triggered manually through a web browser (unless your security settings have been changed). Once executed, the output from the script (`http://yoursite/admin/cron.php`) is shown on screen and you have to navigate back to your Moodle system manually.

Most control panels allow you to set up scheduled tasks via a cron job management tool. Bear in mind that this is not part of Moodle but a part of your hosting package. The following screenshot is from the widely-used Plesk system, which executes the script every 5 minutes:

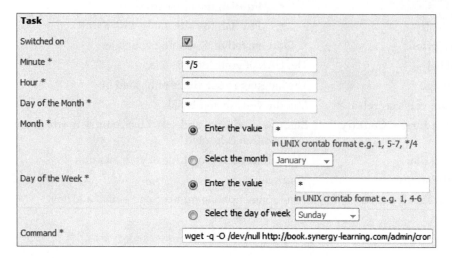

There are a number of ways to call the cron script. `wget -q -O /dev/null http://<yoursite>/admin/cron.php` is the most popular option in a Linux environment (see **Command** in the preceding screenshot). However, if this does not suit your setup, check out `docs.moodle.org/en/Cron` for alternatives.

The interface shown earlier creates an entry in the `crontab`, a file located in the `/etc` directory that contains all system-wide cron entries. This file can also be edited manually using `crontab -e`, but be careful to get the syntax right!

This concludes the installation process for Moodle in a LAMP environment. If you have come across any problems that have not been covered in these instructions, or if your setup differs from the one described, go to `docs.moodle.org/en/Installing_Moodle`, where more installation details are provided and exceptions are covered in greater detail.

# Installation in a Windows environment

XAMPP is a free Apache distribution that contains MySQL and PHP (as well as Perl) and exists for a number of operating systems. The Moodle distribution for Windows makes full use of XAMPP and is located at `download.moodle.org/windows`. The installation works on all the latest Windows PC and server variants.

The XAMPP-based Moodle distribution is only suitable for servers with a small number of users. For larger Windows installations you have to install Moodle manually. This involves installing a database server (MS SQL or any other support system), a web server (Microsoft IIS or Apache), and PHP, separately. You find details about this process at `docs.moodle.org/en/Windows_installation`.

Once downloaded, take the following steps:

1. Copy the distribution to a folder on your PC and unzip the archive in your folder of choice.
2. Make sure any software that uses port 80 is not running or change its settings to point it to an alternative port.
3. Double-click on `Start Moodle.exe`.
4. If you have a firewall installed, allow any shown services to be executed.
5. The XAMPP service will run in the Windows background.
6. Go to your web browser and enter `http://localhost` to your address bar.

7. You will see the same installer being launched as the one described for the LAMP environment. All values have already been populated; all you have to do is navigate through all the screens until you see the familiar **Setup administrator account**. This process will take a few minutes.

8. Enter the administrator details and select **Update profile**.

9. Enter the **Front Page settings** for your site.

10. Check that no warnings are displayed in the **Notifications** section of the **Site administration** area in the **Settings** block.

That's it! Your Moodle system is now up and running and you are now able to use Moodle locally, or from a web browser on another machine, as long as your IP address is accessible via the network you are on.

To stop using Moodle, double-click on Stop Moodle.exe. If you have a firewall installed, you might have to allow the program to be executed.

Instead of starting and stopping Moodle manually, you can start Apache and MySQL automatically as Windows services. In the server directory of your Moodle system, you find an executable called service.exe which you have to run with the -install parameter as administrator, as in the following example:

```
C:/moodle/server/service.exe -install
```

# Installation in a Mac OS X environment

MAMP is a free distribution that contains Apache, MySQL, and PHP for Mac OS X. Like its Windows counterpart, the Moodle distributions for Mac OS X (10.4 or higher) are only intended for local installations and not for production environments. There is also a link on the download site for Mac server installation.

Moodle4Mac is available as universal binaries in XAMPP and MAMP versions, which are located at download.moodle.org/macosx. The XAMPP version has a smaller footprint and uses the new innoDB engine, but requires an additional installation step. The choice seems to come down to personal preference.

Once downloaded, follow these steps:

1. Double-click on the downloaded DMG file to start the installation. This will open a screen as follows, which explains the remainder of the installation process.

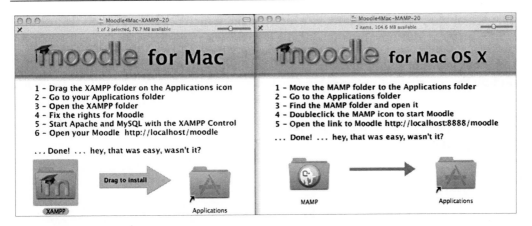

2. Drag the XAMPP or MAMP folder on this screen onto the **Applications** icon which will copy the Moodle system and its required components.

3. Open the XAMPP or MAMP folder in **Applications** where you will find the following relevant icons:

4. This step only applies to the XAMPP installation. Double-click on the **FixRightsForMoodle.sh** icon, wait until a terminal has opened, enter you Mac admin password and close the terminal when the script has completed.

5. Double-click on the **XAMPP** or **MAMP** icon to start Apache and MySQL. There is also a **MAMP** Control Widget in the same directory, which you might want to install.

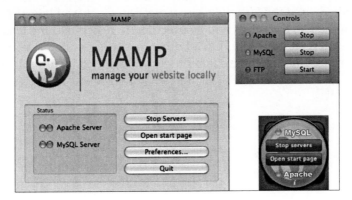

6. Double-click on the **Link to Moodle** icon, which opens your Moodle instance on your localhost in your default web browser.

And that's it! An installation cannot be easier than that! You don't even have to go through the installation process. Moodle is already pre-configured and you are ready to go.

The default password for the admin account is 12345, which you should change in the user profile.

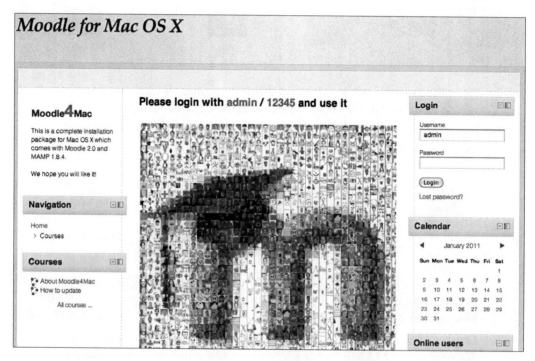

The MAMP folder also includes a shell script called `UpdateMoodle20.sh` (requires CVS to be installed — see the *Updating Moodle* section discussed later). When you double-click on the file, the script will be executed to download the latest version of Moodle and install it on your Mac. On all other operating systems, you will have to go through a more cumbersome update process which will be described further.

# Installation via the Command Line Interface

Moodle 2 has introduced a **Command Line Interface (CLI)**, which lets you perform a number of administrative tasks from the Unix shell prompt. There is no CLI for Windows-based systems. CLI-based installations are useful if you need to automate setups, for example, in an environment where you have to host multiple Moodle instances.

The CLI is not for the faint-hearted, so be careful when using it. You have to execute the installation script as the same user used for the web server, usually wwwroot or apache. You can run the installation script install.php in interactive mode (you will have to enter any parameters by hand) or in non-interactive mode, where the script will run silently.

From your dirroot, you can initiate the interactive script as follows:

```
sudo -u www-root /usr/bin/php admin/cli/install.php
```

More interesting is the non-interactive mode as this can be used for scripting and automation purposes. The list of all available parameters is displayed using the --help command.

```
sudo -u www-root /usr/bin/php admin/cli/install.php --help
```

```
Options:
--chmod=OCTAL-MODE      Permissions of new directories created within dataroot.
                        Default is 2777. You may want to change it to 2770
                        or 2750 or 750. See chmod man page for details.
--lang=CODE             Installation and default site language.
--wwwroot=URL           Web address for the Moodle site,
                        required in non-interactive mode.
--dataroot=DIR          Location of the moodle data folder,
                        must not be web accessible. Default is moodledata
                        in the parent directory.
--dbtype=TYPE           Database type. Default is mysqli
--dbhost=HOST           Database host. Default is localhost
--dbname=NAME           Database name. Default is moodle
--dbuser=USERNAME       Database user. Default is root
--dbpass=PASSWORD       Database password. Default is blank
--dbsocket              Use database sockets. Available for some databases only.
--prefix=STRING         Table prefix for above database tables. Default is mdl_
--fullname=STRING       The fullname of the site
--shortname=STRING      The shortname of the site
--adminuser=USERNAME    Username for the moodle admin account. Default is admin
--adminpass=PASSWORD    Password for the moodle admin account,
                        required in non-interactive mode.
--non-interactive       No interactive questions, installation fails if any
                        problem encountered.
--agree-license         Indicates agreement with software license,
                        required in non-interactive mode.
-h, --help              Print out this help
```

An example command line would look like the following, where you will have to adjust the parameters to your local setup:

```
sudo -u www-root /usr/bin/phpinstall.php --wwwroot=http://123.54.67.89/
moodle --dataroot=/var/moodledata/ --dbtype=mysqli --dbhost=localhost
--dbname=moodle --dbuser=moodle --dbpass=Password123! --fullname=moodle2
--shortname=moodle2 --adminpass=Password123! --non-interactive --agree-
license
```

There are more Moodle tasks that can be administered via the CLI, for example, resetting passwords or putting Moodle in maintenance mode. We will show the relevant syntax at the appropriate places throughout the book.

 If your installer crashes, you might have to increase your PHP `memory_limit` and `post_max_size` settings.

# Updating Moodle

Moodle is updated constantly, which is common practice in open source development environments. A new version containing resolved bug fixes is created every night and, as mentioned earlier, a fully-tested version is released on a weekly basis. There is usually no need to install updates every week. However, you should upgrade your Moodle system when:

- Security patches have been issued
- New features have been added
- Bugs have been fixed that affect your setup
- A major new update is released (every 6 months)

There are two ways Moodle systems can be updated. You can either run updates manually (using the web interface or the CLI) or stay up-to-date using the CVS or GIT commands. Both procedures are described in this section.

Either way, before you start, make sure you put Moodle in maintenance mode to ensure that no other user is logged in during the update. Go to **Server | Maintenance mode**, enable the **Maintenance mode**, and enter a maintenance message.

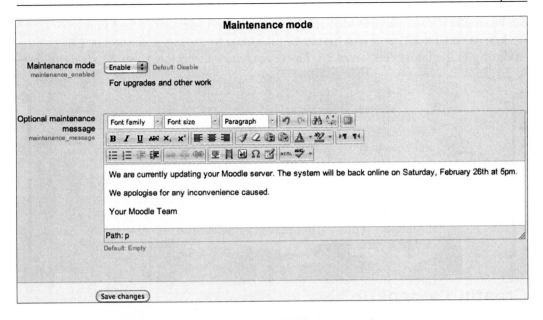

You can also put Moodle in maintenance mode using its CLI as follows:

```
sudo -u www-root /usr/bin/php admin/cli/maintenance.php --enable
```

To change back to normal mode use the `--disable` parameter instead of `--enable` as follows:

```
sudo -u www-root /usr/bin/php admin/cli/maintenance.php --disable
```

# Manual update

The high-level process for updating a Moodle system is as follows:

1. Creating a backup.
2. Creating a new Moodle system.
3. Installing the update.

If you are updating from a previous version of Moodle, the process is the same. However, double-check the *Upgrading* document at `docs.moodle.org/en/ Upgrading` for any version-specific issues.

 You cannot jump major versions when updating Moodle.

For example, if your current Moodle system is still on version 1.8 and you wish to update to version 2.1, you will first have to update to the latest version of 1.9 before updating to the latest version of 2.1. However, you can update from 2.1 straight to 2.1.5.

Updating from Moodle 1.x to Moodle 2 is a big version jump that has some serious implications. For example, some theme elements will have to be re-created, custom code will need adjusting and, most importantly, your staff is likely to require training before the new version is put into production.

Moving from Moodle 1.x to Moodle 2 is more a migration from one system to another than an update. Setting up a separate system to test the migration process has proven valuable. You will have to plan and budget for this.

# Creating a backup

Before you install a new update, it is highly recommended that you create a backup of your Moodle system. While most updates will run smoothly, the backup will be required if you have to revert the system to the pre-update version. There are three parts that have to be backed up:

- **Database**: There are two ways you can create a so called database dump from a MySQL database, either via command line or via Moodle's optional database interface.

  The simplest syntax for the command line tool is:

  ```
  mysqldump -u <user> -p <database>>backup.sql
  ```

  To restore the database you need to use the `mysql` command line tool as follows:

  ```
  mysql -u <user> -p <database><backup.sql
  ```

  The interface for the database tool is accessed via **Server | phpMyAdmin**. This is an optional module and has to be installed separately (it is the MySQL Admin add-on—see *Chapter 14, Installing Third-party Add-ons* for more details).

Click on the **Export** link on the front page, select the database to export, and click on **Go**, as shown in the following screenshot. The output of the command will be displayed on screen:

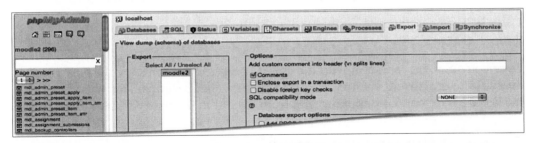

- **Data directory**: This is the `moodledata` directory. Create a copy of this elsewhere on the server (using `cp -R`) or create an archive using the `tar` command (`tar -cvf moodledata`).

- **Moodle**: This is the Moodle software itself. Create a copy of the directory elsewhere on the server. While only some parts of this backup are required (`config.php`, added themes, modified language packs, and so on), it is good practice to create a backup of the entire software. Finally, rename your Moodle system from `moodle` to say, `moodle.old` (`mv moodle moodle.old`).

 For more information on backups, check out *Chapter 13, Backup and Restore*.

# Creating your new Moodle system

Once you have created a backup, it is time to download the new version of Moodle. This is done in the same way as described earlier, during the installation process.

First, create a new `moodle` directory (`dirroot`) and copy the new version to that location (using the same `unzip` or `tar` command as during the installation). Also, make sure the permissions, as well as user and group, are correct.

Now, copy the following files and directories from your `moodle.old` directory to your new `dirroot`. Existing files and directories will have to be overwritten:

- `config.php`
- `.htaccess` (only if present)
- Any theme folders that have been created

- Any modified language packs
- The content of the `local` directory
- Any third-party modules and custom code that are not located in `local`

That's it! The next time you start Moodle, the update script will kick in. We'll go through that next.

Once you are more confident with the update process, you can copy the new version, overwriting the current version, after you have created backups. This will save you the last steps of manually copying files from the old to the new versions.

# Running the update script

Once you go to the location of your Moodle site and login in as administrator, the system will recognize that a new version is available and kick off the installer automatically.

The first screen displays the build of the new version (here, 2.0.1+) and asks you to confirm that you wish to go ahead with the upgrade.

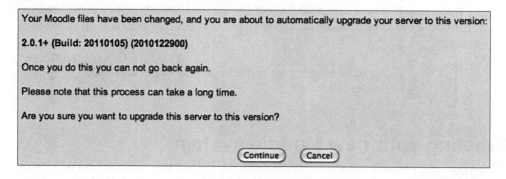

Your Moodle files have been changed, and you are about to automatically upgrade your server to this version:

**2.0.1+ (Build: 20110105) (2010122900)**

Once you do this you can not go back again.

Please note that this process can take a long time.

Are you sure you want to upgrade this server to this version?

Continue    Cancel

Next, a screen is displayed that provides a link to the release notes and performs the same server check as the one described during the installation.

Moodle plugins, whether core or third-party, sometimes cause problems when upgrading Moodle. The installer lists all components and states whether they are **Standard, Non-Standard, Extension,** or **Incompatible**. The **Status** column highlights any actions required or problems found. You will need to resolve any issues that have arisen. See *Chapter 14, Installing Third-party Add-ons*, for more details.

This page displays plugins that may require your attention during the upgrade. Highlighted items include new plugins that are about to be installed, updated plugins that are about to be upgraded and any missing plugins. Contributed plugins are also highlighted. It is recommended that you check whether there are more recent versions of contributed plugins available and update their source code before continuing with this Moodle upgrade.

**Number of plugins requiring attention during this upgrade: 3**

Display the full list of installed plugins

| Plugin name | Directory | Source | Current version | New version | Status |
|---|---|---|---|---|---|
| Activity modules | | | | | |
| ? Feedback | /mod/feedback | Standard | 2010112302 | 2011051600 | To be upgraded |
| Text filters | | | | | |
| mod/wiki | /mod/wiki | Extension | | | Missing from disk! |
| Themes | | | | | |
| packt | /theme/packt | Extension | | | No database |

Once this screen has been confirmed, the actual installation starts, during which new database fields are created and data is modified if and when necessary. Any new system settings that have been added to Moodle are shown and can be changed straightaway. For example, in the following screenshot, a new **Path to dot** parameter has been added to the **System paths** section.

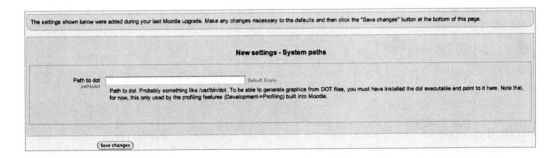

Once the upgrade process has been completed, make sure you check the **Notifications** page as earlier. Also, don't forget to turn off the **Maintenance mode**!

# Updating Moodle via CLI

As you would expect, Moodle updates can also be run using the already-discussed CLI. Once you have backed up your data and updated to the latest version, all you need to do is run the following script:

```
sudo -u www-root /usr/bin/php admin/cli/upgrade.php --non-interactive
```

Updating Moodle via CLI is even more powerful when combined with the CVS or GIT checkout of the Moodle source code. That is what we will look at next.

# Updating Moodle via CVS and GIT

An alternative approach exists to keep a current version up-to-date. It uses open source versioning systems which are supported by Moodle, namely, CVS and GIT. All checked-in Moodle code is made available via this method, which allows you to update only the modules that have actually changed.

The repository `cvs.moodle.org` is a read-only version of `git.moodle.org`. First, we are going to describe the basics of how to set up CVS. CVS has to be installed on your Moodle server. The first time you use CVS, you have to download the full version of Moodle, as follows:

```
cvs -z3 -d:pserver:anonymous@cvs.moodle.org:/cvsroot/moodle co -d
<directory> -r <version>Moodle
```

`<directory>` is the location where your Moodle system is installed and `<version>` specifies the version you wish to install, for example, `MOODLE_21_WEEKLY` or `MOODLE_20_STABLE`.

Once this has been successful, go to your Moodle site and you will be guided through the same update process as discussed earlier. If this fails, check that the user and group permissions are set correctly and adjust them accordingly (`chown -R <user>:<group> moodle`).

For further updates you should use the following command, which remembers your previous settings, such as the chosen mirror site:

```
cvs update -dP
```

For further options of how to use CVS from the command line and in operating systems other than Unix, check out `docs.moodle.org/en/CVS_for_Administrators`.

Setting up GIT is a cumbersome process, which is beyond the scope of this book. You can find details at `docs.moodle.org/en/Git`. However, once set up, GIT is a very streamlined system to use, particularly in conjunction with the CLI we discussed earlier.

The following is a sample script which gets the latest version of the source code, puts Moodle in maintenance mode, merges the old code with the new, runs the upgrade script, and disables the maintenance mode.

```
git fetch
sudo -u www-root /usr/bin/php admin/cli/maintenance.php --enable
git merge origin/cvshead
sudo -u www-root/usr/bin/php admin/cli/upgrade.php
sudo -u www-root/usr/bin/php admin/cli/maintenance.php --disable
```

```
root@debian:/var/www/moodle2# git fetch
remote: Counting objects: 2674, done.
remote: Compressing objects: 100% (560/560), done.
remote: Total 1891 (delta 1326), reused 1850 (delta 1297)
Receiving objects: 100% (1891/1891), 694.97 KiB | 161 KiB/s, done.
Resolving deltas: 100% (1326/1326), completed with 316 local objects.
From git://git.moodle.org/moodle
   fb8642b..9251e27  MOODLE_19_STABLE -> origin/MOODLE_19_STABLE
   eb9d692..06ede85  MOODLE_20_STABLE -> origin/MOODLE_20_STABLE
   6b14adf..804ebc7  master           -> origin/master
 * [new tag]          v2.0.3           -> v2.0.3
```

If you have changed any core code, potential conflicts might arise and will have to be resolved (CVS and GIT will prompt you to do so).

You might also come across some conflicting advice on whether to use CVS or GIT for production sites or not. The advantages are that your system is always up-to-date and that the updates are carried out automatically. The disadvantages are that the update process might require intervention to resolve any conflicts or it might fail, especially when a lot of third-party add-ons have been employed.

# Summary

In this chapter, you have learned how to install Moodle on the most popular operating systems and also how to upgrade the VLE. You have also learned how to use the powerful command line interface.

The fact that Moodle uses a portable software architecture and facilitates standard open source components allows the installation on multiple platforms. However, this also means that different idiosyncrasies have to be considered in different environments.

Now that your system is up and running, let's have a look at the components of Moodle which will provide you with a better understanding of the system and how to administer it.

# 2
# The Moodle System

Now that your Moodle system is up and running, we will be looking at the building blocks of the learning platform. Think of these as the foundation on which Moodle is built. The subjects we will cover are:

- **Moodle architecture**: In this section, you will learn what the main components of Moodle are and where its data is stored.

- **Finding your way around in Moodle**: Moodle has an intuitive user interface that takes a little time to get used to. You will learn the main navigation and also where to find help if it is required.

- **File management**: Dealing with files in web-based applications is not always straightforward. You will learn the different options available to deal with this, which will cover:
    - Moodle's file management
    - Web host file management
    - File management via the File system repository

## Moodle architecture

We will first look at the overall LAMP architecture on which Moodle is based, before we cover the internal components of the VLE layer.

# The LAMP architecture

Moodle has been developed on the open source LAMP framework consisting of Linux (operating system), Apache (web server), MySQL (database), and PHP (programming language). Due to the portability of these components and the modularity of Moodle itself (that's what the "M" stands for), it can support a wide range of operating systems, database systems, and web servers. The following diagram shows a simple overview of the overall architecture:

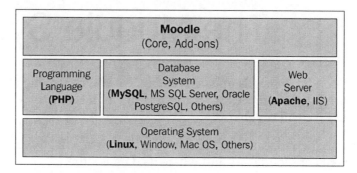

The lowest level is the operating system. While Linux is the preferred platform, other Unix derivatives such as Solaris and AIX are supported, along with Windows and Mac OS X (preferably the server variants for production sites). Certain libraries will have to be installed—see *Chapter 1, Moodle Installation*.

PHP is the programming language in which Moodle is developed (accompanied by HTML, JavaScript, and CSS files). It is the only component that cannot be replaced with any other counterpart.

MySQL is the database of choice for most open source applications, but other database systems such as Microsoft SQL Server, Oracle, and PostgreSQL work without problems. Some details have been provided in the previous chapter but, as mentioned before, the focus in this book will be on MySQL.

Apache has become the de facto standard for large-scale web applications, closely followed by Microsoft IIS. Both web servers are supported like any others offering PHP support. In this book, we will focus on Apache as it is the most popular option for Moodle setups.

The following diagram shows the interaction of the elements in the Moodle architecture:

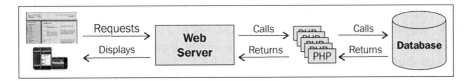

The user makes requests via the web browser interface or a mobile Moodle application (for example, to display a learning resource). The web browser passes the request on to the web server, which calls the PHP module that is responsible for the call. The PHP module calls the database with an action (query, update, insert, or delete operation) that returns the requested data. Based on this information, the PHP module returns data (usually in the form of HTML or JavaScript code) to the web server, which passes the information to be displayed back to the user's browser or application.

# The Moodle layer

Now, let's look at the Moodle layer in more detail. Moodle's main building blocks are shown in the following diagram:

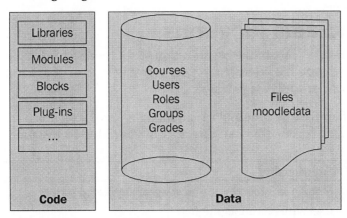

Moodle distinguishes between code (mostly written in PHP, HTML, and CSS) and data (mostly values added via the Moodle interface).

Moodle libraries, modules (such as resources and activities), blocks, plugins, and other entities are represented in code. It is always stored in the filesystem in a Moodle directory referred to as `dirroot`, which has been specified during the installation process in the previous chapter. The code includes all elements that deal with the backend (server) and frontend (user interface) operations.

Moodle courses, users, roles, groups, grades, and other data such as learning resources added by teachers, forum posts added by students, and system settings added by the administrator are mostly stored in the Moodle database. However, files such as user pictures or uploaded assignments, are stored in another Moodle directory, known as moodledata, which is located in a directory called dataroot. Information about files (metadata such as the name, location, last modification, license, and size) is stored in the database, which references the respective files.

 Moodle manages its files internally and it is important to stress that interfering with any files in moodledata will break the application.

Even copying a file from one folder to another or adding a file manually will break the consistency of your system and further behavior cannot be predicted. Internally, Moodle uses a mechanism called SHA1 hashing. Moodle fully supports Unicode file names and also avoids redundant storage when the same file is used twice (even by different users). Again, unlike in previous Moodle versions, you must not modify any Moodle files at system level!

Now let's have a closer look how the Moodle files area—the directory structure—is organized.

## Code and data locations

Though Moodle takes care of the organization—of its code and data, it is usually good to know where a file is located in your learning system; for example, when installing add-ons or applying patches.

System files—files that are required to run Moodle—are located in a number of directories under dirroot (the root directory of your Moodle installation):

| Directory | Functionality | Chapter |
| --- | --- | --- |
| admin | Moodle administration and some unsupported scripts | All |
| auth | User authentication plugins | 5 |
| backup | Backup and restore operations | 13 |
| blocks | Blocks placed in courses and the front page | 7 |
| blog | Internal and external blogging functionality | 9 |
| calendar | Calendar and event management | 9 |
| cohort | Handling of sitewide groups (cohorts) | 4 |
| comment | Comments used in courses | 9 |

| Directory | Functionality | Chapter |
|---|---|---|
| course | Management of courses and categories plus course formats | 4 |
| enrol | User enrolment plugins | 4 |
| error | Error handling; mostly used by developers | - |
| files | File management | 2 |
| filter | Moodle filters applied to text authored in the editor | 7 |
| grade | Grade and grade book management as well as reports | 9 |
| group | Groups and groupings handling | 4 and 5 |
| install | Moodle installation and update scripts | 1 |
| iplookup | Look up of IP addresses | - |
| lang | Localization strings; one directory per language | 9 |
| lib | Libraries of core Moodle code | 2 |
| local | Recommended directory for local customizations | 14 |
| login | Login handling and account creation | 5 |
| message | Messaging tool supporting multiple channels | 9 |
| mnet | Peer-to-peer and hub networking | 16 |
| mod | Core Moodle course modules | 9 |
| my | Users' personal dashboards, known as myMoodle | 7 |
| notes | Handling of notes in user profiles | 11 |
| pix | Generic site graphics | - |
| plagiarism | Plagiarism detection plugins | 8 |
| portfolio | Portfolio plugins allowing users to export data | 8 |
| question | Question and question bank handling plus question types | 9 |
| rating | Ratings used in forums, glossaries, and databases | - |
| repository | Repository plugins allowing users to import and load data | 8 |
| rss | RSS feeds | 9 |
| search | Local course searches and global site searches | 9 |
| sso | Single sign-on operations | 5 |
| tag | Tagging | 9 |
| theme | Themes to change branding of site | 7 |
| user | User management | 5 |
| webservice | Web services functionality | 15 |

The `moodledata` directory (`dataroot`) is organized as follows:

| | |
|---|---|
| `cache` | Caching data |
| `filedir` | That is the actual user content—files that have been uploaded |
| `repository` | External location accessible from within Moodle (see *File management via the File system repository* section) |
| `search` | Temporary files when carrying out searches |
| `temp` | Temporary files |
| `trashdir` | Deleted files |

If problems occur before carrying out an update, it is sometimes necessary to delete caching data and any temporary information Moodle has created. This data is located in the respective directories in the structure shown in the preceding table. In other words, once everybody has logged out, you can safely delete any files in the directories named `cache` and `temp`. This can either be done manually or via **Development | Purge all caches** in the Moodle interface, which we will cover next.

# Finding your way around in Moodle

As an administrator, you will be performing most tasks from the **Site administration** section in the **Settings** block as shown in the following screenshot, which you will see once you log in to Moodle. We will cover all aspects of the menus and submenus throughout the remainder of the book.

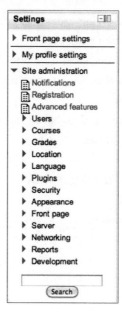

The items displayed in the preceding screenshot will change, depending upon where in Moodle it is shown. For example, inside a course, an additional **Course administration** section will be displayed. As administrator, you will always see the **Site administration** section; other users with lesser rights will only see the menu items that they have access to.

You can dock the **Settings** block (like any other block) to the left to save space by clicking on the **Move this to the dock** icon on the top-right corner of the block. Once you hover over the docked block it will pop out.

# Breadcrumbs

Moodle uses the so-called breadcrumb trail interface for its navigation; the name has been derived from the *Hansel and Gretel* fairy tale. Once you select a menu or submenu item, Moodle displays the respective crumbs in your navigation bar. These crumbs can be used to jump back to any previous menus. In the following menu, the trail consists of five crumbs:

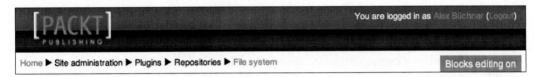

The first crumb is always the name of the site and represents your Moodle front page (here called **Home**). So, if you ever get lost, click on the first crumb and you will be back in familiar territory. Throughout the book, we will be referring to the location of menu items in the **Site administration** section via a consistent notation, for instance, go to **Plugins | Repositories | File system** for the trail shown in the preceding screenshot.

# Administrator search facility

To simplify the identification of any settings in the administration section, a search facility is provided, which is located below the hierarchical **Site administration** menu.

When searching for any term, Moodle displays the results in an expanded form that allows you to change settings immediately. For example, when searching for "calendar", numerous sections appear as a result, which can be changed in each section straightaway, rather than navigating to each separate section to make changes.

The search facility is also highly beneficial when upgrading from older versions of Moodle where configuration settings have been re-organized and their location is difficult to trace.

# Moodle bookmarks

Bookmarks are shown in the **Admin bookmarks** block, which has to be added by clicking on **Turn editing on** and selecting the block from the **Add a block** pull-down list. They allow the bookmarking of any admin menu for easy access to the pages that you require regularly. Select **bookmark this page** to add a bookmark and **unbookmark this page** to delete it. Moodle automatically displays the latter option, when you are on a bookmarked page.

In the preceding screenshot, two pages have already been bookmarked (**Browse list of users** and **Add/edit courses**) and the mentioned link is provided to add more bookmarks.

# Moodle Docs and Help

The entire Moodle documentation is online at docs.moodle.org. If you wish to provide your own documentation, modify the **Moodle Docs document root** setting in **Appearance | Moodle Docs**. On this screen, you can also enable the **Open in new window** option, if you want the documentation pages to be opened in a new window. A link at the bottom of each page provides a reference to the relevant page in the Moodle Docs. In addition to the actual online documentation, some features provide inline help, which is indicated by a question mark symbol. When it is clicked, a help window will appear providing assistance relevant to the respective topic.

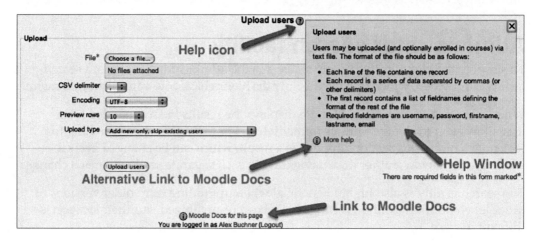

For instance, when clicking on the **Moodle Docs for this page** link in the **Upload users** section, the following article will be opened:

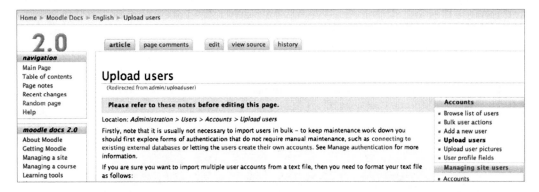

For each version of Moodle, separate Moodle Docs are published. The preceding screenshot is from version 2.0. New Docs will be created for Moodle version 2.1, 2.2, and so on.

The Moodle community is growing continuously and, at the time of writing, had well over 1 million registered users (yes, that's 1 million!) of which 5 percent to 10 percent are active. If you cannot find a solution to any of your Moodle problems in the Moodle Docs, use the **Search moodle.org** functionality at the top of the screen at moodle.org. In order of priority, the search brings forth the already mentioned Moodle Docs, the most active user forums, and the Moodle Tracker, which keeps track of all issues and feature requests (tracker.moodle.org). A search in the Moodle forums can often result in a large number of links. To narrow down the search space, use the **Advanced search** in the **Search forums** block. If you still cannot find the solution to your problem, which is relatively rare, post a question on the relevant forum and somebody is likely to assist you further.

# File management

Dealing with files in web-based applications is not always straightforward. While Moodle provides a user interface to perform this task, it is sometimes necessary that, as the administrator, you will have to bypass this mechanism and use other means. First though, let us look at the built-in file handling that is also the one used by students and teachers.

# Moodle file management interface

Moodle offers a basic file management interface which lets you upload, move, delete, and rename files and directories. We have already talked about how Moodle stores files at system level — the ones we are not to touch! At application level, it arranges files according to Moodle's structure.

 In Moodle, a file is always connected to the particular bit of Moodle that uses it.

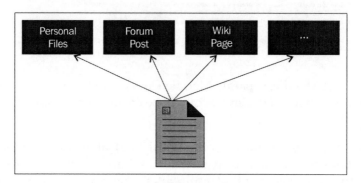

Files are organized in a tree-like structure, which has three types of main branches:

- Categories/Courses/Activities and Resources
- Users (private files and personal backups)
- Front Page (Moodle's home page)

We will be dealing with all those concepts at later stages so, for now, let us just take them for granted. Courses are arranged in categories (and subcategories) and consist of activities and resources. There are usually further subdirectories inside activities and resources.

There are multiple users on your system, each with a dedicated file area that can be accessed from anywhere in Moodle, but there is only a single Front Page. Remember, a file is always connected to the particular bit of Moodle content that uses it, which is reflected in the directory-like structure.

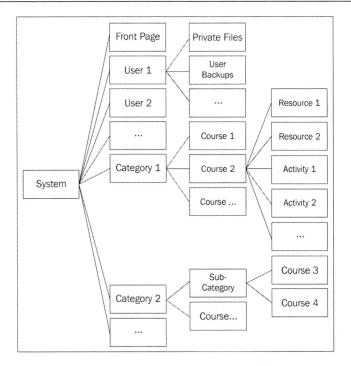

Uploading files takes place in the **File picker**. The **File picker** is a tool that is utilized whenever files have to be added to a particular object in Moodle (usually via the **Add...** button).

 Files in Moodle are (almost) always copied and never linked!

A user can choose from multiple file sources, known as repositories. We will be dealing with them in *Chapter 8*, *Moodle Plugins* and will only cover the basic aspects here.

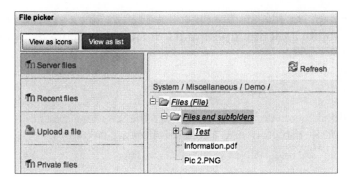

In the preceding screenshot, you can see a sample files area viewed as a list. It shows two files, **Information.pdf** and **Pic 2.PNG** and a **Test** folder located at **System / Miscellaneous** (category) **/ Demo** (course) **/ Files** (resource of type **File**). Moodle has created a subdirectory, **Files and subfolders**. The view from within the content section of the same resource looks as follows:

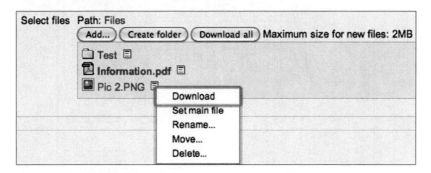

The **Add...** button opens up the **File picker**, the **Create folder** button lets you create a directory, and **Download all** puts all files in a ZIP file and copies it to your local drive. Beside each file, a context-sensitive menu is shown with the following possible options:

- **Download**: Copy file to local drive
- **Unzip**: Extract all files from a ZIP archive (for uploading multiple files)
- **Set main file**: The file that is shown to the viewer of the resource/activity
- **Rename**: Change name of file
- **Move**: Move file to another destination
- **Delete**: Delete file. This irreversible operation has to be confirmed first

Each site and course has a file upload limit, which is set to 2 MB by default. If you need to support files larger than the 2 MB threshold, you will have to increase the limit as follows:

- In your php.ini file, modify the following two lines; <value> represents the maximum limit (multiple input formats are supported, for example, 20M or 20971520):

```
upload_max_filesize = <value>
post_max_size = <value>
```

- If you don't have access to the php.ini file, create a .htaccess file in your main Moodle directory and add the following two lines:

```
php_value upload_max_filesize = <value>
php_value post_max_size = <value>
```

On some systems, you will also have to increase the LimitRequestBody parameter, which is usually found in the Apache configuration file httpd.conf.

Once these changes have been applied, make sure the **Maximum uploaded file size** in **Security | Site policies** is set to **Server limit**. Underneath this parameter, you can also change the **User quota** for private files (specified in bytes). When changing these two values, bear in mind that they could potentially have an impact on bandwidth and disk space.

Alternatively, you can use other file management operations, which we will cover next.

# Web host file management

Most web hosts offer a web interface that provides a file management facility; for example, cPanel and Plesk. These interfaces often allow you to upload files and directories in a more flexible way than by using the Moodle file interface.

The advantages of using a web interface are:

- Ability to upload multiple files
- Usually no upload limit
- Often a more user-friendly interface than the Moodle File picker

The disadvantages of using a web interface are:

- File management is not very flexible
- Uploading large files will still be slow because they are copied over HTTP

It has to be stressed again that you should only modify files in dirroot; for instance, to install third-party add-ons. Unless you know SHA1, do not change any files in moodledata. If you do, Moodle will not function correctly afterwards.

For very large files such as high-quality learning resources, it would be useful to be able to upload the content via (secure) FTP and then use the built-in unzip functionality in the File picker. However, unlike in previous versions of Moodle, it is not possible to upload files directly via FTP anymore. Instead, you have to make use of the file system repository, which is discussed in the following section.

# File management via the File system repository

The objective is to make the files appear in the **File picker** in a separate section; Moodle calls them repositories. To achieve this, we have to go to **Plugins | Repositories | Manage repositories**. Activate the **File system** plugin via **Enabled and visible**. Click on **Settings** and check the first box to allow access from courses before saving the settings (to grant access from users' personal files also, check the second box).

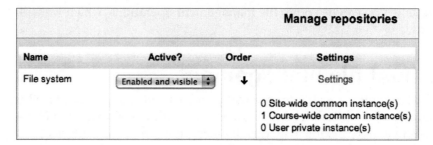

| Manage repositories | | | |
|---|---|---|---|
| **Name** | **Active?** | **Order** | **Settings** |
| File system | Enabled and visible ⬍ | ↓ | Settings |
| | | | 0 Site-wide common instance(s) |
| | | | 1 Course-wide common instance(s) |
| | | | 0 User private instance(s) |

You might have spotted the `repository` directory when we looked at the data locations in the Moodle layer earlier. Any subdirectories in `dataroot/repository` can be read from within Moodle. First, create a subdirectory in that folder and copy or transfer (using FTP) some data into it.

Now go to a course where you wish to allow access to the folder, select the **Repositories** link in the **Settings** block, and click on **Create "File system" instance**. Give the new repository a name and select a folder, in case you have created more than one (we have created three).

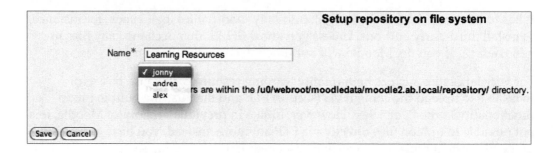

Setup repository on file system

Name* Learning Resources

✓ jonny
andrea
alex

rs are within the **/u0/webroot/moodledata/moodle2.ab.local/repository/** directory.

Save  Cancel

From now on, any user with access to the **File picker** in that particular course has read-only access to the material. How cool is that! You can also grant access to directories at user level. Go to a user's profile settings where you will see the same **Repositories** link as in courses.

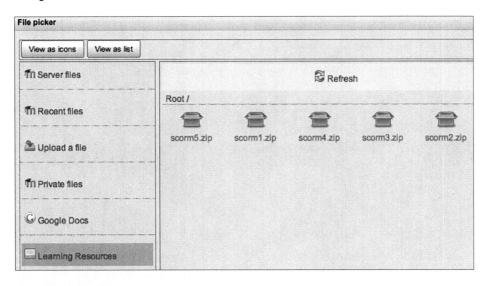

We will be dealing with repositories in more detail in *Chapter 8, Moodle Plugins* and have only focused on the files-related ones for now. For more details on the file system repository, check out `docs.moodle.org/en/File_system_repository_configuration`.

# Summary

In this chapter, we have learned what the building blocks of Moodle look like and where they are located. Furthermore, we have dealt with a number of options for managing files including the basics of some file repositories.

As we found out in the previous chapter, Moodle can be installed on multiple operating systems, supports a wide range of database systems, and can be used with different web servers. Due to the openness of Moodle, it should have come across in this chapter that all its components can be accessed without any restrictions. This allows the management of files via a number of channels that we have covered; such as, Moodle's file management, web host file management, and file management via the File system repository for FTP access.

Now that your system is up and running and you know what its insides look like, it's time to add courses and users.

# 3

# Courses, Users, and Roles

The objective of this chapter is to give an overview of Moodle courses, users, and roles. The three concepts are inherently intertwined and any one of these cannot be used without the other two. We deal with the basics of the three core elements and show how they work together. Let's see what they are:

- **Moodle courses**: Courses are central to Moodle as this is where learning takes place. Teachers upload their learning resources, create activities, assist in learning and grade work, monitor progress, and so on. Students on the other hand read, listen to or watch learning resources, participate in activities, submit work, collaborate with others, and so on.

- **Moodle users**: These are individuals accessing our Moodle system. Typical users are students and teachers, but also other types such as managers, parents, assessors, examiners, or guests. Oh, and the administrator, of course!

- **Moodle roles**: Roles are effectively permissions that specify which features users are allowed to access and, also, where and when (in Moodle) they can access them.

Bear in mind that this chapter only covers the basic concepts of these three core elements. The dedicated chapters — *Chapter 4, Course Management*, *Chapter 5, User Management*, and *Chapter 6, Managing Permissions: Roles and Capabilties* — will then deal with the three concepts in great detail.

# A high-level overview

To give you an overview of courses, users, and roles, let's have a look at the following diagram. It shows nicely how central the three concepts are, and also how other features are related to them. Again, all of their intricacies will be dealt with in due course so, for now, just start getting familiar with Moodle terminology.

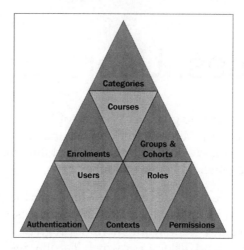

Let's start at the bottom left and cycle through the pyramid clockwise. Users have to go through an *Authentication* process to get access to Moodle. They then have to go through an *Enrolments* step to be able to participate in *Courses* which themselves are organized into *Categories*. *Groups & Cohorts* are different ways to group users at course level or sitewide. Users are granted *Roles* in particular *Contexts*. Which role is allowed to do what and which isn't depends entirely on the *Permissions* set within that role.

The diagram also demonstrates a Catch-22 situation. If we start with users, we have no courses to enrol them in to (except the front page); if we start with courses, we have no users who can participate in them. Not to worry though. Moodle lets us go back and forth between any administrative areas and, often, perform multiple tasks at once.

# Moodle courses

Moodle manages activities and stores resources in courses, and this is where learning and collaboration takes place. Courses themselves belong to categories, which are organized hierarchically, similar to folders on our local hard drive. Moodle comes with a default category called Miscellaneous, which is sufficient to show the basics of courses. We deal with categories in more detail in the dedicated chapter, *Chapter 4, Course Management.*

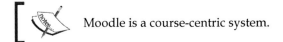 Moodle is a course-centric system.

To begin with, let us create the first course. To do so, go to **Courses | Add/edit courses**. Here, you will see the **Miscellaneous** category. Select the **Add a new course** button and you will be directed to the screen where course details have to be entered. For now, let us focus on the two compulsory fields, namely **Course full name** and **Course short name**. The former is displayed at various places in Moodle, whereas the latter is used to identify the course and is also shown in the breadcrumb trail.

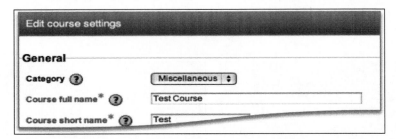

We leave all other fields empty or at their default values and save the course by clicking the **Save changes** button at the bottom.

The screen displayed after clicking **Save changes** shows enrolled users, if any. Since we just created the course, there are no users present in the course yet. In fact, except for the administrator account we are currently using, there are no users at all on our Moodle system. So, we leave the course without users for now and add some users to our VLE before we come back to this screen.

# Moodle users

Moodle users, or rather their user accounts, are dealt with in **Users | Accounts**. Before we start, it is important to understand the difference between authentication and enrolment.

Moodle users have to be authenticated in order to log in to the system. Authentication grants users access to the system through login where a username and password have to be given (this also applies to guest accounts where a username is allotted internally). Moodle supports a significant number of authentication mechanisms, which are discussed later in detail.

Enrolment happens at course level. However, a user has to be authenticated to the system before enrolment to a course can take place. So, a typical workflow is as follows (there are exceptions as always but we will deal with them when we get there):

1. Create your users.

2. Create your courses (and categories).

3. Associate users to courses and assign roles.

Again, this sequence demonstrates nicely how intertwined courses, users, and roles are in Moodle. Another way of looking at the difference between authentication and enrolment is how a user will get access to a course. Please bear in mind that this is a very simplistic view and ignores supported features such as external authentication, guest access, and self-enrolment:

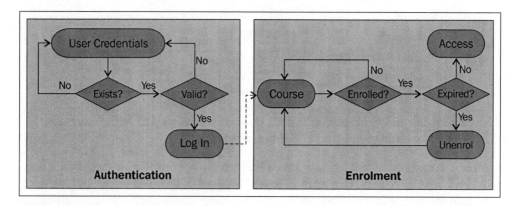

During the authentication phase, a user enters his credentials (username and password). If the account exists locally and the password is valid, he is granted access to Moodle. The next phase is enrolment. If the user is enrolled and the enrolment hasn't expired, he is granted access to the course. You will come across a more detailed version of these graphics later on but, for now, it hopefully demonstrates the difference between authentication and enrolment.

To add a user account manually, go to **Users | Accounts | Add a new user**. As with courses, we will only focus on the compulsory fields, which should be self-explanatory:

- **Username** (has to be unique)

- **New password** (if a password policy has been set, certain rules might apply)

- **First name**

- **Surname**
- **Email address**
- **City/town**
- **Select a country**

Make sure you save the account information by selecting **Update profile** at the bottom of the page. If any entered information is incorrect, Moodle will display error messages right next to the field.

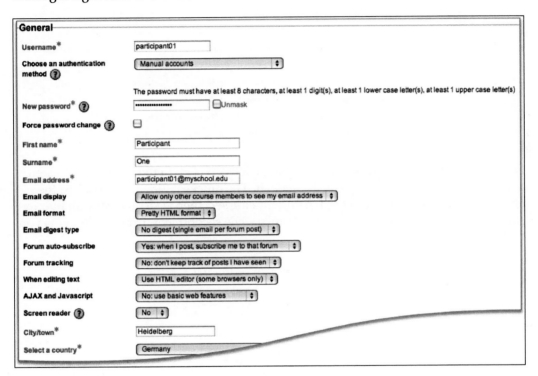

I have created a few more accounts; to see who has access to your Moodle system, go to **Users | Accounts | Browse list of users** where you will see all users. Actually, I did this via batch upload, which will be dealt with in *Chapter 5, User Management*.

| First name / Surname | Email address | City/town | Country | Last access | | |
|---|---|---|---|---|---|---|
| Alex Büchner | packt@synergy-learning.com | Belfast | United Kingdom | 51 secs | Edit | |
| participant 01 | participant01@myschool.edu | Heidelberg | United Kingdom | Never | Edit | Delete |
| participant 02 | participant02@myschool.edu | Heidelberg | United Kingdom | Never | Edit | Delete |
| participant 03 | participant03@myschool.edu | Heidelberg | United Kingdom | Never | Edit | Delete |
| participant 04 | participant04@myschool.edu | Heidelberg | United Kingdom | Never | Edit | Delete |
| participant 05 | participant05@myschool.edu | Heidelberg | United Kingdom | Never | Edit | Delete |
| participant 06 | participant06@myschool.edu | Heidelberg | United Kingdom | Never | Edit | Delete |
| participant 07 | participant07@myschool.edu | Heidelberg | United Kingdom | Never | Edit | Delete |
| participant 08 | participant08@myschool.edu | Heidelberg | United Kingdom | Never | Edit | Delete |
| participant 09 | participant09@myschool.edu | Heidelberg | United Kingdom | Never | Edit | Delete |
| participant 10 | participant10@myschool.edu | Heidelberg | United Kingdom | Never | Edit | Delete |
| Tommy Teacher | tommy@myschool.edu | Holywood | United Kingdom | Never | Edit | Delete |

Now that we have a few users on our system, let's go back to the course we created a minute ago and enrol new participants to it. The quickest way to get back to the enrolments screen is via **Courses | Add/edit courses**, then select the **Miscellaneous** category where you will see our demo course. The second icon from the left gets you to the **Enrolled users** screen.

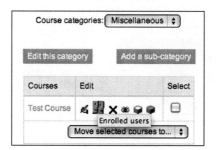

As expected, the list of enrolled users is still empty. Click on the **Enrol users** button to change this. To grant users access to the course, select the **Enrol** button beside them and close the window. In the following screenshot, two users, **participant 01** and **participant 02** have already been enrolled to the course. Two more users, **participant 03** and **participant 04** have been selected for enrolment.

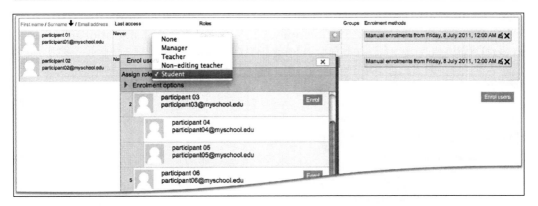

You have probably spotted the **Assign roles** drop-down menu at the top of the pop-up window. This is where you select what role the selected user has once he/she is enrolled in the course. For example, to give Tommy Teacher appropriate access to the course, we have to select the **Teacher** role first, before enrolling him to the course.

This leads nicely to the third part of the pyramid; namely, roles.

# Moodle roles

Roles define what users can or cannot see and do in your Moodle system. Moodle comes with a number of pre-defined roles—we already saw Student and Teacher—but it also allows us to create our own roles; for instance, for parents or external assessors.

Each role has a certain scope (called **context**), which is defined by a set of permissions (expressed as **capabilities**). For example, a teacher is allowed to grade an assignment whereas a student isn't. Or, a student is allowed to submit an assignment, whereas a teacher isn't.

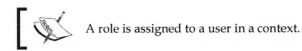

A role is assigned to a user in a context.

Okay, so what is a context? A context is a ring-fenced area in Moodle where roles can be assigned to users. A user can be assigned different roles in different contexts; where the context can be a course, a category, an activity module, a user, a block, the front page, or Moodle itself. For instance, you are assigned the **Administrator** role for the entire system, but additionally, you might be assigned the **Teacher** role in any courses you are responsible for; or, a learner will be given the **Student** role in a course, but might have been granted the **Teacher** role in a forum in order to act as a moderator.

To give you a feel of how a role is defined, let us go to **Users | Permissions**, where roles are managed and select **Define roles**. Click on the **Teacher** role and, after some general settings, you will see a (very) long list of capabilities:

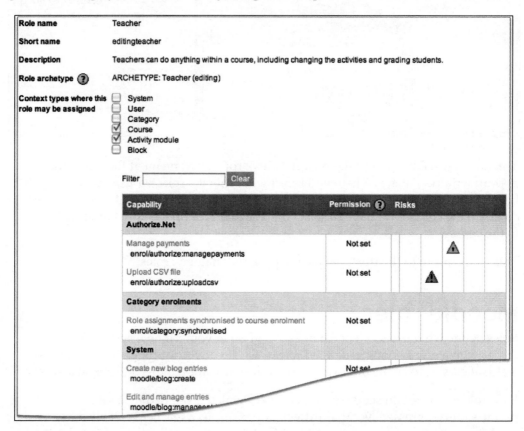

We will deal with all this in great detail in *Chapter 6, Managing Permissions: Roles and Capabilities* so don't panic!

For now, we only want to stick with the example we used throughout the chapter. Now that we know what roles are, we can slightly rephrase what we have done. Instead of saying, "we have enrolled the user **participant 01** in the demo course as a student.", we would say, "we have assigned the **Student** role to the user **participant 01** in the context of the demo course."

In fact, the term enrolment is a little bit of a legacy and goes back to the times when Moodle didn't have the customizable, fine-grained architecture of roles and permissions that it does now. One can speculate whether there are linguistic connotations between the terms *role* and *enrolment*.

# Summary

In this chapter, we have very briefly introduced the concepts of Moodle courses, users, and roles. We have also seen how central they are to Moodle and how they are linked together. Any one of these concepts simply cannot exist without the other two and this is something you should bear in mind throughout. Well, theoretically they can, but it would be rather impractical when you try to model your learning environment.

If you haven't fully understood any of the three areas, don't worry. The intention was only to provide you with a high-level overview of the three core components and to touch upon the basics.

There are dedicated chapters to each concept which will hopefully clarify any outstanding issues and will also go significantly into more detail. As we did earlier, let us start with courses.

# 4
# Course Management

Moodle stores learning resources and activities in courses, which belong to categories. In the first part of this chapter, you will learn to:

- Organize courses in categories and sub-categories
- Create and manage courses
- Deal with course requests

In the second part of the chapter, we will cover different ways of enrolling users to courses. The enrolment mechanisms covered are:

- Internal enrolment (manual, self, and guest)
- Cohort enrolment and synchronization
- Database-driven enrolment (LDAP, external databases, flat files, and IMS Enterprise files)
- Meta courses
- Payment-driven enrolment (PayPal)

## Course categories

The role of the Moodle administrator is to manage categories and courses. It is possible to delegate these tasks to non-administrators and we will deal with this in *Chapter 6, Managing Permissions: Roles and Capabilities*. Let's start with an overview of course categories.

# Course categories—an overview

Categories act as containers for courses. They can have sub-categories, which can also have sub-sub-categories, and so on. The arrangement is similar to that of files and folders on a disk drive, where courses are like files and categories are like folders. This hierarchical structure can be visualized as follows:

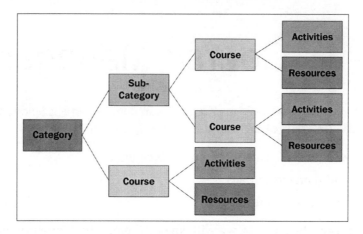

A course always belongs to a single category. It cannot belong to multiple categories and also cannot be without a category. There is one exception to this rule, namely; the front page. Internally, the front page is treated as a course that neither belongs to a category, nor can it be deleted.

There are different ways of organizing course and category hierarchies, for instance; by faculty, by subject area, by intake year, and so on. The following figure shows the positioning of the same course in hierarchies of two different categories representing the same organization.

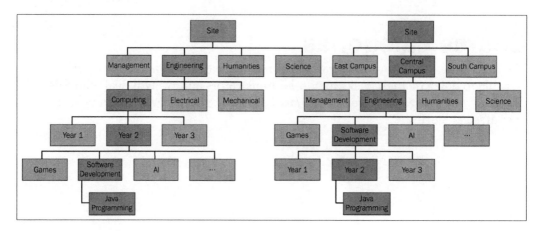

As you can see, each hierarchy represents the same information, but in different forms. There is no right or wrong way when it comes to organizing your courses. The structure depends on:

- The size of your organization
- The number of courses you offer
- The type of courses you run
- The frequency of course commencement (once a term, once a year, roll-on/ roll-off, and so on)

It is highly advisable to get the structure right the first time around, as changing it is time consuming and potentially irritating for users. Also, try to plan ahead, thinking about whether the structure will work in the future, for example; when changing from one academic year to another.

As mentioned before, different organizations apply different categorization approaches. Some examples of the category levels are:

- Campus | Department/School | Year | Subject
- Year of Entry | Topic | Subject
- Customer | Subject | Proficiency Level
- Trainer | Module

Sometimes, deep levels of categories can be off-putting, as their management is cumbersome. However, bear in mind that only you, as the administrator, will see the entire category structure. The students and teachers will only see the courses they are enrolled in or assigned to.

# Managing course categories

Once you have planned your category hierarchy structure, it is time to model the organization in Moodle. Categories are administered in **Courses | Add/edit courses**, as shown in the following screenshot:

Initially, Moodle comes with a single category called **Miscellaneous**. You can see in the previous screenshot that two courses have already been created in that category in our system.

# Adding course categories

To add a new category, click on the **Add new category** option and enter a new name in the **Category name** field. The **Parent category** drop-down menu indicates where in the hierarchy the course is located. We will leave this at **Top** and come back to it shortly. It is good practice to provide the optional **Description** (as shown in the following screenshot). You can force a theme that will be applied to all courses in the category. This requires category themes to be enabled in **Appearance | Themes | Theme settings** (see *Chapter 7, Moodle Look and Feel*).

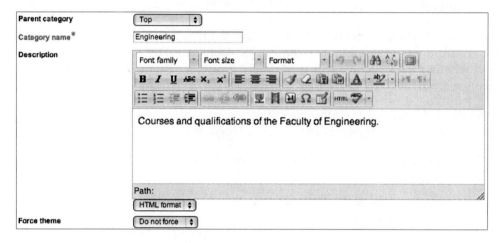

# Course sub-categories

As mentioned earlier, to improve the organization of courses, Moodle allows the creation of sub-categories. You can create a sub-category by choosing an existing category or adding a new category (as shown in the preceding screenshot), and then moving it into a parent category using the drop-down menus on the **Course categories** page. For example, to create sub-categories called **Computing-Year 1**, **Computing-Year 2**, and **Computing-Year 3** in **Computing**, first create the sub-categories and then, one by one, move them into **Computing** using the drop-down menu. Alternatively, you can select the correct parent category when you create the sub-category, as shown in the following screenshot:

| Course categories | Courses | Edit | Move category to: |
|---|---|---|---|
| Computing | 0 | ✎ ✗ ❀ ⊞ ↓ | Top |
| Computing - Year 1 | 0 | ✎ ✗ ❀ ⊞ ↓ | Computing |
| Computing - Year 2 | 0 | ✎ ✗ ❀ ⊞ ↑ ↓ | Computing |
| Computing - Year 3 | 0 | ✎ ✗ ❀ ⊞ ↑ | Computing |

# Deleting course categories

When deleting a course category using the cross symbol, any courses belonging to the category will be moved to the parent category, if one exists, or in the next top-level category. If there are no higher-level categories, the courses will be moved to the **Miscellaneous** category.

The **Miscellaneous** category can be deleted as soon as other categories are added. If the last category is deleted from the system, Moodle automatically re-creates the **Miscellaneous** category as it cannot operate without categories.

 You cannot delete courses by deleting categories. The courses must be deleted manually, one by one, or via custom scripts.

# Organizing courses

Use the up and down arrows to change the position of a course category. When you move a parent category, all the child categories will move with it. Unfortunately, there is no option to automatically arrange categories alphabetically.

You can hide categories using the eye icon. This is usually done when courses within a category are undergoing development or if you want to create an experimental area (sandpit) that is not to be seen by anybody but yourself:

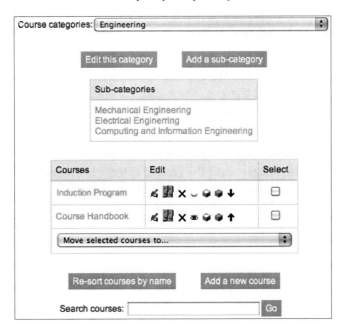

On clicking a course category, you are directed to a screen that shows all sub-categories and courses belonging to that category. When a sub-category is selected, a similar screen is shown with the content of that sub-category. When a course is selected, you are directed to the actual course content.

You also have options to carry out a number of actions. When you choose the **Edit this category** option, you can rename its title and change its description. Furthermore, the **Add a sub-category** option lets you add a new category, which Moodle positions automatically in the current category.

There are a number of icons besides each course that trigger the following actions:

| Icon name | Description |
| --- | --- |
| **Settings** | Link to course settings (see the *Creating courses* section) |
| **Assign roles** | Link to course roles (see *Chapter 6, Managing Permissions: Roles and Capabilities*) |
| **Delete** | Remove the course and its content |
| **Show/Hide** | Make the course visible/invisible to students |
| **Backup** | Link to course backup facility (see *Chapter 13, Backup and Restore*) |
| **Restore** | Link to course restore facility (see *Chapter 13, Backup and Restore*) |
| **Up/Down** | Move courses up and down; to rearrange courses alphabetically, click on the **Re-sort courses by name** button |

To move a course or a number of courses to another category, first select the course(s) and then the target course location in the **Move selected courses to...** drop-down menu.

On sites with a large number of courses, it is sometimes quicker to search for courses by their name or part thereof. After clicking on **Go**, the courses found, their respective categories, and the same course actions (as in the preceding screenshot) are shown.

When you click on **Turn editing off** in the **Settings** block, you are directed to a non-editable view of the courses and the course categories, which the students and teachers see. Lastly, you can add a new course to the current category by clicking on the **Add a new course** button, which is dealt with in the following section.

# Creating courses

Once the **Add a new course** button has been clicked from within the **Course categories** screen, Moodle directs you to the screen where course details have to be entered. We already came across this screen during earlier chapters. These details are identical to the course settings that can be edited from within a course by a user with teaching rights. The only difference is that, by default, the teacher does not have the right to change the category to which the course belongs.

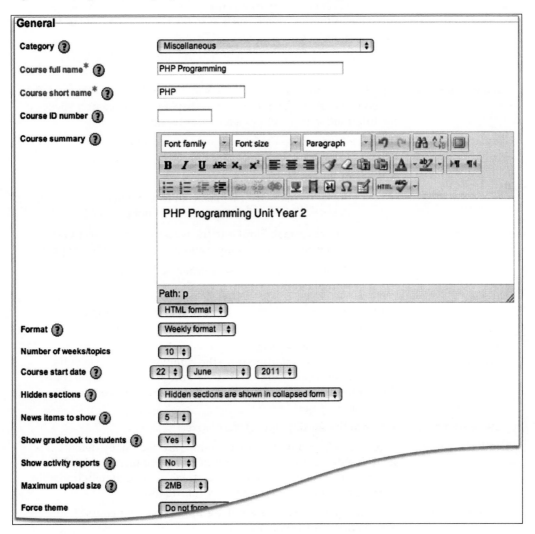

The following settings are available:

| Setting | Description |
| --- | --- |
| Category | Category to which the course belongs. |
| Course full name | The full name of the course (displayed at the top of the screen and in the course listings). |
| Course short name | Many organizations have a short form for referring to a course. This field is compulsory as it is used in several places where the full name is inappropriate (such as in the breadcrumb trail or when uploading users in batch files). |
| Course ID Number | Course code (often used in conjunction with external systems). |
| Course summary | It is recommended to write a concise paragraph that explains what the course is about. The summary is displayed when a user clicks on the information icon, and when the course appears in a list. |
| Format | By default you can select four formats for a course:<br><br>• **SCORM format**: Shows a SCORM package at the beginning of the course<br><br>• **Social format**: One main (social) forum, which is listed on the main course page, for example a notice board<br><br>• **Topics format**: Similar to the weekly format, except that each week is called a topic and no time restriction applies<br><br>• **Weekly format**: Course is organized week-by-week, with a start and a finish date<br><br>Additional course formats might have been installed in your Moodle instance. |
| Number of weeks/topics | In the weekly course format, it is the number of weeks that the course will run for, starting from the commencement date of the course. In the topics format, it is the number of topics in the course. Both of these translate to the number of boxes in the center column of the course page. |
| Course start date | Refers to the starting date of the course. |
| Hidden sections | Determines how hidden course sections are shown. By default, it is set to **Hidden sections are shown in collapsed form, invisible** to the learners. When set to **Hidden sections are completely invisible**, learners are not presented with any information. |
| News items to show | Determines how many recent items appear on your course home page in the news section (if any). |
| Show gradebook to students | Determines whether students are shown the **Grades** link in their **Settings** block. You can set this to No and still grade your activities. |

| Setting | Description |
| --- | --- |
| **Show activity reports** | Determines whether students can see their own activity reports (see *Chapter 10, Moodle Reporting*) via their profile page. |
| **Maximum upload size** | This setting limits the size of a file a user can upload into this course. |
| **Force theme** | A theme that is to be used for this course is forcibly applied through this option. Requires course themes to be enabled in **Appearance | Themes | Theme Settings** (see *Chapter 7, Moodle Look and Feel*). |

The fields **Course full name**, **Course short name** and **Course ID number** can be modified by a teacher, by default. You can disallow this by changing the appropriate permissions for the **Teacher** role by navigating to **Users | Permissions | Define roles** (search for capabilities starting with **moodle/course:change**, using the **Filter** box). We are going to deal with this in *Chapter 6, Managing Permissions: Roles and Capabilities*.

The remaining settings cover **Guest access**, **Groups**, **Availability**, **Language**, **Student progress**, and **Role renaming**, as shown in the following screenshot:

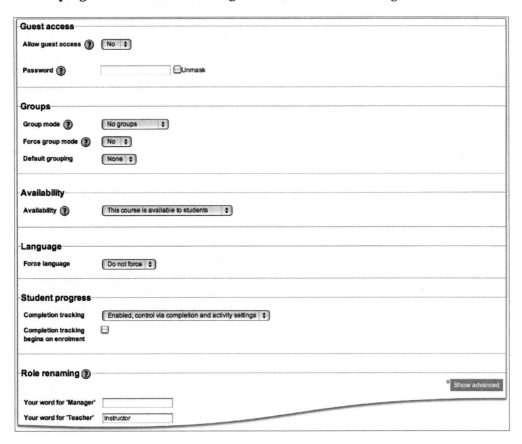

| Setting | Description |
| --- | --- |
| **Allow guest access** | Allows guest (read-only) access to the course (has to be allowed sitewide). |
| **Password** | If guest access is allowed, you can specify an optional password. |
| **Group mode** | Sets group mode of the course to:<br><br>• **No groups**: There are no sub-groups. Everyone is part of one big community or class.<br>• **Separate groups**: Users can only see their own group, while other groups are invisible.<br>• **Visible Groups**: Users work in their own group, but can also see other groups. |
| **Force group mode** | If set, the selected group mode is used for every activity and group settings in individual activities are ignored. This is useful when the same course is run multiple times with separate batches of students. Also, if group mode is forced and set to **No groups**, the **Groups** link will not be shown in the course administration menu. |
| **Default grouping** | If grouping is enabled and used within the course, the one that is to be used as default can be selected. |
| **Availability** | If set to **This course is not available to students**, the course is hidden. Except for the course teachers and administrators, no one else will be able to view it in any course listings. |
| **Force language** | If set, the selected language is used throughout the course and cannot be changed. |
| **Completion tracking** | If completion tracking is enabled sitewide, it has to be activated at course level. |
| **Completion tracking begins on enrolment** | If enabled, lets you specify whether the tracking will start automatically when students are enrolled or if it has to be initiated manually. |

Once a course has been created, you can assign users to various roles in the course (such as enrolling students and assigning teachers); we have briefly covered this in *Chapter 3, Courses, Users, and Roles* and cover roles management in the dedicated *Chapter 6, Managing Permissions: Roles and Capabilities*, and will therefore be ignoring the **Role renaming** part, for now.

For most parameters, you can specify the course default settings when creating new courses; you can find these in **Courses | Course default settings** (as shown in the following screenshot). The fields and values are identical to the ones we have described in the preceding screenshots.

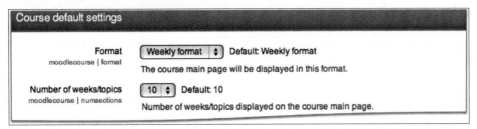

# Course requests—enabling teachers to ask for new courses

Only the administrators or course creators (or any other role with course creation rights) are allowed to create new courses. In order to streamline the procedure for requesting courses, especially in larger organizations, Moodle offers a course requesting facility. This is enabled by going to **Courses | Course request**.

You have to specify a **Default category for course requests**, which is where the courses created upon request will be placed. As the courses have to be approved, you can specify who will receive a **Course request notification**:

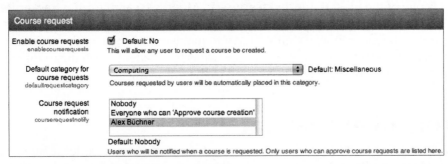

As soon as the feature is enabled, each teacher has the ability to request new courses (via the **Request a course** button on the **All courses** screen). The information that has to be provided is:

- Course short name
- Course full name
- Summary
- Reasons for course request

A new item **Courses | Pending approval** appears in the **Site administration** section. On selection, a list of requested courses is shown, which you can then **Approve** or **Reject...** by selecting the appropriate button:

| Course short name | Course full name | Requested by | Summary | Reason for course request | Action |
|---|---|---|---|---|---|
| Extreme | Extreme Programming | Tommy Teacher | eXtreme Programming Unit | Part of 2nd Year Computer Science degree | Approve Reject... |

When you approve a screen, the familiar course settings screen appears. This screen already contains the provided values of the course as well as the default category specified in the system settings. If you reject a course, a reason has to be given, which is then e-mailed to the requester.

# Creating courses and categories in bulk

So far, all operations in this chapter have been carried out manually. However, in an organization with a large number of courses and categories, this process should be automated. Unfortunately, at the time of writing (Moodle 2.1), Moodle does not yet provide a bulk upload feature for courses or categories. There is also no CLI for creating and deleting courses and categories as yet.

As this is one of the most requested features in Moodle (search for the tracker item *MDL-13114* at tracker.moodle.org), it is expected to appear sooner or later, as part of its core. In the meantime, we either have to make use of some of the scripts and patches floating around on moodle.org, or use an enrolment mechanism that also supports course creation, which is covered in the following section.

# Forms of enrolment

We have already touched upon enrolment in the introductory chapter, *Chapter 3, Courses, Users, and Roles*. Now, we will go into more detail and look at the different mechanisms that can be set up to grant users access to courses. You may recall the basic enrolment workflow presented in the earlier chapter. Let us have a look at a more complete version:

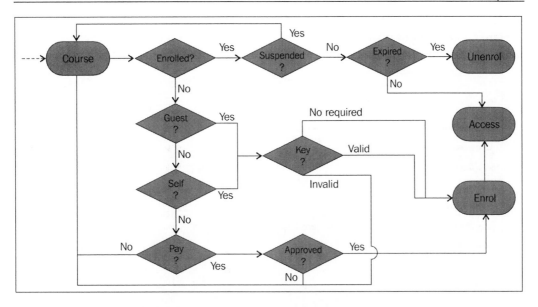

Let's start from the top-left, where the user attempts to access a course. If he/she is already enrolled and the enrolment has not expired yet, he will be granted access. If he/she is suspended, access will be denied. If he/she is not enrolled, Moodle checks if guest or self enrolment access is allowed. If either is the case, the enrolment key will be checked. If it is correct or not required, enrolment will take place and access will be granted. Lastly, it is checked if payment has been accepted and, if approved, the user will be enrolled to the courses. You might come back to this diagram when we deal with a specific enrolment mechanism.

Students need to be given access to a course before they are allowed to use it. Or, in Moodle-speak, users need to be assigned a role within the course context. They can be assigned the role automatically via cohorts or external enrolment facilities, by self-enrolling, or manually via **Users | Enrolled users** in the **Course administration** section in a course.

Granting access is performed via an enrolment mechanism. Moodle supports a wide range of enrolment options, which are discussed in the remainder of this chapter.

The actual enrolment of students does not require administrator rights, and is a task that can be performed by teachers. The role of the administrator is to set up the enrolment mechanisms available sitewide.

You can access the course enrolments configuration page via **Plugins | Enrolments | Manage enrolment plugins**. Each supported enrolment mechanism is represented by an enrolment plugin that can be enabled and configured separately:

| Available course enrolment plugins | | | | | |
|---|---|---|---|---|---|
| Name | Instances / enrolments | Enable | Up/Down | Settings | Uninstall |
| Manual enrolments | 4 / 6 | 👁 | ↓ | Settings | Uninstall |
| Guest access | 3 / 0 | 👁 | ↑ ↓ | Settings | Uninstall |
| Self enrolment | 4 / 0 | 👁 | ↑ ↓ | Settings | Uninstall |
| Cohort sync | 0 / 0 | 👁 | ↑ ↓ | Settings | Uninstall |
| LDAP enrolments | 0 / 0 | 👁 | ↑ | Settings | Uninstall |
| Category enrolments | 0 / 0 | 👁 | | Settings | Uninstall |
| External database | 0 / 0 | 👁 | | Settings | Uninstall |
| Flat file (CSV) | 0 / 0 | 👁 | | Settings | Uninstall |
| IMS Enterprise file | 0 / 0 | 👁 | | Settings | Uninstall |
| Course meta link | 0 / 0 | 👁 | | Settings | Uninstall |
| MNet remote enrolments | 0 / 0 | 👁 | | Settings | Uninstall |
| PayPal | 0 / 0 | 👁 | | Settings | Uninstall |

For every plugin, the number of instances and enrolments are shown. Each plugin can be enabled or disabled separately and multiple plugins can be enabled simultaneously (multi-enrolment). The arrangement of plugins dictates in which order user enrolments are checked when a user attempts to enter a course. It is recommended to give the plugins that are used by the majority of users higher priority over the ones that are only used sporadically, as this will benefit system performance.

All plugins have to be configured; we will deal with those settings when we cover the individual enrolment mechanisms. While it is possible to uninstall plugins, it is not recommended. If they are required at a later stage, they will have to be installed manually. It is preferable to simply leave them disabled.

> Students need to have a user account before they can be enrolled in a course.

Each enrolment type is now covered in some detail except **MNet remote enrolments** (Moodle Networking), which is covered in *Chapter 16*, *Moodle Networking* and **Category enrolments**, which is a legacy solution and has been replaced by cohort synchronization. The type of enrolment mechanism you choose depends entirely on the infrastructure you have in place, that is; where and in what format learners' enrolment data is stored.

Once an enrolment form has been set up, it has to be configured inside the course in which it will be used. Go to **Users | Enrolment methods** in **Course administration**, where you will see a list of all enrolment plugins that are active (shown) and not active (hidden) as in the following screenshot. Each enrolment method comes with a number of settings (except **Guest access**), which we will cover as part of the plugin itself.

Any non-database enrolment method that has been enabled and configured at site level can be added via the **Add method** drop-down menu (as shown in the preceding screenshot). Whether a plugin automatically appears in the list of new courses depends on the **Add instance to new courses** parameter. Some plugins, for example, **Self enrolment** or **PayPal**, can be added multiple times in the same course, which is useful if you need to support multiple roles.

# Internal enrolment

Moodle supports three types of internal enrolment:

- Manual enrolment
- Self enrolment
- Guest access

# Manual enrolment

Manual enrolment is the default enrolment mechanism when Moodle is installed. The sitewide settings are set at **Plugins | Enrolments | Manual enrolments**:

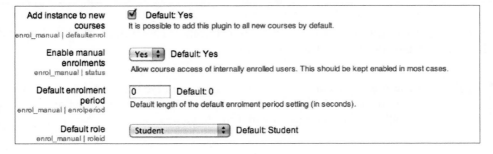

| Setting | Description |
|---|---|
| **Add instance to new course** | Every newly-created course will contain this plugin by default. |
| **Enable manual enrolments** | The plugin is enabled by default. |
| **Default enrolment period** | Default time, for how long users are enrolled in a course. Oddly, this has to be specified in seconds. |
| **Default role** | The role that manually enrolled users will have by default. |

Once the plugin has been set up, you will see a very similar-looking screen under **Users | Enrolment methods | Manual enrolments**, in the **Course administration** section. Here, a more user-friendly way to specify the default enrolment period has been implemented.

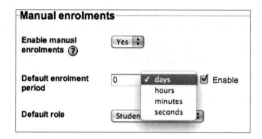

The actual enrolment of users takes place in **Users | Enrolled users**, as we have already covered in the previous chapter. What we haven't covered yet are the suspension and expiry of enrolments. You can change these via the edit symbol in the **Enrolment methods** column of your enrolled course users:

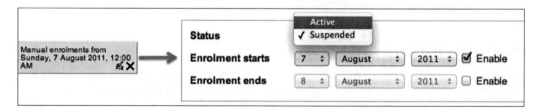

A teacher can carry out all of these steps, but often their role will be modified so that only the administrator can deal with enrolments.

If you need to unenrol multiple users from a course, select the **Enrol users** icon in the **Edit** column of **Enrolment methods** where you can select multiple users and remove them from the course.

# Self enrolment

The concept of self enrolment is relatively simple. Users choose which courses they want to participate in. A course can contain a password, known as the enrolment key. Anyone who knows this key is able to add himself or herself to a course. An opened-door icon is shown besides courses that allow guest access without a password; a closed-door icon is shown otherwise.

The enrolment key is set at course level. The teacher has to inform the students about the key and ideally limit the enrolment period to an appropriate time frame to avoid any misuse.

Once the enrolment key has been set, learners will have to enter it when they access the course for the first time. If the key is entered correctly, access will be granted, otherwise it will be denied.

 Self enrolment requires manual enrolment to be enabled.

The sitewide settings for self enrolments are found in **Plugins | Enrolments | Self enrolment**:

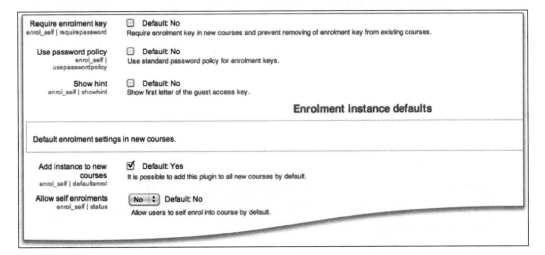

| Setting | Description |
|---|---|
| **Require enrolment key** | If enabled, new courses must have an enrolment key. Enrolment keys set in existing courses cannot be removed, but can be modified. |
| **Use password policy** | If enabled, the password policy (see *Chapter 11, Moodle Security and Privacy*) will be applied to enrolment keys. |

| Setting | Description |
|---|---|
| **Show hint** | If enabled, the first letter of the enrolment key is shown. |
| **Add instance to new courses** | Every newly created course will contain this plugin by default. |
| **Allow self enrolments** | This plugin is disabled by default and has to be enabled inside the course where it will be used. |
| **Use group enrolment keys** | If enabled, users can self enrol via a group enrolment key which also makes them a member of that group. |
| **Default role assignment** | The roles that self-enrolled users will have by default. |
| **Enrolment period** | Default time (in seconds), for how long users are enrolled in a course. |
| **Unenrol inactive after** | Number of days after which users will be unenrolled due to their inactivity. |
| **Max enrolled users** | Maximum number of users who can enrol in the course (0 means no limit). |
| **Send course welcome message** | If enabled, a welcome message will be sent to the user by e-mail. |

Once the plugin has been set up, you will be able to instantiate it at **Users | Enrolment methods | Self enrolment** inside a course:

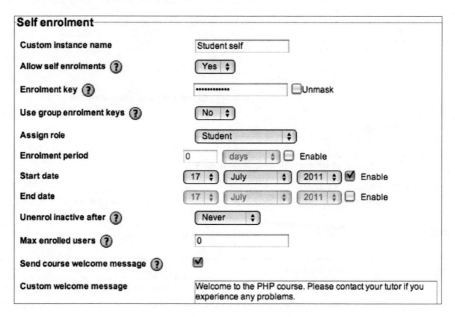

You can create multiple instances of the self enrolment method inside a course, which is why you have to assign a **Custom instance name**. This is useful if you need to give different user roles access to the same course, for instance, Students and Teachers. In addition to the sitewide default settings, you can specify a course **Start date** and **End date** as well as **Custom welcome message** which will be sent out to newly-enrolled users by e-mail.

# Guest access

Guest access can be seen as temporary enrolment. Users who are not authenticated on the system will be granted controlled (read-only) access to a course via the **Login as a guest** button on the login screen. Internally, they are allocated a temporary user ID, which will be disposed of afterwards. The guest icon is shown beside courses that allow guest access.

The sitewide settings for guest access are found in **Plugins | Enrolments | Guest access**:

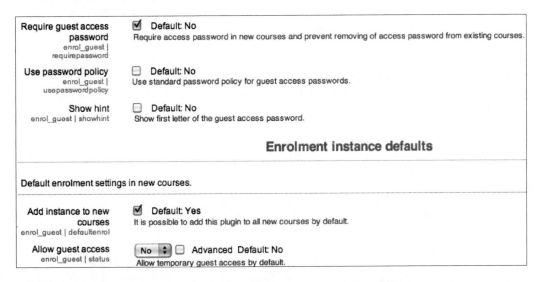

It is possible to specify a password in the course settings for guest access. If you wish to make this compulsory, select **Require guest access password**. For newly created courses, a random password will be generated (unmask the password in the course settings to view it). It will not be possible to remove guest access passwords from courses but they can be changed.

The **Enrolment instance defaults** are the same as for the manual and self enrolment methods.

The guest access enrolment method can only be allowed or disallowed inside a course. Surprisingly, the plugin does not have any local settings. Instead, you have to go to the course settings where you can set **Allow guest access** to **Yes** and also specify the **Password** already described. I guess this is for legacy reasons and might be changed in the future.

# Cohort enrolment and synchronization

Cohorts are sitewide or global groups. Once cohorts have been created and members have been allocated, it is possible to enrol an entire cohort to a course or to synchronize the membership of a cohort with that of a course.

For example, in a school you might have a class called 7c with 24 pupils. The same class has to be enrolled in eight different courses, where each course represents a subject. We only have to create the cohort 7c once and then we can enrol all members of that cohort to each course one-by-one. Alternatively, we can activate cohort synchronization with the eight courses and Moodle will take care of the rest. Also, if a new pupil joins the class, we only have to add his or her account to the cohort and the enrolment will be done automatically. Similarly, if a cohort member is removed, the pupil will be unenrolled.

Cohorts are also great for organizations where groups move together between classes, like an elementary school. Instead of moving individual users from one year to the next, you will be dealing with cohorts of users, which is less time-consuming and more fault-tolerant.

The **Cohort sync** plugin (**Plugins | Enrolments | Cohort sync**) only contains a single parameter, the **Default role** that is given to users when they are enrolled:

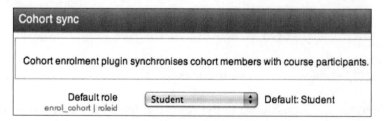

To see cohort synchronization in action, we have to create a cohort and assign some members to it. Go to **Users | Accounts | Cohorts** and add a cohort by clicking on the **Add** button. Give the cohort a **Name** (in our case, **7c**) and, from the **Context** drop-down menu, select the category in which all courses belong to class 7c. Select **System**, if that doesn't apply. The **Cohort ID** and **Description** are optional fields. Once saved, you can assign members to the cohort by clicking on **Assign**.

At the time of writing (Moodle 2.1), it is not possible to create or populate cohorts in batch mode. Similarly, it is not possible to perform either task via CLI scripts. However, as this is a highly sought-after feature, it is most likely that this functionality will be added in the near future, probably to Moodle 2.2 (search for the tracker item *MDL-26965* at `tracker.moodle.org`).

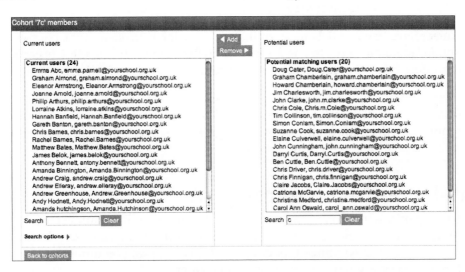

Once this has been successful, we can synchronize the cohort with our first course. This can be done as a one-off exercise or as a permanent arrangement. Inside a course, go to **Users | Enrolled users** and click on the **Enrol cohort** button:

You can see our cohort **7c** and two options.

If we click on **Enrol cohort**, all 24 users of the cohort will be enrolled and synchronized. Moodle will automatically create an enrolment method instance for the course and populate the two fields (**Cohort** and **Role**) accordingly. We could have added the enrolment method as before, but going via the list of already-enrolled users is a viable alternative. As with self enrolment, cohort sync allows multiple instances inside a course.

If we select **Enrol users**, all 24 users of the cohort will be enrolled to the course in a way similar to manual enrolment. However, no further synchronization is carried out. It is effectively the same as manually enrolling all 24 users, but in a single step.

Cohort synchronization is a great way to organize your users if you have groups that have to be enrolled in multiple courses. Whether to use one-off or permanent synchronization depends on the turnover of group members and whether courses have to be kept in sync with those groups.

# Database-driven enrolment

In larger organizations, it is common to store certain user-related information on a separate database or directory. If this information contains course-related information it should be utilized for enrolment. In doing so, you minimize the effort that is necessary when using manual enrolment.

 Unlike internal enrolment methods, database-driven enrolment cannot be configured at course-level. They are applied across the site once set up.

## LDAP

**Lightweight Directory Access Protocol (LDAP)** is an application standard for querying and modifying directory services running over TCP/IP. It is used by many organizations to store learner details and is therefore well suited as an enrolment source for Moodle.

It is necessary that the PHP LDAP extension is installed on the server for the enrolment to work. If it is not installed, Moodle will display an error message. The module also supports Microsoft's implementation of LDAP, called Active Directory, as well as OpenLDAP, an open source implementation of the authentication mechanism. Most sites that use LDAP enrolment also use LDAP for authentication, which is discussed in great detail in *Chapter 5, User Management*.

The principle of the enrolment method is rather simple, but effective. The information stored in the data source about students, teachers, and courses is mapped to the Moodle counterparts. Enrolments are updated when a user logs in. All we have to provide are the mappings.

Moodle makes a number of assumptions when working with LDAP enrolment:

- Your LDAP tree contains groups that map to courses
- Each group has multiple membership entries to map to students
- Users have a valid **ID number** field

The LDAP settings are located in **Plugins | Enrolments | LDAP enrolments**. They have been annotated with detailed explanations hence I will not repeat them; instead, I will provide additional information where applicable. If you are not sure where to locate some of the required information, contact your system administrator.

There are six sections of parameters that have to be provided:

- The **LDAP server settings** establish the connection to the directory. LDAP servers with SSL encryption are also supported
- The **Bind settings** specify details about the credentials to access the LDAP server, that is, the provided username and password
- The **Role mapping** specifies how user-related information is stored in the LDAP server. The roles, which contain a context (usually the same as the one in the server settings) and the member attribute (user IDs), have to be set. It is important to set the **Search subcontexts** correctly. If it is set to **No**, sub-contexts will not be searched, but the search is potentially faster and vice versa. Also make sure that the **User type** is set to the type of server you use, for example MS ActiveDirectory.
- The **Course enrolment settings** specify how course and module information is stored on the LDAP server. It also provides options for different forms of unenrolment.
- The **Automatic course creation settings** are a potentially time-saving feature. A course is created for each entry on the LDAP server in the category specified. To expedite the process and to guarantee consistency among courses, you should create a course with the preferred settings and use it (its course ID) as a template for all newly-created courses.

- The **Nested groups settings** let you to configure support for groups of groups inside your LDAP server

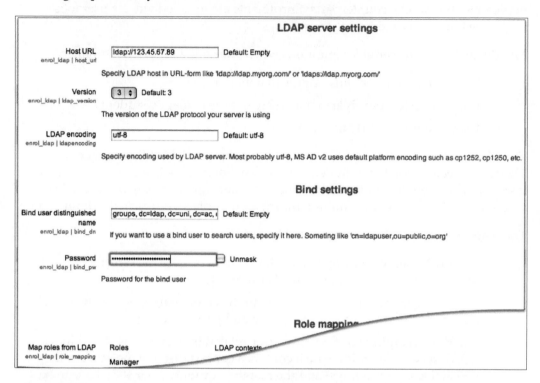

Working with LDAP enrolments often requires a degree of trial and error. It is recommended to create a number of sample courses and enrolments in a playpen, before applying the mechanism to your production server.

# External database

A lot of organizations use a **Management Information System (MIS)**, either proprietary or developed in-house, that holds information about staff and/or learners and the courses that they are enrolled in. It makes perfect sense to utilize this data for enrolment to Moodle. As all MISs use a database at their core, all we have to do is to get access to the relevant data.

The bad news is that there is a plethora of database systems out there that need to be supported, from the big players such as Oracle and Microsoft SQL Server to the lesser-known systems such as Informix or Sybase. The good news is that there exists a layer called ADO, the successor to ODBC, which does all of the hard work for us. We only have to talk to the ADO layer and its internals will deal with the rest, no matter what database it is talking to.

The database has to contain course ID and user ID fields. These two fields are compared with fields that you choose in the local course and user tables.

 Get your database administrator to set up a read-only view of the relevant data and provide you with the details. That way, your enrolment mechanism is nicely decoupled from the database itself.

To configure database-driven enrolment, go to **Plugins | Enrolments | External database**:

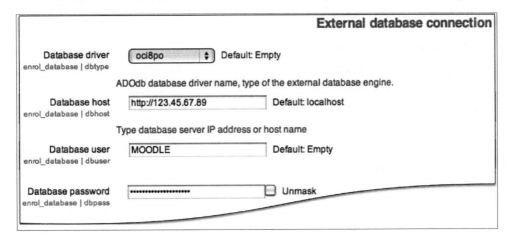

The database connection settings have been annotated on the screen with good explanations, which I will not repeat. If you are not sure where to locate some of the required information, contact your database administrator.

 Some databases, such as Oracle, are case-sensitive, that is, field names have to be provided with the correct casing for the database link to work properly.

# Flat file

Moodle provides a flat file enrolment mechanism that is configured at **Plugins |
Enrolments | Flat file (CSV)**. The method will repeatedly (via the Moodle cron
process) check for and process a specially-formatted **Comma Separated Value (CSV)**
file in the location that you specify. The format of the file is as follows:

| Field | Description |
| --- | --- |
| **operation** | add (to add an enrolment) or del (to remove it). |
| **role** | See **Flat file mapping** in the lower part of the same screen, for example student or editingteacher. |
| **idnumber (user)** | ID number of the user to be enrolled (optional). |
| **idnumber (course)** | ID number of course in which the user is to be enrolled (optional). |
| **starttime/ endtime** | Start/end time in seconds since epoch (January 1, 1970) (optional). |

Below is a sample file snippet:

```
add, teacher, 5, Psychology1
add, student, 12, Psychology1
del, student, 17, English2
add, student, 29, English, 1207008000, 1227916800
```

The start time and end time have to be provided together. To generate the numbers
since epoch, it is best to use an online converter.

In the text file settings in **Plugins | Enrolments | Flat file (CSV)**, you have to
provide the absolute file location on the server. Moodle has to be able to read
the file and delete it once it has been processed.

You can choose to send a logfile to the administrator and a notification to teachers and students. The default roles (**Flat file mapping**) can be overridden with other values, if required:

# IMS Enterprise file

The IMS Global Learning Consortium has specified an XML file format that represents student and course information. Moodle is capable of using any file that conforms to the format as its enrolment source. Like the flat file format, Moodle checks regularly for its presence and, if found, it will process the file and delete it. You can find details of the basic structure of the format at docs.moodle.org/en/ IMS_Enterprise.

The plugin is also able to create user accounts if they aren't yet created, or change user details if requested. Furthermore, new courses can also be created if they are not found on Moodle.

All other fields, including role mappings, are self-explanatory. They can be found at **Plugins | Enrolments | IMS Enterprise file**:

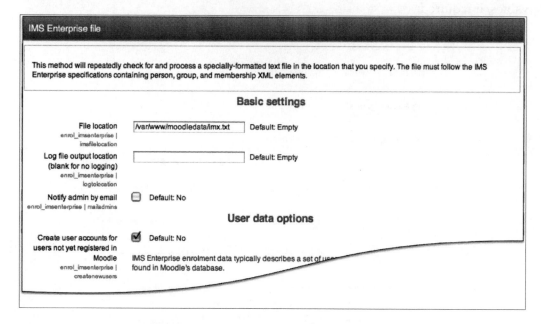

# Meta courses—sharing enrolment across courses

Meta courses are courses that take their enrolment from other courses. They populate many courses from one enrolment, or one course from many enrolments. There are two main scenarios when this is useful, which are as follows:

- When multiple courses want to share information or resources (meta course)
- When a course is part of a qualification where students have to be enrolled in a number of courses; each course is set up as a meta course

Both scenarios are depicted in the following diagram:

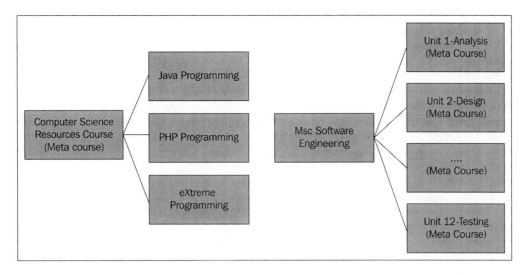

Go to **Plugins | Enrolments | Course meta link**. The list contains any roles that are not synchronized, that is, users with those roles in child courses will also be given access to their parent courses:

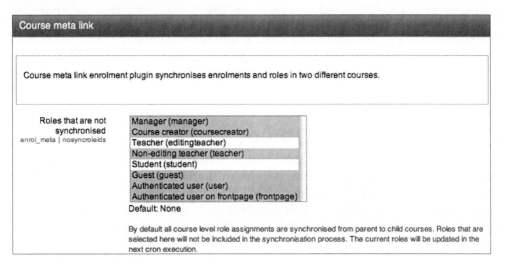

Teachers have the right to set up meta courses and to manage their dependents via the **Course meta link** under **Enrolment method** in the **Users** section of a course. While it is the role of the teacher to manage meta courses, experience has shown that the administrator is frequently asked to set these up on behalf of others.

A child course gives its enrolments to the parent course. Create a link from the parent course to the child course.

To set up the first scenario, as shown in the diagram earlier, where the meta course holds shared resources, you have to create all four courses first and create three separate course meta link instances from within the Computer Science Resources course. Each instance has to link to a separate child course:

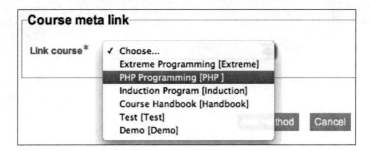

To model the second scenario, you will have to create all 13 courses (one course for MSc Software Engineering and a course for each unit) and add a course meta link method in each of the 12 parent courses to the MSc Software Engineering course.

Meta courses are a great way to synchronize users across courses. There are scenarios where you can achieve the same with cohorts and cohort synchronization. If this is the case, it is usually the preferred option to work with cohorts as they are easier to manage, especially on larger sites.

# Enrolment with payment

Moodle comes with a single enrolment plugin that enables you to set up paid courses. There exist other third-party plugins fulfilling the same purpose, but they have not been incorporated into the core Moodle system. Popular examples are Course Merchant (a fully-featured e-commerce service, dedicated to e-learning applications) and Authorize.net (a payment gateway which supports credit card and electronic check payments).

## PayPal

Moodle supports payments for courses, a feature that has been implemented as an enrolment plugin. Simply put, once the payment has been successful, the user will be enrolled in the course.

You have to specify the default cost and currency at site level (**Plugins | Enrolments | PayPal**). This amount can be overridden in the course. If the amount for any course is zero, students are not asked to pay for entry. If you enter an enrolment key in the course settings, then students will also have the option to enrol using a key. This is useful if you have a mixture of paying and non-paying learners.

You require a valid PayPal account that can be set up at no cost at `www.paypal.com`. The notification parameters indicate who is going to be sent an e-mail once a user has enrolled via a PayPal payment. The language encoding has to be set to **UTF-8/Unicode** in the **More Options** area of your PayPal account.

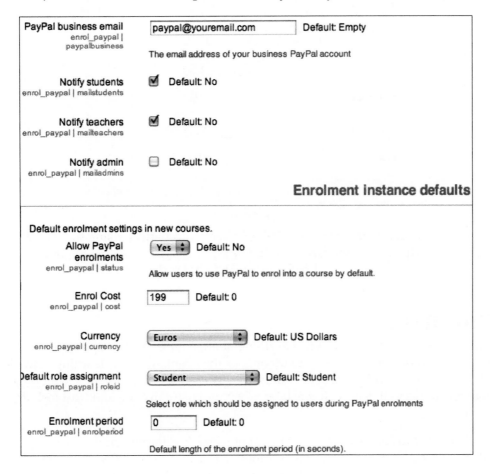

Inside a course you can create multiple instances of PayPal enrolment methods. This allows you to charge different amounts to different user groups/roles or in different currencies.

Moodle has the ability to test the PayPal enrolment mechanism using the PayPal developer sandbox. You will have to add `$CFG->usepaypalsandbox` to your `config.php` file (see *Appendix, Configuration Settings* for details).

# Summary

In this chapter, you have learned everything about courses and categories. As we have discovered, courses are key to Moodle as they contain all the learning activities and content prepared by teachers and used by students. Even Moodle's front page is a course, but we will deal with this later when we customize the look and feel of your VLE.

Closely related to courses is the enrolment of users. It is important that you understand the difference between enrolment, which we've covered in this chapter, and authentication, which we will discuss in great detail in the following chapter.

# 5
# User Management

In this chapter, you will learn how to manage users in your Moodle system. We will first look at what information is stored for each user and how we can extend their profiles. We will then perform a number of standard user actions. Finally, we will deal with a wide range of user authentication mechanisms, before concluding the chapter with a best practice section. To summarise; we will cover the following topics:

- User profiles
- Standard user actions (manual and bulk)
- Manual accounts (including batch upload)
- User authentication
- Usernames — best practice

A lot to take in, so we'd better get going!

## User profiles

Other than guest users, each user has a profile that contains information about him or her. We will first deal with the information that is stored for each user and how it is organized in Moodle.

You can view or change your own profile by clicking on your name, which is usually found in the header or footer of your system. Click on the **Edit profile** link in the **Settings** block to view the most commonly used fields. To modify the profiles of other users, click on the **Edit** link besides their name in **Users | Accounts | Browse list of users**.

# Profile fields

Moodle user profiles are divided into a number of categories, of which the first four cannot be changed via the Moodle user interface:

- **General**: Standard user fields
- **User picture**: Image of the user
- **Interests**: Tags for social networking activities
- **Optional**: Additional user information
- **User-defined**: Newly created fields

## General category

The following screenshot shows the profile fields of the **General** category:

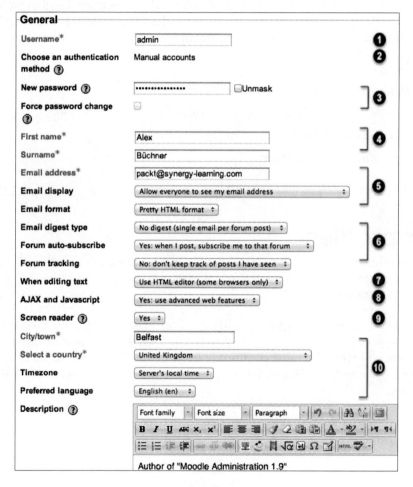

Most of these items are self-explanatory; but there are a few things you need to know about each of them. Here is a brief description of each profile element, along with tips on how to use them effectively:

1. **Username**: A unique username has to be provided. By default, only alphanumeric lowercase characters, underscores (_), hyphens (-), periods (.), or the at symbol (@) are allowed. If you also want to use other characters in usernames, such as umlauts(ˇ), you will have to enable this by turning on the **Allow extended characters in usernames** in **Security | Site Policies**. It is important to remember that you should have administrator rights to change the username.

2. **Authentication method**: This menu allows changes to the authentication method for the user. Oddly, it is possible to choose from the list of all installed authentication plugins, even though only a subset has been configured and enabled.

> Selecting the incorrect authentication method will prevent users from logging in or even delete their account completely!

3. **Password information**: A password should be provided for security reasons. If the user should change the given (default) password on their first login, the **Force password change** option has to be selected. You can unmask (show) your own password, but not that of other users. However, you can override the existing password of a user.

   If the **Password policy** is enabled (**Security | Site policies**), the password has to adhere to that policy.

> For more details on password policy, see *Chapter 11, Moodle Security and Privacy*.

4. **First name** and **Surname**: These are compulsory fields for users, for which diacritical marks are fully supported.

5. **E-mail information**: By default, there are three entries dictating how Moodle and other users can communicate with the current user through e-mail:

| | |
|---|---|
| **Email address** | This is a compulsory field and has to be unique in Moodle. It is important that the address is correct, as Moodle makes regular use of it; for example, to notify when new posts have been added to a forum. |
| **Email display** | Choices can be made as to who exactly can see the user's e-mail address. The choices are: **Hide my email address from everyone**, **Allow everyone to see my email address**, and **Allow only other course members to see my email address**. Administrators and teachers (with editing rights) will always be able to see e-mail addresses, even if they are hidden. |
| **Email format** | This setting dictates whether e-mails sent from Moodle is formatted using pretty HTML (default) or is sent in plain text. Most modern e-mail clients have the ability to receive and display HTML content. |

6. **Forum information**: There are three forum-related entries:

| | |
|---|---|
| **Email digest type** | This setting determines how a user receives posts from forums to which a subscription exists. There are three possible choices, which are: **No digest (single email per forum post)**, which is the default, **Complete (daily e-mail with full posts)**, or **Subjects (daily e-mail with subjects only)**. |
| **Forum auto-subscribe** | This setting dictates whether a user is automatically subscribed to forums in which he or she posts. |
| **Forum tracking** | If enabled, posts that have not yet been read will be highlighted, which improves forum navigation. |

7. **When editing text**: This option determines whether to use plain text or the native HTML text editor in Moodle. It can usually be left to **Use HTML editor (some browsers only)**, which allows for text formatting options. If a user is experiencing difficulties when editing text, the setting should be changed to **Use standard web forms**.

8. **AJAX and JavaScript**: Moodle has a drag-and-drop interface that is used at various places making use of AJAX and JavaScript; for example, arranging items in courses. If a user's web browser does not support these technologies (older or unsupported browsers, some Linux browsers, and browsers on handheld devices and games consoles have occasional problems with this new technology), the option should be set to **No: use basic web features**.

9. **Screen reader**: If enabled, pages will be rendered accessible via screen readers that are used by visually-impaired users.

 For more information on screen readers, see the *Accessibility* section in *Chapter 7, Moodle Look and Feel*.

10. **Location, Timezone**, and **Language**: **City/town** and **Country** are used to further identify users by geographical location. They are all compulsory fields.

    **Timezone** is used to convert time-related messages on the system (such as assignment deadlines) from the local time (typically, the server time) to the correct time in whichever zone the user has selected. This is necessary as your users may be geographically spread across a number of time zones. The default city, country and time zone can be specified in **Location | Location settings**.

    The default language of the system is shown and can be changed to the **Preferred language** of the user. We will deal with localization in *Chapter 9, Moodle Configuration*.

Also, a **Description** field is shown, which is used to provide additional information about the user. As an administrator, you can leave the field empty. However, when a user logs in to his or her profile, populating the field is compulsory.

A number of additional options might appear in the user's profile, for example; **Preferred theme** or **Email charset**, but this requires settings to be changed elsewhere. We will mention these when the respective topics arise.

# User picture category

The second category is called **User picture** and, as the name suggests, deals with the image attached to a user profile.

To upload a new picture, click on the **Choose a file...** button and upload or select the image from the file picker. The image cannot be larger than the maximum size listed (here, 2 MB) or it will not be uploaded. If your image is too large, we recommend reducing its size to a minimum of 100x100 pixels. Supported formats are JPG and PNG, however, be careful with transparent backgrounds as they are not supported by older browsers.

The **Picture description** field is used as alt tag, to conform to accessibility guidelines.

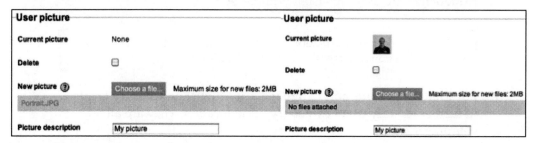

Once a picture has been assigned, it will be shown in place of the **None** label. To remove the picture, check the **Delete** checkbox and the picture will be removed when the profile information is updated.

Moodle will automatically crop the image to a square and resize it to 100 x 100 pixels for the larger view, and 35 x 35 pixels for the smaller thumbnail view.

Both of these small images are created by Moodle in the upload process, which also reduces the file size to around 4K. All uploaded user pictures can be viewed by a logged-in administrator via the URL `<moodleurl>/userpix`.

If you suspect that your learners are likely to misuse this feature by uploading unsuitable pictures, you can disallow the functionality. Go to **Security | Site policies** and check the **Disable user profile images** checkbox. Bear in mind that once this feature is disabled, pictures cannot be assigned to any users (except the administrator), nor will it be possible for teachers to represent groups in courses with images.

# Interests category

Interests, such as hobbies or professional activities, can be entered and have to be separated by commas. The given **List of interests** represents tags, which are used by Moodle activities such as the **Flickr** and **Youtube** blocks. You can find more information about tagging at `docs.moodle.org/en/Tags` and in the *Collaboration* section in *Chapter 9, Moodle Configuration*.

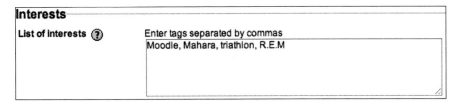

## Optional category

More personal details are grouped under the **Optional** category:

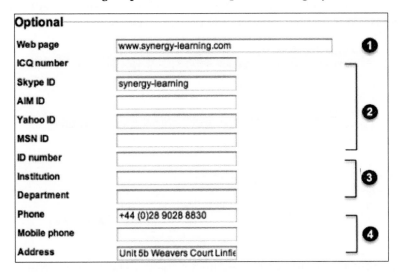

1. **Web page**: This is the URL of the user's web or home page.
2. **Messenger Information**: Moodle supports a range of popular messenger services. These are: ICQ, Skype, AOL Instant Messenger (AIM), Yahoo Messenger, and Microsoft's MSN. When entering any of the services' IDs, Moodle will make use of their functionalities, if possible (for instance, displaying the user's Skype status information in their profile).
3. **ID number, Institution, and Department**: This contains IDs of students or staff and information on school and department.
4. **Contact Details**: It has the user's phone numbers and postal address.

Some organizations rename some of these fields to ones that are required in their setup. For more information on how to do this, see the *Localization* section in *Chapter 9, Moodle Configuration*.

# Creating user-defined profile fields

Moodle allows new arbitrary fields to be added to the user profile. This feature can be found in **Users | Accounts | User profile fields**.

## Profile categories

The profile fields are organized into categories (**General**, **User picture**, **Interests**, and **Optional**). Additional categories can be created and user-defined fields can then be placed within this new categories. A default category called **Other fields** is already present, which can be deleted or renamed via the standard Moodle icons. To create a new category, click on the **Create a new profile category** button.

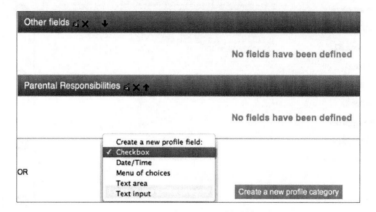

You will be asked to provide a unique category name. The category will be displayed at the bottom of the user profile, once profile fields have been added to the category.

## Profile fields

Once a category has been created, five types of profile fields can be added to Moodle via the **Create a new profile field** pull-down menu:

- **Checkbox** (values can be true or false/yes or no/on or off)
- **Date/Time** (date and an optional time field)
- **Menu of choices** (selection of a value from a pre-defined list)
- **Text area** (multiline formatted text)
- **Text input** (single line of text or a number)

Once you have chosen your field type, you will be taken to a settings screen for that field. It has two sections. The **Common settings** section deals with parameters that apply to all fields and the **Specific settings** section deals with parameters that apply only to the chosen field type.

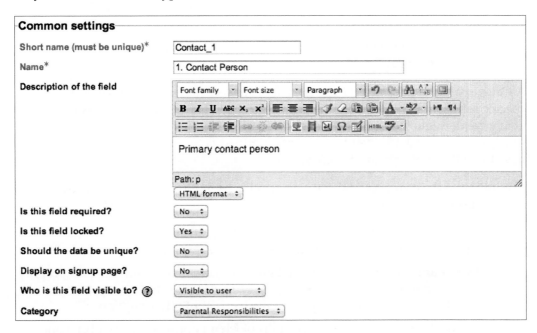

The **Short name** is a unique identifier of the field that is accompanied by the **Name** textbox, in which the name specified is the label displayed in the profile. An optional description of the field can be given in **Description of the field**.

If the field is to be made compulsory, the **Is this field required?** option has to be set to **Yes**. The field can be locked. That is, the user can be prevented from modifying it. If the value entered needs to be unique, the **Should the data be unique?** field must be changed accordingly.

When self-registration is enabled, a number of default fields have to be provided at signup. If the new field is also to be displayed on the signup page, the **Display on signup page?** option has to be set to **Yes**. This can be very useful in a commercial training setting, when additional information such as the address of the learner or previous qualifications are required.

The custom field can be given one of the following three visibility settings:

- The **Not visible** setting is typically set by an administrator who wants to hold private data on the users

- The **Visible to user** setting is normally selected for fields that hold sensitive information

- The **Visible to everyone** setting is used for any other type of information This is the default setting.

A **Category** has to be selected from the list of created values entered before the specific settings can be provided for each field type. It is only possible to select newly-created categories; unfortunately, default categories cannot be selected. For example, if you wish to extend the existing address field with a zip code, you will have to do this in a separate category.

In addition to the common field settings, specific settings also need to be provided for each profile field type:

- **Checkbox**: This type has only a single setting. It specifies whether the checkbox will be checked by default in new user profiles, or not.

- **Date/Time**: The **Start year** (by default, the current year) and the **End year** (by default, the current year + 30) have to be specified. Additionally, an optional time field can be included by checking the **include time?** option.

- **Menu of Choices**: For this type, a list of **Menu options (one per line)** and an optional **Default value** have to be provided. The list consists of a single item per line. In the following screenshot, three options (**Father, Mother,** and **Carer**) have been entered, with **Mother** being the default value:

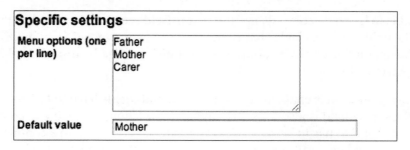

If you wish to allow empty values, leave the first entry empty.

- **Text Area**: This type allows users to define a **Default value** in a free-form textbox.

- **Text Input**: For this type, a **Default value**, the **Display size** (size of textbox), and the **Maximum length** have to be provided. Additionally, it has to be specified if the field is a password field, which will lead to masking being turned on, if enabled.

  The **Link** field lets you create dynamic links, where a $$ represents the parameter that will be replaced with the entered text. In the following screenshot, we have specified **http://twitter.com/$$**. The transformed link will be shown in the user profile. The **Link target** specifies where this link will be opened once selected.

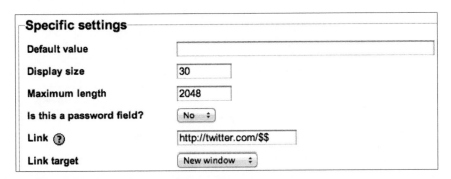

Once all the required fields have been added, the order in which they will be displayed in the user profile can be changed by using the up and down arrows, as shown in the following screenshot:

| Parental Responsibilities | |
| --- | --- |
| Profile field | Edit |
| 1. Contact Person | ✍ ✕ ↓ |
| Relationship | ✍ ✕ ↑ ↓ |
| Parent at work? | ✍ ✕ ↑ ↓ |
| Comment | ✍ ✕ ↑ ↓ |
| Expiry date | ✍ ✕ ↑ ↓ |
| Twitter ID | ✍ ✕ ↑ |

These fields will now be shown in the user profile in the same way as generic Moodle fields:

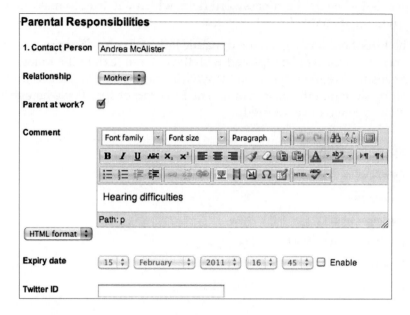

# Standard user actions

So far, you have learned what type of user information Moodle holds and how to extend the information that is stored in each profile. Now, it is time to work with existing users on your system.

## Browsing users

The quickest way to get access to your Moodle users is via **Users | Accounts | Browse list of users**. Initially, a list of users is displayed (as in the following screenshot), ordered by **First name**. Thirty users are shown at a time and, if applicable, you can navigate via the **(Next)** and **(Previous)** links or jump directly to another page by clicking on the respective number. Each column can be sorted in ascending or descending order by clicking on the column header:

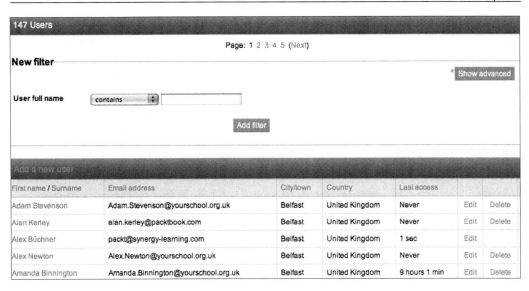

You can view an individual's profile information by clicking on a user's name in the first column. Here, you are looking at your own (admin) profile and not the profile of another user:

The profile provides detailed information about the user. Hyperlinks are provided to e-mail, web pages, and some messaging services. For instance, in the preceding screenshot a link is provided to launch Skype, indicating that the user is currently unavailable.

When you look at the profile of another user account, you will see a **Login as** link in the **Settings** block, which lets you masquerade as another user. This is useful when tracking down issues, which you cannot locate as administrator. To view all user profile fields of a user or to modify any of them, as discussed earlier, click on the **Edit profile** link.

You can specify which information about a user is shown on a user's public profile and thus is visible to others. Go to **Users | Permissions | User policies** and select the fields that should not be shown in the **Hide user fields** list.

To delete a user, go back to the user list and click on the **Delete** link in the right-hand column. A confirmation screen has to be answered before the user is irreversibly removed from Moodle. Actually, the user is irreversibly removed only from Moodle's user interface. Internally, the user is still retained in the database with the deleted flag turned on. This is necessary so that certain contributions of that user don't disappear, for instance, forum posts.

# Filtering users

Very often, we may be required to search for a particular user or for a number of users. Moodle provides a very powerful and flexible filtering mechanism to narrow down the list of displayed users. In basic mode, you can filter by full name, that is, first name and last name combined. The following filter operations are available, all of which are case-insensitive:

| Filter operation | Description |
| --- | --- |
| **contains** | The provided text has to be contained in the field |
| **doesn't contain** | Opposite of contains |
| **is equal to** | The provided text has to be the same as the value of the field |
| **starts with** | The field has to begin with the provided text |
| **ends with** | The field has to end with the provided text |
| **is empty** | The field has to be empty |

For example, when adding a filter **Full name starts with "chr"**, all users whose name begins with "chr" are displayed. See the following screenshot:

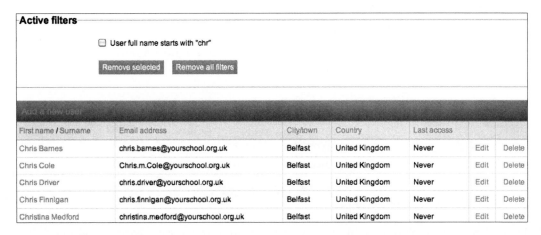

You can see at the top that the added filter is now active. This becomes more useful once multiple filters have been added, which is done in the advanced mode (the **Show Advanced** button). Now, we have the ability to apply filters to a wide range of fields:

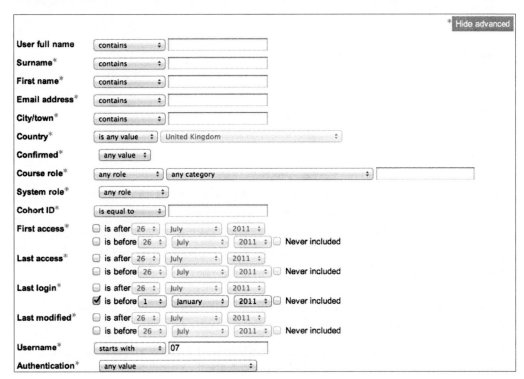

For instance, in the preceding screenshot, we were looking for all users whose username starts with **07**, (our naming scheme starts with the year of entry) and who haven't used the system this year. Using this mechanism, it is possible to add as many filters as required.

Every time a filter is added, it will be shown in the **Active filters** frame and will be applied to the user data in Moodle:

Here, three self-explanatory filters have been added. It is now possible to either delete individual filters (select the filter and click on the **Remove selected** button) or **Remove all filters**.

The filter criteria for text fields have been described earlier in this section. Depending on the field type, there are a number of additional operations that can be used, as listed in the following table:

| Filter Operation | Field Type | Description |
| --- | --- | --- |
| **is any value** | Lists | All values are acceptable; filter is disabled |
| **is equal to** | Lists | List value has to be the same as the one selected. |
| **isn't equal to** | Lists | Opposite of **is equal to**. |
| **any value** | Yes/No | Value can be either **Yes** or **No**; filter is disabled. |
| **Yes** | Yes/No | Value has to be **Yes**. |
| **No** | Yes/No | Value has to be **No**. |
| **is defined** | Profile fields | The field has to be defined for the user. |
| **isn't defined** | Profile fields | Opposite of **is defined**. |
| **is after** | Date | All dates after specified day, month, and year. |
| **is before** | Date | All dates before specified day, month, and year. |
| **Never included** | Date | Users who have never logged in. |

The **Authentication** criterion offers a selection of all authentication methods supported. We will deal with these later in the chapter.

If user profile fields have been specified, an additional **Profile** criterion is shown, offering a choice of all user-defined fields (as specified earlier).

The current filter settings are saved and can be used the next time you log in. Not only that, they are also saved for bulk uploading, which is covered next.

# Bulk user actions

There are several actions that Moodle allows you to take on many users at a time. You can:

- Confirm registration
- Send a bulk message
- Delete users
- Display a summary of their profile
- Download their profile details to a file
- Force a password change

As an administrator, you can apply these operations, which Moodle calls bulk user actions. They are accessed at **Users | Accounts | Bulk user actions**.

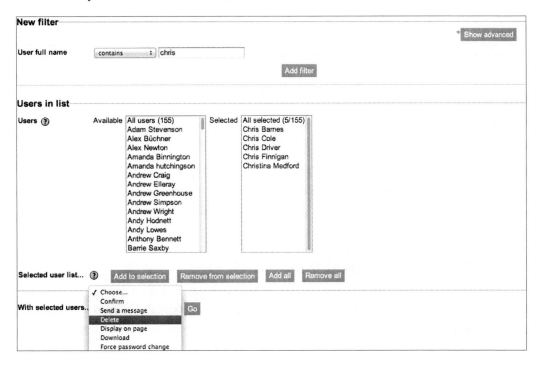

The screen contains two main parts. The first part is the familiar filter and is identical to the one in the **Browse list of users** submenu. Interestingly, filters that are already created will also be displayed in this screen, as they have been saved.

The second part displays the users that match the specified filter criteria in the **Available** list. Before you can do anything with the users, you will have to move them into the **Selected** list using the **Add to selection** button. In the preceding screenshot, five users have been moved across. To move them back to the **Available** list, select the users and press the **Remove from selection** button. Two shortcut buttons exist, which allow you to **Add all** users from the **Available** list to the **Selected** list and to **Remove all** users (move them in the opposite direction).

The advantage of this approach is that you can apply a number of filters in succession and select the respective users. For example, if you wish to select all users from two entry years, you can create a **User full name starts with "07"** filter for all usernames starting with "07" and select all the users that show up in the results. You can then delete the filter and create another filter for all usernames starting with "08". For the theorists amongst you, this is the equivalent of a logical UNION operator.

When the **Go** button for the **With selected users...** drop-down menu is clicked, the operation selected will be performed on the users from the **Selected** list. The available operations are shown in the following table:

| Action | Description |
| --- | --- |
| **Confirm** | After a confirmation screen, pending user accounts will be confirmed. This is only applicable to self-registrations. |
| **Send a message** | You are asked to write a message body, which will be sent to the selected users. |
| **Delete** | After a confirmation screen, users will be irreversibly removed from the system (see information about user deletion in the *Browsing users* section discussed earlier). |
| **Display on page** | User information is shown on screen. The fields displayed are **Full name**, **Email address**, **City/town**, **Country**, and **Last access**. |
| **Download** | You can choose between three download formats:<br><br>• **Text**: Comma-separated text file<br>• **ODS**: Open Document Format<br>• **Excel**: Microsoft Excel<br><br>The fields that are included are (Moodle's internal user) **id**, **username**, **email**, **firstname**, **lastname**, **idnumber**, **city**, and **country**. |
| **Force password change** | Users will have to change their password next time they log in to Moodle. |

Now that we know how to deal with existing users, let's have a look at how they are added to the system.

# Manual accounts

There are two ways for users to manually access an existing Moodle system and its courses. This can be done by:

- Adding individual users
- Uploading users in bulk

You will learn how to perform and support each type in the two sections that follow.

## Adding individual users

To add user accounts manually, go to **Users | Accounts | Add a new user**. You will be confronted with the same screen as when you edit a user's profile.

You should avoid adding individual users as much as possible as it is a very time-consuming, cumbersome, and potentially error-prone procedure. However, there are situations when you cannot avoid it. For example, when a pupil joins the school halfway through the term.

If you have more than one user to add, use Moodle's batch uploading facility, which we will look at next.

## Bulk uploading and updating users and their pictures

Uploading users in bulk allows you to import multiple user accounts from a text file or you can update user accounts that already exist in your system.

Student information is often available in existing applications, such as the internal student management information system, which can export data to an Excel spreadsheet or directly to a text file.

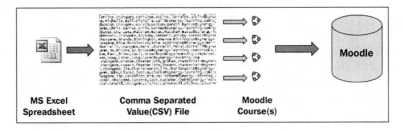

| MS Excel Spreadsheet | Comma Separated Value(CSV) File | Moodle Course(s) |

You will find good documentation on uploading and updating users in batch mode at `docs.moodle.org/en/admin/uploaduser`.

# Text file format

Before uploading users, you have to generate a text file that must conform to a certain format. Its general format is that of a **Comma Separated Value (CSV)** file, which is a flat text file format. You can create such a CSV file in Excel or any other spreadsheet application. Use the first row to provide field names, and then fill in each cell with the required data. Then save the file as CSV, making sure that you specify that the top row contains field names.

The format of a text file has to be as follows:

- Each line of the file must contain a single record
- Each record must be a series of data separated by commas or other delimiters
- The first record of the file must contain the list of field names that will define the format of the rest of the file.

An example of a valid input file is as follows:

```
username, password, firstname, lastname, email
galmond, pwd, Graham, Almond, graham.almond@yourschool.ac.uk
earmstrong, pwd, Eleanor, Armstrong, eleanor.armstrong@yourschool.ac.uk
jarnold, pwd, Joanne, Arnold, joanne.arnold@yourschool.ac.uk
```

The first line contains the list of fields that is provided, while the remaining three lines represent individual users to be uploaded.

Moodle's upload function supports five types of data fields:

- **Required**: Compulsory fields which have to be included
- **Optional**: If no value is provided, specified default values will be used
- **Custom**: User-defined profile fields
- **Enrolment**: Deals with courses, roles, and groups
- **Special**: Used for changing or removing users

## Required fields

When adding new users, only the `firstname` and `lastname` are compulsory. When updating records, only the `username` is required. You might recall that the user profile has a few more compulsory fields, such as the e-mail address. If these fields are not provided, a default value has to be specified via a template. We will deal with this a little later.

The sample file is an example of a valid input file containing five fields, including the required `firstname` and `lastname`.

# Optional fields

Optional fields do not have to be specified. If they are not included in the text file, default values are taken, if present. These are listed as follows:

| Field | Values |
|---|---|
| address | Text |
| ajax | 0: No, 1: Yes |
| auth | Text (from existing list) |
| autosubscribe | 0: No, 1: Yes |
| city | Text |
| country | Text (from existing list) — two letter code in capitals |
| department | Text |
| description | Text |
| emailstop | 0: enabled, 1: disabled |
| htmleditor | 0: standard web forms, 1: HTML Editor |
| icq | Text |
| idnumber | Text |
| institution | Text |
| lang | Text (from existing list) |
| maildisplay | 0: Hide, 1: Allow everyone, 2: Allow course members |
| mailformat | 0: Pretty, 1: Plain |
| password | Text |
| phone1 | Text |
| phone2 | Text |
| timezone | Text (from existing list) |
| url | Text |

Let us assume that the default city has been set to Birmingham. In order to override the field for users who are not living in the default town, the following sample file can be used:

```
username, password, firstname, lastname, city, email
galmond, changeme, Graham, Almond, London, graham.almond@yourschool.
ac.uk
earmstrong, changeme, Eleanor, Armstrong, , eleanor.armstrong@
yourschool.ac.uk
jarnold, changeme, Joanne, Arnold, York, joanne.arnold@yourschool.
ac.uk
```

In the preceding sample file, a city field has been added. After uploading the file, city for Graham Almond is set to London and that for Joanne Arnold is set to York. The city for Eleanor Armstrong has been left empty and will be set to the default value of Birmingham.

It is important to include empty fields in the data when the default setting is used. It must be left empty even if it is the last field in each record. An empty field is represented by two consecutive commas (as shown in the preceding sample file).

If you set the password to changeme, the user will be forced to change the password when they log in for the first time. This only works if the password policy has been deactivated. A better way to do this is by using the **Force password change** in **Bulk user actions**.

If no password is set, Moodle will generate one and send out a welcome e-mail.

In fields that have numeric values, the options are numbered in the same order as they appear in the Moodle interface; the numbering starts with 0. For instance, **Email display** allows the following settings:

0.  **Hide my email address from everyone**
1.  **Allow everyone to see my email address**
2.  **Allow only other course members to see my email address**

For Boolean fields, such as **Forum auto-subscribe,** use 1 for Yes and 0 for No.

If any fields in your upload file contain commas (for example, in the **Description**), you have to encode them as &#44; the upload function will automatically convert these back to commas.

## Custom fields

Any user-defined fields you specify (in our case, the ones for parental responsibilities) can also be used as part of the batch upload process. Each field has to be preceded by profile_field_, for instance, the field representing the Twitter ID would be called profile_field_twitter.

Custom fields are treated in the same way as optional fields. If they are specified, the values are taken, otherwise default values will be used, if present.

# Enrolment fields

Enrolment fields allow you to assign roles to users, that is, you can enrol them to courses and also groups. Groups are created by teachers in courses. Roles will be covered in great detail in *Chapter 6, Managing Permissions: Roles and Capabilities.*

Each course has to be specified separately by `course1`, `course2`, `course3`, and so on. The course name is the short name of the course. Each corresponding type, role, and group has to have the same postfix, that is; `role1` and `group1` has to correspond to `course1`.

It is possible to set the role of a user in a course. Each role has a role short name and a role ID, either of which can be specified. If the type is left blank, or if no course is specified, the user will be enrolled as Student.

If you want to assign users to groups in a course (`group1` in `course1`, `group2` in `course2`, and so on) you have to specify the group name or ID. If a specified group does not exist, it will be created automatically.

The following example demonstrates some of the enrolment features:

```
username, course1, role1, course2
galmond, Advanced, editingteacher, Staff
earmstrong, Advanced, examiner, Staff
jarnold, Basic, 3, Staff
```

As before, the first line specifies the fields in the file. `course1` and its corresponding `role1` as well as `course2` are optional enrolment fields. `Graham Almond` will be assigned the `editingteacher` role in the `Advanced` course and a `student` role in the `Staff` course (no role has been specified and hence the default is set). `Eleanor Armstrong` will be assigned the `examiner` role and also a `student` role in the `Staff` course. `Joanne Arnold` will be an `editingteacher` (the role ID is 3) in the `Basic` course and a `student` in the course labeled `Staff`.

# Special fields

Two special fields are supported that allow you to change user names or delete users. The former is represented with the field name `oldusername`, while latter is called `deleted`.

# Uploading users

In order to upload or update users in batch mode, go to **Users | Accounts | Upload users**:

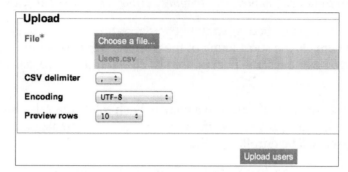

The following settings are available:

| Setting | Description |
| --- | --- |
| **File** | The name of the comma-delimited text file selected from the file picker. |
| **CSV delimiter** | Specify whether the delimiter is a comma (default), semi-colon, colon, or tab. In most European locales, for instance, German, French, and Dutch, the default delimiter is a semi-colon! |
| **Encoding** | Encoding scheme of your uploaded file, which specifies the locale in which it has been saved (default is **UTF-8**). |
| **Preview rows** | The number of rows that will be displayed on the preview screen. |

Once this screen has been confirmed, you will see the following four sections:

- A preview of specified number of rows that will be uploaded. Records to be skipped will not be shown.
- **Settings**, which will depend on the selected upload type.
- All user fields for which default values can be set.
- Any user-defined fields grouped by category, if present.

| CSV line | username | course1 | role1 | course2 | Status |
|---|---|---|---|---|---|
| 2 | galmond | Advanced | editingteacher | Staff | |
| 3 | earmstrong | Advanced | examiner | Staff | |
| 4 | jarnold | Basic | 3 | Staff | |

**Settings**

| | |
|---|---|
| Upload type | Add new only, skip existing users |
| New user password | Create password if needed |
| Existing user details | No changes |
| Existing user password | No changes |
| Allow renames | No |
| Allow deletes | No |
| Prevent email address duplicates | Yes |
| Standardise usernames | Yes |
| Select for bulk operations | No |

Bear in mind that not all settings exist for all upload types; they will remain grayed out if they are not applicable. The following settings have to be applied:

| Setting | Description |
|---|---|
| **Upload type** | There are four self-explanatory upload types:<br><br>• **Add new only, skip existing users**<br>• **Add all, append number to usernames if needed**<br>• **Add new and update existing users**<br>• **Update existing users only** |
| **New user password** | Moodle either requires a password to be in the file (**Field required in file**) or the upload process will generate a password automatically if none is specified (**Create password if needed**). This has to be changed by the user via the lost password mechanism. |
| **Existing user details** | Specifies what is done with the existing user details when an account is updated. The options are:<br><br>• **No changes**<br>• **Override with file**<br>• **Override with file and defaults**<br>• **Fill in missing [fields] from file and defaults** |

| Setting | Description |
|---------|-------------|
| Existing user password | Specifies what is done with users' passwords when the user details are updated. The password can either be left unchanged (**No changes**) or be overridden (**Update**). |
| Force password change | This item will only appear if there are empty or weak passwords in the CSV file. The options are **Users having a weak password**, **None**, and **All**. |
| Allow renames | Specifies whether changing of usernames is allowed. This only applies to the special field `oldusername`. |
| Allow deletes | Specifies whether removing of users is allowed. This only applies to the special field `deleted`. |
| Prevent email address duplicates | Specifies whether the same e-mail address is allowed for multiple users. This should be set to **Yes** to avoid any conflicts. |
| Standardise usernames | Removes any invalid characters from usernames (extended characters, unless allowed, as well as spaces) and ensures that all characters are lowercase. |
| Select for bulk operations | You can specify if **New users**, **Updated users** or **All users** should be selected for bulk operations. You will see the respective names in the **Selected** list for **Bulk user actions**. |

# Setting default values and templates

As mentioned earlier, the Moodle batch upload function supports default values that are used instead of optional fields, if no value has been set. This includes all the values in the user profile that can be uploaded and also any user-defined custom fields.

Each text-based field can be populated using a template. This is useful for some fields, for instance; the URL of students' websites, and is compulsory for required fields if not specified in the CSV file. For example, `username` and `email`. Moodle will warn you if the latter is the case. For example, in the following screenshot, the **Username** has not been provided which is indicated by the red warning message:

**Default values**

| Username* | Required. You may use template syntax here (%l = lastname, %f = firstname, %u = username). See help for details and examples. |
|-----------|---------------------------------------------------------------------------------------------------------------------------------|
| Email display | Allow only other course members to see my email address |

The template (or pattern) will create a value based on the values of other fields and the standard characters you specify. For example, if the username should be the first name of a user, followed by a period, and then the surname; the template you will have to specify would look like this: `%f.%l`.

Four replacement values can be used:

- `%f` will be replaced by the `firstname`
- `%l` will be replaced by the `lastname`
- `%u` will be replaced by the `username`
- `%%` will be replaced by `%` (required if you need a percentage sign in the generated text)

Between the `%` sign and any of the three code letters (`%l`, `%f` and `%u`), the following four modifiers are allowed:

- `-`: value will be converted to lowercase
- `+`: value will be converted to UPPERCASE
- `~`: value will be converted to Title Case
- `#`: value will be truncated to that many characters (where the hash represents a decimal number)

For instance, if `firstname`(`%f`) is *Caroline* and `lastname`(`%l`) is *Gordon*, the following values will be generated:

| Pattern | Value |
|---|---|
| `%f%l` | `CarolineGordon` |
| `%l%f` | `GordonCaroline` |
| `%l%2f` | `GordonCa` |
| `%-f_%-l` | `caroline_gordon` |
| `http://www.youruni.edu/~%-1f%-l/` | `http://www.youruni.edu/~cgordon/` |

The last template is an example of embedding the replacement values inside other text, in this case a URL that represents a user's homepage.

# Loading of data

Once all settings have been specified, all the default values have been set, and the **Upload users** button has been pressed, Moodle will finally start the actual importing process.

Moodle displays a large table that contains all the user fields that have been added and/or changed. It also displays a status for each field, including any problems or errors that have occurred.

At the end of the user upload process, a short message is displayed, summarizing the upload process. It contains the number of users created, the number of users updated, the number of users having a weak password (according the password policy), and the number of errors occurred, as in the following screenshot:

| User not updated - error | 142 | 285 | jwatts | John | Watts | John.Watts@yourschool.org.uk | Missing password or invalid password policy for internal authentication |
|---|---|---|---|---|---|---|---|
| User updated | 143 | 286 | dwilliams | David | Williams | David.Williams@yourschool.org.uk | |
| New user | 144 | 293 | pkennedy | Peter | Kennedy | Peter.Kennedy@yourschool.org.uk | changeme |
| User updated | 145 | 287 | pwilliams | Paul | Williams | paul.williams@yourschool.org.uk | |
| User updated | 146 | 288 | nwilson | Nigel | Wilson | Nigel.Wilson@yourschool.org.uk | |
| User updated | 147 | 289 | awright | Andrew | Wright | Andrew.w.wright@yourschool.org.uk | |

Users created: 1
Users updated: 138
Users having a weak password: 0
Errors: 7

Continue

It is recommended that you identify the respective users immediately and modify their user settings manually.

# Uploading user pictures

The process to upload users, described so far, does not support user profile pictures. These have to be uploaded separately at **Users | Accounts | Upload user pictures**, as in the following screenshot:

The pictures to be uploaded have to be archived in a ZIP file. The name for each image file has to conform to the format `user-attribute.extension`. The **User attribute to use to match picture** field is set to any one of these values — **username**, **idnumber**, or the **id** of the user. This attribute is used to match the picture to an existing user and you will have to select the attribute in the respective pull-down menu. The extension is the filename extension (`.jpg` or `.png`). Names for image files are not case-sensitive.

For example, if the username consists of an initial and a surname (`%1f%l`, if expressed in template style), valid filenames are `asmith.png`, `ejones.png`, and `mstripe.png`. If the users exist, the pictures will be added to their profile. If a picture already exists for a user, it will only be replaced if you have enabled the **Overwrite existing user pictures?** option.

# Manual account settings

You have the ability to lock fields for manually created accounts or uploaded via batch files at **Plugins | Authentication | Manual accounts**. This is useful whenever you do not want users being able to change certain data in their user profiles; young students may misuse the **Description** field, the **ID number** may be used by Moodle for linking to other systems, the **Email address** might have been provided by the company, and so on.

If a field is **Locked**, the user will not be able to change its value. If you lock any compulsory fields, you will either have to make sure that they are populated correctly or you set its lock state to **Unlocked if empty**. This will force the user to enter the value and then it will be locked. In the following screenshot, this has been done for the **Email address** field. If a required field is locked and not populated, Moodle will not operate correctly:

Unfortunately, the locking mechanism is only available for a certain number of user fields as you can see in the screenshot:

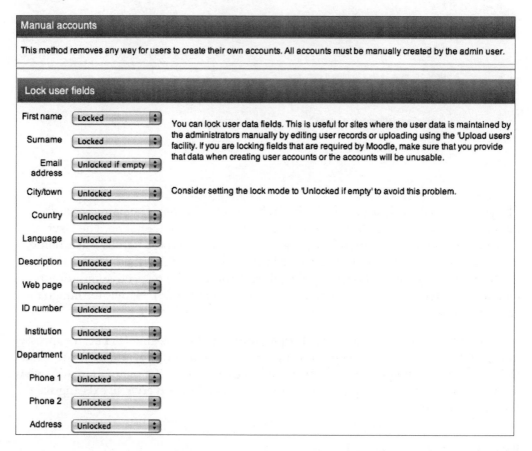

# User authentication

Now that you know everything about users and the information that is stored about them, let's look at how to authenticate them with Moodle. So far we have only dealt with manual accounts, which are activated by default after the installation of Moodle.

Moodle supports a significant number of authentication types. Furthermore, Moodle supports *multiauthentication*; that is, concurrent authentication from different authentication sources. For example, your organization might use an LDAP server containing user information for all your full-time students and staff, but wishes to manage part-time users manually.

Remember the basic authentication workflow we looked at in *Chapter 3, Courses, Users, and Roles*? Now, we can have a look at a more complete picture shown in the following diagram:

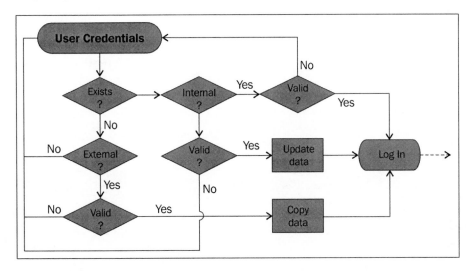

Let's start at the top where the user enters his or her user credentials. That is; username and password. Bear in mind that this could take place automatically; for example, in a single sign-on setup. Moodle checks whether a profile exists for the user. If it does and the account is authenticated via an internal mechanism, Moodle only has to check that the password is valid.

If it doesn't exist, which is usually the case the first time a user attempts to log in, Moodle checks for any enabled and configured external authentication mechanisms. If there is a valid entry, an account will be created and any existing data for which a mapping exists will be copied to the local user profile and access will be granted.

Once the profile exists and authentication is external, Moodle checks whether the credentials are valid for the set authentication method. If this is the case, any modified data in the source will be updated and access will be granted.

To access all authentication plugins go to **Plugins | Authentication | Manage authentication**. You can see a list of **Available authentication plugins**. Each plugin can be activated by clicking on the closed-eye icon. If you click on the opened-eye icon, it will be deactivated again. Settings for each type, which are discussed in this section, are accessed by their respective links or directly through the **Site administration** block, once the settings are active.

You can also change the order in which Moodle attempts to authenticate users, via the up and down arrows. The order in which authentication plugins are applied will have an impact on how long it takes for users to login, so make sure that the main ones are at the top:

| Available authentication plugins | | | |
|---|---|---|---|
| Name | Enable | Up/Down | Settings |
| Manual accounts | | | Settings |
| No login | | | Settings |
| Email-based self-registration | 👁 | ↓ | Settings |
| LDAP server | 👁 | ↑↓ | Settings |
| MNet authentication | 👁 | ↑ | Settings |
| CAS server (SSO) | 👁‍🗨 | | Settings |
| External database | 👁‍🗨 | | Settings |
| FirstClass server | 👁‍🗨 | | Settings |
| IMAP server | 👁‍🗨 | | Settings |
| NNTP server | 👁‍🗨 | | Settings |
| No authentication | 👁‍🗨 | | Settings |
| PAM (Pluggable Authentication Modules) | 👁‍🗨 | | Settings |
| POP3 server | 👁‍🗨 | | Settings |
| RADIUS server | 👁‍🗨 | | Settings |
| Shibboleth | 👁‍🗨 | | Settings |
| Web services authentication | 👁‍🗨 | | Settings |

Please choose the authentication plugins you wish to use and arrange them in order of failthrough.
Changes in table above are saved automatically.

Additional authentication methods are supported by external plugins on `moodle.org`; for example, OAuth and SAML. Once installed (see *Chapter 14, Installing Third-party Add-ons*), they will appear in the list alongside all core mechanisms.

# Common authentication settings

First of all, let's have a look at the common authentication, which you will see underneath the list of available plugins. Whatever your preferred authentication system(s) are, there are a number of common settings which apply across all mechanisms:

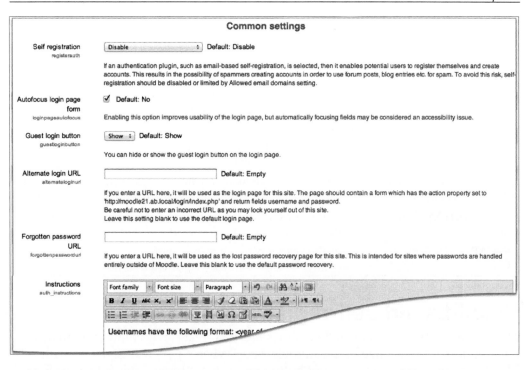

| Setting | Description |
|---|---|
| **Self registration** | Here you specify which plugin is used for self-registration (see next section for details). |
| **Autofocus login page form** | When enabled, the cursor on the login page will always jump directly to the username input field, if empty, or to the password field otherwise. |
| **Guest login button** | By default, guest access to your Moodle system is allowed. If you disable this, which is recommended for most educational and commercial sites, the guest login button will not be shown on the login screen. |
| **Alternate login URL** | By default, users have to log on to Moodle via the standard login screen. However, to change the source of the login credentials (username and password), enter the correct URL here. This is necessary if you wish to have a login block on a separate web page, such as your home page. Details of this mechanism are shown in *Chapter 7, Moodle Look and Feel*. |
| **Forgotten password URL** | Moodle has a built-in mechanism to deal with lost or forgotten passwords. If you use an authentication method that has its own system to do this, you will have to enter its URL here. |

| Setting | Description |
|---|---|
| **Instructions** | It is good practice to provide information on how to sign up for the system and what format the username should have (only applies to self-registration). |
| **Allowed email domains** | You can restrict the e-mail domains that are allowed on your system when new user accounts are created; for example, `yourschool.ac.uk` or `.edu`. |
| **Denied email domains** | Similarly, you can specify which e-mail domains are not allowed on your system. |
| **Restrict domains when changing email** | If enabled, the two e-mail domain settings, mentioned earlier in the table, will be applied when an e-mail address is changed. |
| **ReCAPTCHA public key** | This is the key for displaying the reCAPTCHA element on the signup form (see the *Email-based self-registration* section). |
| **ReCAPTCHA private key** | This is the key for communicating with the reCAPTCHA server (see the *Email-based self-registration* section). |

# Email-based self-registration

Moodle supports a mechanism that allows users to create an account without any intervention or knowledge of the administrator. When a new user signs up with Moodle via the **Create new account** button on the login screen, she or he can choose her or his own new username and password. Once this step has been completed, a confirmation mail is sent to the user's e-mail address containing a secure link to a page where the user has to confirm the account. The signup screen looks as follows:

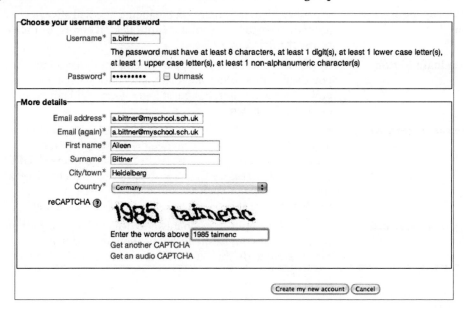

When dealing with user-defined profile fields, we saw how to add more items to the signup screen (**Display on signup page** option) in the *Profile fields* section. This is often invaluable in commercial training settings when additional data, such as the address of the learner, has to be gathered.

Moodle supports a CAPTCHA mechanism that has been activated on the signup screen as shown in the preceding screenshot. The facility is used to avoid automated signups by bots. In order to activate this facility, you will have to sign up for a free account at www.google.com/recaptcha, add the public and private key provided in the **Common settings** in the **Manage Authentication** area, and enable the reCAPTCHA element, as shown in the *Common authentication settings* section.

> The PHP cURL extension has to be installed for reCAPTCHA to work.

The same locking settings can be set for self-registration as for manual accounts (**Plugins | Authentication | Email-based self-registration**). Also, the same restrictions apply as described earlier. Additionally, you have the option to **Enable reCAPTCHA element**.

If a site policy has been specified in **Security | Site policies**, a link to the agreement with the confirmation checkbox — **I understand and agree** — is shown on the signup screen.

# LDAP server

We have already seen a basic introduction to LDAP in the previous chapter when we dealt with enrolments. Now, let's look at how it can be utilized for authentication. We will only cover basic LDAP settings and exclude advanced setups; such as, multiple LDAP servers and secure LDAP. These are discussed in greater detail in the Moodle Docs at docs.moodle.org/en/LDAP_authentication.

The principle of the authentication method is rather simple, but effective. If the entered username and password are valid, Moodle creates a new user account in its database, if it doesn't already exist. Once it does exist, the credentials are checked against LDAP for validity.

> It is necessary for the PHP LDAP extension to be installed on the server for the authentication to work.

Go to **Plugins | Authentication | LDAP server** to see the settings, which also cover Microsoft's implementation of LDAP, Active Directory. There are a significant number of parameters that you have to set to communicate with an LDAP server. The settings have been amended with detailed explanations (which I will not repeat). I will only provide additional information when applicable. If you are not sure where to locate some of the required information, contact your system administrator.

There are two types of parameters that must be populated to make Moodle work in your LDAP setup, namely; settings and mappings, which are discussed in the sections that follow.

# LDAP Settings

There are nine sections of LDAP settings that must be provided:

- The **LDAP server settings** establish the connection to the directory. LDAP servers with SSL encryption are also supported

- The **Bind settings** specify details about the credentials to access the LDAP server. If you have multiple contexts, it is recommended to put them in order of importance as Moodle stops searching once it has found an entry. For example, if you have ou=Students and ou=Staff and your students make up 90 percent of the logins, we recommend putting them before their lecturers, unless staff are given priority.

- The **User lookup settings** describe how and where a user is stored on your LDAP directory. Make sure you select the correct **User type**. For multiple contexts, the same applies as for the distinguished name in the bind settings. It is important to set **Search subcontexts** correctly. If it is set to **No**, subcontexts will not be searched, but the search is potentially faster, and vice versa.

- **Force change password** specifies whether and how passwords can be changed by users on their first access to Moodle

- **LDAP password expiration settings** are concerned with passwords lapsing and how this is dealt with

- **Enable user creation** lets you activate a mechanism similar to self-registration but, in addition to that, an account is created with values from your LDAP

- **Course creator** specifies which LDAP user groups will have course creator permissions in Moodle

- The **Cron synchronization script** setting specifies what Moodle should do with local user accounts when these have been deleted on the LDAP server

- **NTLM SSO**: In a Windows-based environment with MS-AD active, NTLM, if configured correctly, supports single sign-on. That is, users logged in via the Windows domain do not have to re-enter their credentials when accessing Moodle. Check out `docs.moodle.org/en/NTLM_authentication` for details.

# Data field mappings

User profile information is stored in the LDAP server. In order to connect the two, a mapping must be provided where a counterpart in the directory has to be specified for each field in Moodle. All fields are optional. Default values are used if you leave any of the fields blank:

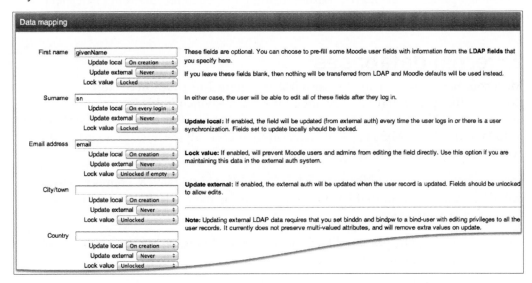

If you provide field information, you will have to set four parameters for each data field, as follows:

| Setting | Description |
| --- | --- |
| **Field name** | Field name in the external database representing the value in Moodle. |
| **Update local** | For each external user, information is stored locally. You can update this information **on creation** (faster, but potentially not up-to-date) or **every login** (a bit slower, but always up-to-date). |
| **Update external** | If a user updates the value of the data field in Moodle, you can decide if you write that information back to the external database (**on update**) or not (**never**). Often, the external database is a read-only view, which will prevent Moodle from updating data in it. |
| **Lock value** | You can specify if the value can be modified by the user. The setting is identical to the lock field explained earlier. |

If you use Microsoft's Active Directory, check out the *Data Mapping* section at `docs.moodle.org/en/LDAP_authentication` for details.

When using LDAP you might come across a situation where you wish to assign courses to users before they have logged in to the system for the first time. This scenario regularly applies before the start of the academic year. The problem is that the local user accounts do not exist yet and you cannot access this information as it is only stored in the external directory. A way around this is to create the user accounts via batch files and set the `auth` field to `ldap`. You effectively mimic the initial logging in of each user.

The same applies to all external authentication mechanisms, including external databases.

# External databases

Most commercial organizations use a **Management Information System (MIS)** — either proprietary or developed in-house — which holds information about staff and learners. It makes perfect sense to utilize this data for authentication in to Moodle. As all MISs use a database at their core, all we have to do is to get access to the relevant data.

MIS departments are usually not too keen for external systems to connect to their database. A mechanism that has proven valuable is the read-only view. This has a number of advantages:

- A view can be prepared for Moodle usage, that is; only required fields are shown in the required format
- No write access to the database
- If the database schema of the MIS ever changes, only the view has to be adapted, not Moodle

The external database authentication method contains two types of parameters that you have to provide at **Plugins | Authentication | External database**, namely; connection settings and data field mappings.

# Connection settings

The database connection settings have been amended with good explanations (which I will not repeat). If you are not sure where to locate some of the required information, contact your database administrator.

Some databases, such as Oracle, are case-sensitive, that is; field names have to be provided with the correct casing for the database link to work properly.

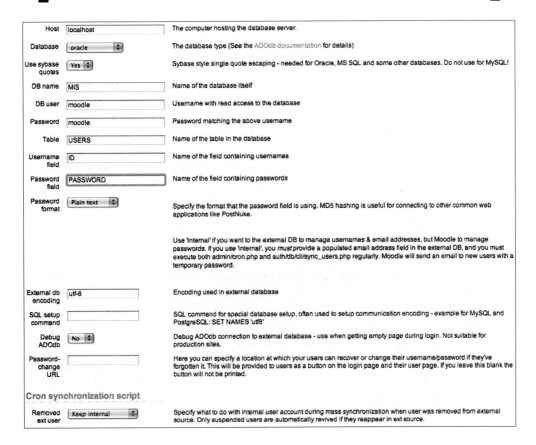

If you experience problems establishing a connection between Moodle and the external database, use the debug mode (**Debug ADOdb**), which will display information that is useful in locating the source of the problem.

# Data field mappings

User profile information is stored in the external database. In order to connect the two, a mapping must be provided where a counterpart in the MIS has to be supplied for each field in Moodle. All fields are optional. Default values are used if you leave the any of the fields blank.

This mechanism is identical to the one for mapping data in the LDAP setup, which we covered prior to this section.

# Other authentication mechanisms

In addition to the popular authentication mechanisms that we have dealt with so far, Moodle supports a number of additional external authentication methods as well as some internal ones, which we will cover in the following sections.

## External Moodle authentication methods

Due to the fact that these external authentication methods are less popular than LDAP and external databases, we will only cover them in brief. I will provide some pointers to web sites for further information.

- **CAS Server (SSO): CAS (Central Authentication Service)** is an open source authentication server based on Tomcat that supports single sign-on in a web environment. CAS is gaining in popularity, in particular in environments that comprise multiple authentication sources and consumers. It utilizes LDAP and therefore requires the PHP LDAP modules to be installed.

  More information on CAS can be found on the JA-SIG website at `http:// www.ja-sig.org/products/cas/overview/cas2_architecture/ index.html`.

- **FirstClass Server: FirstClass**, by Open Text Corporation, is a commercial client/server groupware, e-mail, online conferencing, voice/fax services, and bulletin-board system for Windows, Macintosh, and Linux. The product is used for authentication of pupil accounts. In addition to some FirstClass specific settings, user fields can be locked in the same way as described earlier.

- **IMAP Server: IMAP (Internet Message Access Protocol)** is a standard used by many e-mail servers such as Microsoft Exchange. The user contact information in the server is used for Moodle authentication. In addition to some IMAP-specific settings, user fields can be locked in the same way as described earlier.

  The IMAP consortium has a dedicated website, which can be found at `www.imap.org`.

- **NNTP Server: NNTP (Network News Transfer Protocol)** is mainly used for transferring articles and Usenet messages between news servers. Its user details are used for Moodle authentication.

- **PAM: PAM (Pluggable Authentication Modules)** is yet another authentication scheme that maps user information onto a higher-level application interface. PAM is open source and has been adopted as the authentication framework of the Common Desktop Environment and is currently supported by all main Linux derivatives. The PHP PAM Authentication module has to be installed on the Moodle server.

- **POP3 Server**: POP3 (**Post Office Protocol version 3**) is a standard used by many e-mail servers. The user contact information on the server is used for Moodle authentication. In addition to some POP3-specific settings, user fields can be locked in the same way as described earlier.

- **RADIUS Server**: RADIUS (**Remote Authentication Dial In User Service**) is a protocol for controlling access to various network resources. It supports authentication, authorization, and accounting and is used by Internet Service Providers.

  It is necessary for the Auth_RADIUS module to be installed on the server.

- **Shibboleth**: Shibboleth is an open source middleware that provides Internet single sign-on across organizational boundaries. Privacy and security are at the heart of Shibboleth, which is the main reason for its growing popularity. However, the price to pay is a complicated setup process that has been detailed in the readme file at `auth/shibboleth/README.txt` of your Moodle site.

  More information on Shibboleth can be found at `shibboleth.internet2.edu`.

- **Web services authentication**: This plugin is for users who are being authenticated via external clients communicating with Moodle via web services (see *Chapter 15, Moodle Integration via Web Services* for details). The authentication plugin has no settings.

  Other external authentication modules are available as contributed third-party modules, for instance, OAuth and SAML. These can be found in the **Downloads** section on `moodle.org`. More details on third-party add-ons will be covered in *Chapter 14, Installing Third-party Add-ons*.

# Internal Moodle authentication methods

Moodle provides three authentication methods, which are used by a range of internal operations.

- **No login**: This plugin has no settings and cannot be disabled. Its purpose is to suspend a user from logging in to your Moodle system. This is done in the user's profile, where you have to select the authentication method in the **Choose an authentication method** drop-down list.

- **No authentication**: When this method is enabled, users can create accounts without any kind of authentication and without email-based confirmation. It is highly recommended not to use this method as it creates a very insecure Moodle site, and should only be used for testing or development purposes.

  Only user fields can be locked in the same way as described before.

- **Moodle Network authentication**: Moodle networking allows the connection of multiple Moodle sites in a peer-to-peer or hub style. *Chapter 16, Moodle Networking* has been dedicated to the details of this powerful feature.

# Usernames—best practice

User management in an organization is a critical subject for a range of reasons:

- Once implemented, it is difficult to change (sustainability)
- A system that is too simple is potentially unsafe and not future-proof
- A system that is too complicated is unlikely to be accepted by users and is likely to cause administrative difficulties.

There is no ideal user management scheme, as the preference in every organization is different. However, there are a number of issues that are considered best practice.

Usernames have to be unique. The simplest way to implement this is to give each user a unique number, which is never reused even after students have finished a course. However, such a number-based system will be very difficult for learners to remember, especially younger ones. It is therefore necessary to come up with a more user-friendly scheme considering the following potential issues:

- `firstname.lastname` causes difficulties when the same name exists twice
- `class.firstname.lastname` causes difficulties when the same name exists twice in a class. Also, when learners transfer from one class to another, there is a potential conflict.
- `startyear.firstname.lastname` causes difficulties when the same name exists more than once in a year. Furthermore, students who have to repeat a class or join a school at a later stage will be out of sync with the rest of the learners in the same class. The same holds for the naming scheme `endyear.firstname.lastname`.

A system-compliant naming scheme would therefore be `startyear.firstname.lastname`, with an optional number added in case there is an overlap. Students who repeat or join the school at a later stage would then be changed manually to be in sync with the rest of their peers in the year. Examples are `04.caroline.killen`, `05.jim.smith.1`, `05.jim.smith.2` and `06.caroline.hinds`.

For smaller learning organizations, a system that uses `firstname.lastname` as a scheme with an added number (in case of name duplication) is usually sufficient. The same applies to training providers who have rolling start dates of users.

Some schools still do not make use of e-mail addresses. As it is a compulsory field in Moodle, it is necessary to work around this issue. You will have to come up with a unique dummy e-mail address scheme or void e-mail addresses that have to be used for identification purposes. In order to avoid the usage of the actual e-mail address, it is necessary that you deactivate it in the user's profile.

# Summary

Phew! That was a lot to take in for one chapter. This chapter demonstrated the different ways Moodle provides to manage users. We first looked at what information is stored for each user and how their profiles can be extended. We then performed a number of standard manual and bulk user actions.

We finally dealt with a wide range of user authentication types, before concluding the chapter with a best practice section. The next step is to grant user roles, that is; what they can and cannot do. This will be dealt with in the next chapter.

# Managing Permissions: Roles and Capabilities

We already touched upon permissions in *Chapter 3, Courses, Users, and Roles*. Now we want to cover roles and capabilities fully, which is a complex but powerful subject. Roles define what users can or can't see and what they can or can't do in your Moodle system.

In this chapter, we will:

- Understand how permissions work and how they fit into different contexts
- Assign roles to different users in different contexts
- Modify roles and create new ones, including a role for parents or mentors
- Manage a range of administrative role-related settings.

Let us start with a short definition that should be borne in mind when managing permissions:

 A role is a collection of capabilities.

## Moodle predefined roles

Moodle comes with a number of predefined roles. These standard roles are suitable for most educational setups, but some institutions require modifications to the roles system to tailor Moodle to their specific needs.

Each role has capabilities for a number of actions that can be carried out. For example, an administrator and a course creator are able to create new courses, whereas all other roles are denied this right. Likewise, a teacher is allowed to moderate forums, whereas students are only allowed to contribute to them.

The description of each standard role and the short names that are used, internally and in operations such as user batch upload, given by Moodle, are listed in the table that follows:

| Role | Description | Short Name |
|------|-------------|------------|
| **Administrator** | Administrators have full access to the entire site and to all courses. | `admin` |
| **Course creator** | Course creators can create new courses, but not participate or teach in them. | `coursecreator` |
| **Manager** | Managers can access courses and modify them, without participation. | `manager` |
| **Teacher** | Editing teachers can do anything within a course, including changing activities and grading students. | `editingteacher` |
| **Non-editing teacher** | Non-editing teachers can teach in courses and grade students, but not alter any activities. | `teacher` |
| **Student** | Students can participate in courses. | `student` |
| **Guest** | Guests have minimal privileges and usually cannot enter any content. | `guest` |
| **Authenticated user** | All logged-in users. | `user` |
| **Authenticated user on frontpage** | All users logged in to the frontpage course. | `frontpage` |

Before we can actually do anything with roles, we need to understand contexts, which are dealt with in the following section.

# Contexts

**Contexts** are the areas in Moodle where roles can be assigned to users. A role (remember, a collection of capabilities) can be assigned within different contexts. A user has a role in any given context; a context can be a course, a course category, an activity module, a user, a block, or Moodle itself. Moodle comes with seven contexts that you will come across a lot in this chapter:

| Context | Scope |
|---------|-------|
| **System** | Entire Moodle system (also known as core or global context) |
| **Course category** | Categories and sub-categories organizing courses |

| Context | Scope |
| --- | --- |
| Course | Courses |
| Activity module | Course activities and resources |
| Block | Moodle blocks |
| User | Users |
| Front page | Front page and files that can be accessed outside courses |

Each context is like a ring-fenced area in which certain actions can be carried out. It is also sometimes referred to as a *scope*. You can compare this to a large company with multiple divisions and departments. A manager of the finance division has certain rights and responsibilities for every department in his division, but these do not apply to departments in other divisions of the organization.

To implement such a structure, it is important that role assignments to users be made at the correct context level. For example, a **Teacher** role should be assigned at **Course** context level, a moderator for a particular forum should be assigned at **Activity** context level, an administrator should be assigned at **System** context level, and so on. While it is technically possible to assign any role in any context, some roles just don't make any sense. Unfortunately, Moodle doesn't warn you about this, since it cannot distinguish between intentional and unintentional assignments.

Contexts are hierarchical; that is, permissions are inherited by lower contexts from higher contexts. Rights in a higher context are more general, whereas the ones at a lower context are more specific. The same applies in the company structure mentioned earlier. A sales manager at country level would have the same rights at regional level, whereas the opposite is not true.

The following diagram shows the contexts that exist in Moodle and how they are arranged hierarchically:

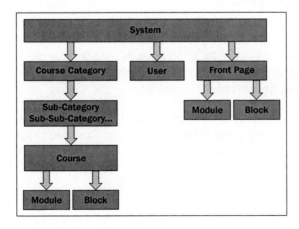

The *System* context is the root node of the hierarchy, that is, every role assigned in this context will apply to any other context below it. The *Course Category* context on the next level acts as a parent to the *Course* context. If sub-categories and sub-sub-categories, and so on, have been created, respective contexts will exist. On the lowest level, you can see the *Module* and *Block* contexts, respectively. Like the Course context, the *Front Page* context has a *Module* and *Block* sub-context (the front page is internally treated as a course). The *User* context is a standalone entity that does not have any children in the hierarchy.

For example, Jim is a teacher for a course. He is assigned a **Teacher** role in the relevant context (that is, the class he is teaching). He will have this role in all areas of the course, including blocks and activity modules (that is, activities and resources). If however, Jim had been assigned the **Teacher** role in the **Course category** context instead, he would have the same rights in all courses in this category and all its sub-categories. This also means that he will receive e-mails about all assignments, in all courses, even if he doesn't teach in them.

Organizing contexts hierarchically has a number of advantages that will sound familiar to readers who have knowledge of object-oriented technologies:

- **Inheritance**: Rights and permissions set at one level are passed down to lower levels, which simplifies maintenance.

- **Overriding**: Rights and permissions can be changed at lower levels, which we will deal with later on.

- **Extensibility**: New contexts might be added in future versions of Moodle, for example, *Tenancy* to model the planned multi-tenancy setups, without changing any of the exiting role system.

# Assigning roles

As mentioned before, assigning roles to users is done for, and in, a particular context. The process of the actual role assignment (except for courses) is similar for each context. What is different is the location of each context and the method of its access. The process of assigning roles to users is described first, before outlining how and where to assign them in individual contexts:

1. Navigate to any *Assign roles* screen for the required context, for example, **Front page | Front page roles** (I will explain how to find the *Assign roles* screen for each context later). You will see a screen as follows:

## Please choose a role to assign

| Role | Description | Users with role | |
|---|---|---|---|
| Manager | Managers can access course and modify them, they usually do not participate in courses. | 0 | |
| Teacher | Teachers can do anything within a course, including changing the activities and grading students. | 2 | Matthew Bates Mary Fawcett |
| Non-editing teacher | Non-editing teachers can teach in courses and grade students, but may not alter activities. | 0 | |
| Student | Students generally have fewer privileges within a course. | 18 | More than 10 |

In this preceding screenshot, you can see that there are currently two Teachers assigned (**Matthew Bates** and **Mary Fawcett**) and 18 Students (only up to 10 names are displayed).

2. Select the role to which you wish to assign a user by clicking on the role name or, if there are more than 10 assignees, click on the **More than 10** link. For example, if you wish to allocate more **Student** roles you will be directed to the following screen:

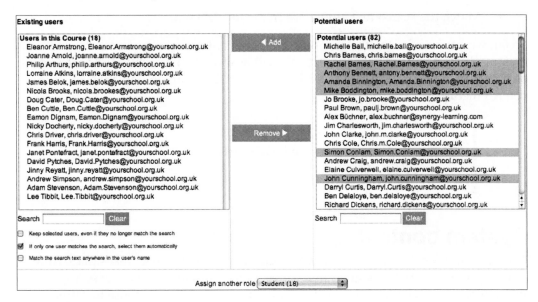

3.  Assign the role to users by selecting their names from the **Potential users** list and moving them to the category using the **Add** button. Hold down the *Shift* key to select a range of users and the *Ctrl* key (*Apple* or *Command* key on a Mac OS) to select multiple users. To revoke users' role assignments, select the person in the **Existing users** list, and move them back to the **Potential users** group by clicking on the **Remove** button.

 Once a user has been assigned a role, permissions will be granted immediately. There is no need to save any changes.

If your list of potential users contains more than 100 entries, no user names are shown and you will have to use the **Search** box to filter the list of accounts. Moodle uses a live search, that is, as soon as you start typing, the list of users is updated immediately. There are a number of self-explanatory **Search options** underneath the left **Search** box. You might have to expand this area if it is collapsed:

*   **Keep selected users, even if they no longer match the search**
*   **If only one user matches the search, select them automatically**
*   **Match the search text anywhere in the user's name**

So far, we have dealt with the general concept of contexts, and looked at how to assign roles to users within a context. We will now deal with each individual context, as shown in the diagram towards the beginning of this chapter, depicting Moodle's context hierarchy.

 Assigning roles in the incorrect context is a common source of problems. It is highly recommended to check the current context regularly to make sure no unintended rights are granted.

# System context

The **System** context covers the entire Moodle system. Assignment takes place from **Users | Permissions | Assign system roles**. In our system, only two roles appear that can be assigned. We mentioned already that it doesn't make sense to assign certain roles in certain contexts. Inside a role, it is possible to specify in which context types may be assigned. Only these two roles have been selected, which is the reason for the limited choice.

| Assign roles in System ⊘ | | |
|---|---|---|
| WARNING! Any roles you assign from this page will apply to the assigned users throughout the entire system, including the front page and all the courses. | | |

**Please choose a role to assign**

| Role | Description | Users with role |
|---|---|---|
| Manager | Managers can access course and modify them, they usually do not participate in courses. | 0 |
| Course creator | Course creators can create new courses and teach in them. | 0 |

You will see this familiar screen that allows the assignment of roles to users. The only difference from the generic screen outlined earlier is the following warning: **WARNING! Any roles you assign from this page will apply to the assigned users throughout the entire system, including the front page and all the courses**.

In most Moodle systems with predefined roles, it only makes sense to assign the **Manager** role if you wish to allow read-only access to a user for all courses; for example, an Inspector or School principal. Assigning the **Course creator** role to a user allows him or her to create new courses in any category. If, for example, a **Teacher** role is assigned in the **System** context, it means that the user would not only be allowed access to every single existing course in the site, but also to all courses created in the future.

There are scenarios when global roles are justified; for instance, in very small organizations, or if Moodle hosts only a very small number of courses that are attended by all users. Also, some new user-defined roles, such as a School Inspector, are designed to be assigned at global level.

One role that should be assigned at system level is the **Administrator** role. This task has been given a dedicated area under **Users | Permissions | Site administrators**. When you installed Moodle, a primary administrator was created, which cannot be modified or deleted. You can, however, create additional administrator accounts. The procedure is identical to assigning users in any other context, with the exception that you have to confirm the assignment.

 Make sure you keep the number of Moodle administrators to a minimum! This will improve consistency of your system, increase security, and avoid potential mismanagement of the site.

# Course category context

The **Course category** context covers all courses within a category and all of its sub-categories. The role assignment takes place under **Courses | Add/edit course**, where you have to select the course category you wish to deal with and click on the **Assign roles** link in the **Settings** block. The same mechanism applies to sub-categories, sub-sub-categories, and so on.

A typical role that is assigned in the **Course category** context is the **Course creator** role. It will allow a dedicated user to create new courses within the specified category, which is very often a department or division. The standard **Course creator** role does not include teacher capabilities, that is, a course creator cannot edit course content. In smaller organizations, it may be required to grant the **Teacher** role access to all courses within the category.

# Course context

As the name suggests, in this context, all role assignments that cover a course are granted. The assignment takes place in the actual course. We have already come across this in *Chapter 4, Course Management*, when we dealt with enrolments. In fact, enrolments in courses are treated as roles in the **Course** context. Because enrolments contain some unique options (start date, end date, and a suspension option) and due to the fact that these enrolments are often carried out by (non-technical) teaching staff, a different user interface has been implemented. However, within a course, when you go to **Users | Enrolment methods** in the **Settings** block, and then click on the **Enrol users** icon in the **Edit** column of the **Manual enrolments** method, you will see a familiar-looking screen. We have already dealt with the additional expiry options in the center of the screen when we covered enrolments.

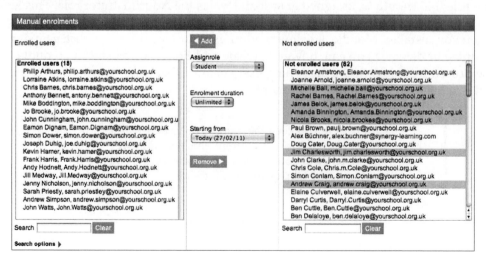

When a student is enrolled in a course, either by self-enrolment or any other enrolment mechanism, Moodle will automatically assign the **Student** role in the relevant **Course** context. This also applies if you upload users in batch mode and specify a course to which a user has to be enrolled.

If you want to assign roles to users who are not enrolled, but have a role in the course, go to **Users | Other users** in the **Settings** block and click on the **Assign roles** button. This applies to the **Manager** role, for instance, or a newly created role, such as Supervisor teacher. The user interface is in line with the enrolment interface, not the general roles interface:

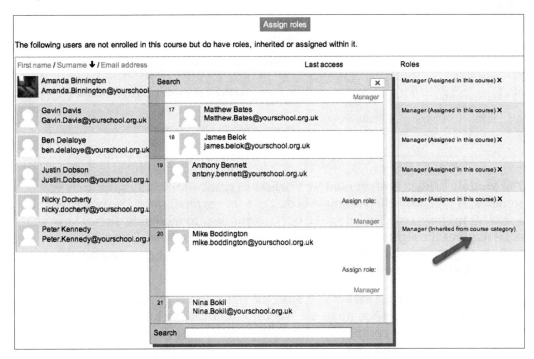

The preceding screenshot also displays any users who have inherited a role in this course; for instance, one user has been assigned in the **Course category** context (see arrow in the screenshot).

# Module context

Once you are inside a course, it is possible to assign roles to users for individual modules; such as the resources and activities. While editing the module properties, you will see three role-related links in the **Settings** block. The one labeled **Locally assigned roles** will lead you to the familiar screen to **Assign roles**. The **Permissions** and **Check permissions** links let you change inherited roles and verify roles of individual users. We will deal with this later in the chapter:

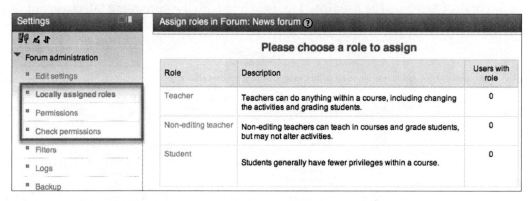

The **Module** context is often used by teachers to grant additional rights to their students. A regularly-cited example is that of a forum moderator. If you wish to put a student in charge of a forum so she or he learns how to moderate discussions, she or he requires the rights to edit and delete posts (among others). These rights are provided by the Teacher role and it is perfectly feasible to assign a **Teacher** role to a student in a single activity.

By default, users with a **Teacher** role have the rights to assign roles in the **Module** context. However, it is often up to the Moodle administrator to carry out the task on their behalf, due to the complexity of the roles system. The same applies to the **Block** context, which is covered next.

# Block context

Similar to the **Module** context, the **Block** context allows the assignment of rights on block level within a course. You will see an **Assign roles** icon at the top-left corner of each block, clicking on which will lead to the **Assign roles** screen (editing has to be turned on).

If your system doesn't contain a role that has been granted rights to be assigned in the **Block** context, you will see a message that reads: **You are not able to assign any roles here**. This is the case, by default. We will deal with modifying roles in the *Roles definitions* section further down.

It is possible to control the users who can view blocks. For example, you might have a block that you don't want guest users to see. To hide that block from guests on the front page, access the roles page of the block by clicking on the **Assign roles** icon. Click on the **Permissions** link, select the **Guest** role from the **Advanced role override** drop-down list, set the **moodle/block:view** capability to **Prevent**, and click on **Save changes**. We will deal with capabilities later on.

The same mechanism also applies to blocks outside courses, whether on the front page, in My Moodle, on the default profile page, or inside activities.

# User context

The **User** context is a standalone context, which has only the **System** context as parent. It deals with all issues relating to a user outside a course. They include the user's profile, forum posts, blog entries, notes and reports, logs, and grades.

The assignment of roles takes place via the **Profile settings for <user> | Roles | This user's role assignments** link in the **Settings** block, on the profile page of that user. This link does not appear by default. You need to have a role that can be assigned in the **User** context. None of the predefined roles make sense to be applied in such a way, which is why this only applies to user-defined roles. An often-cited example of a custom role to be applied in the **User** context is the Parent/Mentor role, which we will deal with in the *Creating custom roles* section.

Roles assigned in the **User** context will only have access to information accessible from the user screen. They will not have access to any courses:

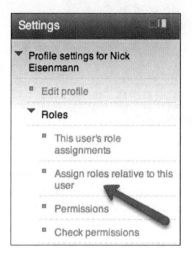

# Front page context

In Moodle, the front page is a course and, at the same time, not like a course. In other words, it is a special course! The **Front page** context has the **System** context as parent and, like the **Course** context, **Module** and **Block** as the sub-contexts. It is accessed via **Front Page | Front page roles**:

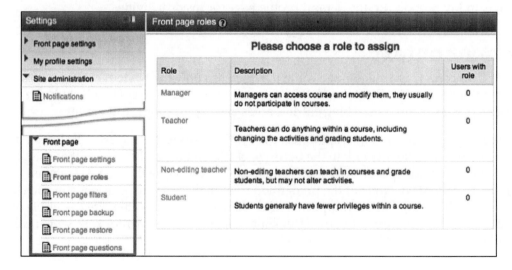

A typical user in the **Front page** context is a designer who is responsible for the layout and content of the front page of the Moodle system. When assigned, only the **Front page** menu and its submenus are accessible. Most sites apply either the **Teacher** role or create a dedicated Designer role.

# Multiple roles

It is common for a user to be assigned more than a single role. For example, a class teacher is also made course creator for the year group he or she is responsible for (Category), or is in charge of the Moodle administration (Site), or acts as a support teacher in a different class (Course), or is the parent of a child (User). In fact, every logged-in user is automatically assigned the **Authenticated user** role in the **System** context. We will deal with this later in the chapter.

A significant part of the roles infrastructure in Moodle is the ability to assign multiple roles to a user at the same time. The equivalent in our initial company example is a member of staff who is in charge of the Marketing department, but is also temporarily in charge of the Sales division.

To specify an additional role, the actual context has to be selected, as discussed earlier. You will then be able to assign additional roles as necessary.

It is technically possible to assign two or more roles to the same user in the same context. Having said this, it is hard to think of situations where such a setup would actually make sense. The real problem is the potential for conflicts, which Moodle has to resolve. For example, if one role has the ability to delete a forum post and another one does not, but a user has been assigned both roles in the same context, which right applies? While Moodle has a built-in resolution mechanism for these scenarios, it is best to completely avoid them.

 If you are desperate to know about the built-in resolution mechanism mentioned earlier, see `docs.moodle.org/en/How_permissions_are_calculated`.

# Capabilities

So far, we have given users existing roles in different Moodle contexts. In the following few pages, we will have a look at the inside of a role where capabilities dictate what functionality is allowed. Remember, a role is a collection of capabilities. Once we have understood these, we will modify existing roles and create entirely new custom ones.

# Role definitions

Existing roles are accessed via **Users | Permissions | Define roles**. The screen that will be shown is similar to the familiar **Assign roles** screen, but has a very different purpose:

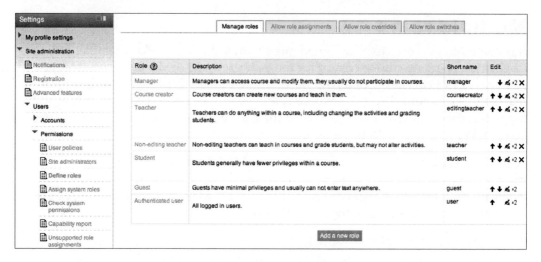

When you click on a role name, its composition is shown. Each role contains a unique **Role name**, a unique **Short name** (used when uploading users), and an optional **Description**:

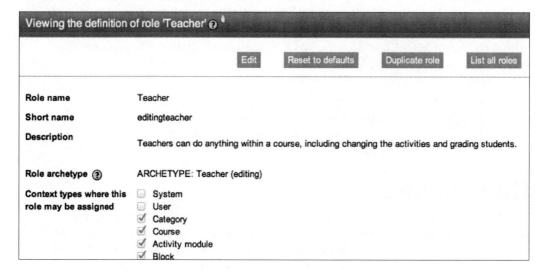

The **Role archetype** specifies which permissions are set if the role is reset to its default value. The setting further determines what values any new permissions will have, when introduced in future versions of Moodle. These settings will then be applied during the update process.

The **Context types where this role may be assigned** field is set to the context in which the role will be allowed as an option. This reduces the risk that roles are assigned in contexts where they shouldn't. We have already come across this when we tried to assign roles in the **Block** context and were told that this is not possible. In the preceding screenshot, we have changed it and added the **Block** as well as the **Category** context as options.

In addition to these five fields, each role consists of a large number of capabilities. Currently, Moodle's role system contains almost 400 of them.

 A capability is a description of a particular Moodle feature.

These include grading an assignment or editing a wiki page. Each capability represents a permissible Moodle action and is displayed as a single row in the list of all capabilities.

To simplify searching for capabilities, use the provided **Filter** mechanism. It only shows the capabilities (with both the name and the description) that match the filter criterion:

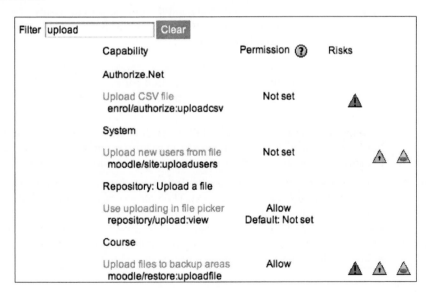

Each capability has the following components:

- **Description**: For example, **Upload new users from file** provides a short explanation of the capability. On clicking a capability, the online Moodle documentation for that capability is opened in a separate browser window.

- **Name**: For instance, **moodle/site:uploadusers** follows a strict naming convention — `level/type:function` — which identifies the capability in the overall role system. The level states to which part of Moodle the capability belongs (such as, `moodle`, `mod`, `block`, `gradereport`, or `enrol`). The type is the class of the capability, and the function identifies the actual action.

- **Permission**: Each capability has to have one of four values, explained in the following table:

| Permission | Description |
| --- | --- |
| Not Set | By default, all permissions for a new role are set to this value. The value in the context where it will be assigned is inherited from the parent context. To determine this value, Moodle searches upward through each context, until it finds an explicit value (**Allow**, **Prevent**, or **Prohibit**) for this capability; that is, the search terminates when an explicit permission is found. |
| | For example, if a role is assigned to a user in a **Course** context and a capability has a **Not set** value, then the actual permission will be whatever the user has at the category level, or, failing to find an explicit permission, at the site level. If no explicit permission is found, then the value in the current context is set to **Prevent**. |
| Allow | To grant permission for a capability, set the permission to **Allow**. It applies in the context in which the role will be assigned and all contexts which are below it (children, grand-children, and so forth). |
| | For example, when assigned in the **Course** context, students will be able to start new discussions in all forums in that course, unless some forum contains an override or a new assignment with a **Prevent** or **Prohibit** value for this capability. |
| Prevent | To remove permission for a capability, set the permission to **Prevent**. If it has been granted in a higher context (no matter at what level), it will be overridden. The value can be overridden again at a lower context. |
| Prohibit | This is the same as the **Prevent** permission, but the value cannot be overridden again at a lower context. The value is rarely needed, but useful when an administrator wants to prohibit a user from certain functionality throughout the site, in which case the capability is set to **Prohibit** and then assigned in the site context. A situation where this applies is when a user is a "bad student" who is not allowed to post to the forums. |

Principally, permissions at lower contexts override permissions at higher contexts. The exception is **Prohibit**, which, by definition, cannot be overridden at lower levels.

- **Risks**: Moodle displays the risks associated with each capability; that is, the risks that each capability can potentially raise. They can be any combination of the following five risk types:

| Risk | Icon | Description |
|------|------|-------------|
| Configuration | ⚠ | Users can change site configuration and behavior. |
| XSS | ⚠ | Users can add files and texts that allow cross-site scripting (potentially malicious scripts which are embedded in web pages and executed on the user's computer). |
| Privacy | ⚠ | Users can gain access to private information of other users. |
| Spam | ⚠ | Users can send spam to site users or others. |
| Data loss | ⚠ | Users can destroy large amount of content or information. |

Risks are only displayed. It is not possible to change these settings as they are only acting as warnings. When you click on a risk icon, the Risks documentation page is opened in a separate browser window.

Moodle's default roles have been designed with the following capability risks in mind:

| Role | Allowed Risks |
|------|---------------|
| **Administrator** | All capabilities, with a few exceptions. |
| **Teacher** | Certain capabilities with XSS and privacy risks, mainly adding and updating content. |
| **Student** | Certain capabilities with spam risks. |
| **Guest** | Only capabilities with no risks. |

# Modifying roles

To edit a role, either click on the **Edit** button at the top of the **Viewing the definition of role** screen or select the appropriate icon in the **Edit** column on the main roles screen.

When editing a role, you can change the standard fields as well as its permissions. For example, some schools change the role name "Student" to "Pupil", while some training organizations change the role name "Teacher" to "Instructor". Bear in mind that this only changes the name of the role, not the corresponding labels used throughout Moodle. You will learn how to do this in the *Localization* section in *Chapter 9, Moodle Configuration*.

When you change capabilities in a role that has been derived from a **Role archetype**, its original values are highlighted when you click on the **Show advanced** button. For example, in the following screenshot, **Manage templates** has been set to **Not set**, but the **Allow** value remains highlighted. Do not forget to save your role changes, once applied:

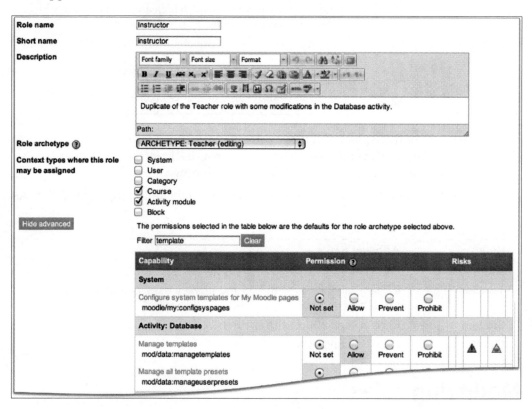

Unless you are confident with your role modifications, we recommend that you duplicate a role first (using the **Duplicate role** button) and then edit it. Keeping the default roles untouched also makes maintenance easier in case multiple administrators work on the same system or a third party provides support.

For example; if, due to privacy or other reasons, your organization decides not to allow users to see the profiles of other users, you could edit the **Student** role, search for the **moodle/user:viewdetails** capability, and change it from **Allow** to **Not set**:

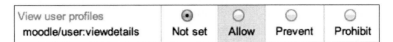

 It is not possible to modify the **Administrator** role via the Moodle interface.

# Overriding roles

It is possible to override permissions of a role in a given context using the **Permissions** link in the role assignment screen. You are shown a screen that describes which role has been given or has inherited permission for any of the capabilities of the current module activity (here, an assignment):

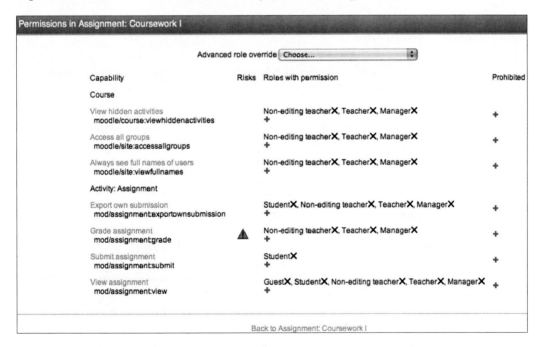

Overrides are specific permissions designed to change a role in a specific context, allowing you to tweak your permissions as required. Tweaking involves granting additional rights or revoking existing rights. Once you select a role from the **Advanced role override** drop-down menu, you will see a familiar screen that shows the details of each activity's capability for this particular role.

For example, while learners with the role of Student in a course are usually allowed to start new discussions in forums, there may be particular forum for which you want to restrict that capability; you can set an override that prevents students from starting new threads in this forum (namely, **mod/forum:startdiscussion**).

Overrides can also be used to open up areas of your site and courses to grant extra permissions to users. For instance, you may want to experiment with giving students the ability to grade some assignments (see the following screenshot) or to peer rate forum posts:

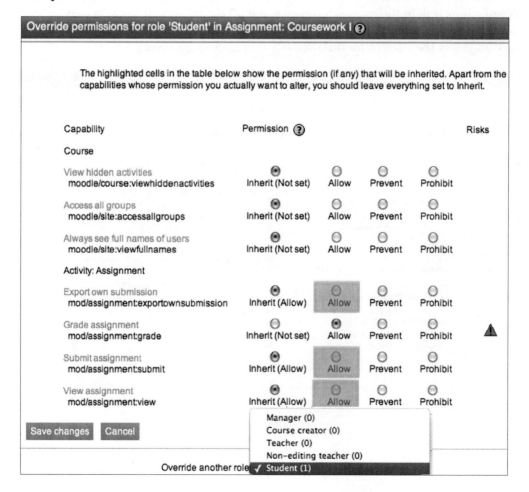

Depending on the context in which permissions are being overridden, only relevant capabilities are shown. In the preceding screenshot, only seven capabilities are displayed. The underlying gray boxes show permissions that have been copied. The highlighted value is that of the permission in this role, in the parent context. In the screenshot, it would therefore make no difference whether the capability values **Submit assignment** and **View assignment** are set to **Allow** or are left to **Inherit**.

# Creating custom roles

Moodle allows the creation of new roles. Examples of such custom roles are Parent, Teaching assistant, Secretary, Inspector, and Librarian. New roles are defined at **Users | Permissions | Define roles** using the **Add a new role** button.

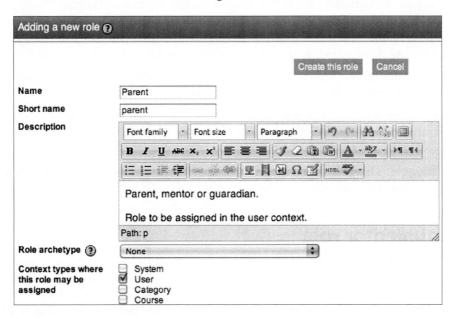

Duplicating a role is a common way of creating a new role. It not only minimizes the amount of work required, but also reduces errors in creating new roles. Alternatively, you can create a new role and use the **Role archetype** of an existing role.

Make sure that you specify the **Context types in which this role may be assigned**. If you miss out a context, it will not be possible to assign the role. If you allow a context that is not suitable for the role, you run the risk that it will be assigned at a later stage and potentially cause problems.

# Example roles

Moodle Docs has provided a number of sample roles that might be relevant to your organization. If not, they offer a good starting point to create other roles, which are listed as follows:

- **Inspector**: This role provides external inspectors or verifiers with the permission to view all courses in Moodle without being required to enrol (for more details on this role, see `docs.moodle.org/en/Inspector_role`)

- **Demo teacher**: This role provides a demonstration teacher with an account that has a password and profile that cannot be changed (for more details on this role, see `docs.moodle.org/en/Demo_teacher_role`)

- **Forum moderator**: This role enables moderation in a particular forum and provides a user with the ability to edit or delete forum posts, split discussions, and move discussions to other forums (for more details on this role, see `docs.moodle.org/en/Forum_moderator_role`)

- **Calendar editor**: This role enables a user to add site events to the calendar (for more details on this role, see `docs.moodle.org/en/Calendar_editor_role`)

- **Question creator**: This role enables students to create questions for use in quizzes (for more details on this role, see `docs.moodle.org/en/Question_creator_role`)

- **Blogger**: This role limits blogging to specific users (for more details on this role, see `docs.moodle.org/en/Blogger_role`)

# Parent/Mentor role

One of the most popular and sought-after custom roles in Moodle is the one of a parent, guardian, or mentor. The idea is to grant permission for users to view certain profile information; such as, activity reports, grades, blog entries, and forum posts of their children, wards, or mentees. This can be achieved with the creation of a new role. Furthermore, the specially-introduced **Mentees** block has to be placed on the front page to give users who have been assigned the role, access to the **User** context.

1. Create new role: For creating a new role, follow these steps:

   a. Go to **Users | Permissions | Define roles**.

   b. Add a new role and name it **Parent** or **Mentor**. Provide an appropriate **Short name** and a **Description**.

   c. Leave the **Role archetype** type set to **None**.

d. Check the **User** checkbox for the **Context types where this role may be assigned** field.

e. Change the capability **moodle/user:viewdetails** to **Allow**. This grants access to the user profile page.

f. Change the following capabilities in the **Users** section to **Allow**, which grants access to individual areas on the user profile page:

- **moodle/user:readuserposts**: to read the child's forum posts.
- **moodle/user:readuserblogs**: to read the child's blog entries.
- **moodle/user:viewuseractivitiesreport**: to view the child's activity reports and grades.

2. Create user account for parent: Each parent requires a separate user account, which is set up as explained in the earlier chapter (go to **Users | Accounts | Add a new user** and add details for the parent or use Moodle's bulk upload facility). In our example, the father is **Roy Harris** and his children are **Frank Harris** and **Paul Harris**, as shown in the following screenshot:

| First name / Surname | Email address | City/town | Country | Last access | | |
|---|---|---|---|---|---|---|
| Frank Harris | Frank.Harris@yourschool.org.uk | London | United Kingdom | Never | Edit | Delete |
| Paul Harris | paul.harris@yourschool.org.uk | London | United Kingdom | Never | Edit | Delete |
| Roy Harris | roy.harris@yourschool.org.uk | London | United Kingdom | Never | Edit | Delete |

3. Link parent to pupil: Each parent has to be linked to each respective child. Unlike the creation of users, this process cannot be automated via batch files yet and so is a potentially time-consuming process. It is expected that this feature will be added to user batch creation in the near future.

a. Access the first child's profile page and click on the **Roles | Assign roles relative to this user** link in the **Settings** block.

b. Choose **Parent** as the role to assign.

c. Select the parent (**Roy Harris**) from the **Potential users** list and add him to the **Existing users** list.

d. Repeat the steps (a) to (c) for the second child, Paul Harris.

4. Add mentee block: A special **Mentees** block has been introduced to facilitate access to user information.

a. Go to your front page and click on the **Turn editing on** link.

b.  Add the **Mentees** block to the front page (it can also be added as a sticky block in My Moodle) and change its title to **Parent access** via the **Configuration** icon.

c.  Login as **Roy Harris** and you should see the following block:

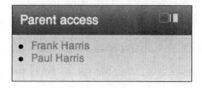

When a name is clicked on, the respective user profile will be shown, which includes any posts sent to forums, blog entries, and activity reports, including logs and grades.

# Testing new roles

After creating a new role, it is recommended to test it thoroughly before it is assigned to any users. To do this, create a test account and assign the new role to it. Log out as administrator and log in as the newly-created user to test the new role or use the **Login as** function to masquerade as the test user. Alternatively, use a different browser to test out the role without logging out as administrator.

If you have modified a predefined role and would like to roll back to its factory settings, go to **Users | Permissions | Define roles**, select a role, and click on the **Reset to defaults** button. This will replace its existing values with those from the built-in capabilities.

The complexity of the roles system and the ability to assign multiple roles to multiple users in multiple contexts calls for a mechanism to verify the correctness of permissions set. This problem is amplified by the fact that permissions can be inherited and then overridden again at lower levels.

Moodle has a built-in permission checker that displays the values of any capabilities in the context in which the checker has been called. This facility is called via the **Check permissions** link in a specific context. For example, in the following screenshot, we have called the permission checker in the **User** context of **Paul Harris** and showed the permissions of user **Roy Harris**. It confirms the settings of the earlier-created **Parent** role:

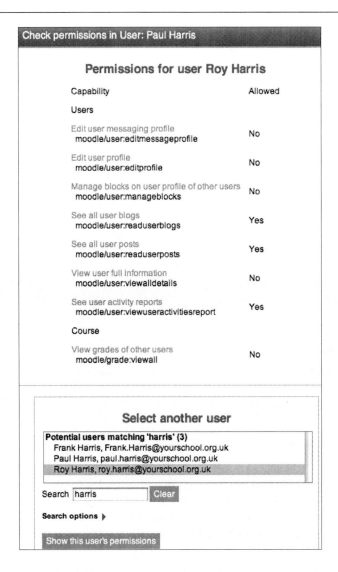

At site level, there are two additional mechanisms that help to identify any potential issues with roles. The capability report (**Users | Permissions | Capability report**) shows, for a selected capability, what permissions it has in the definition of one or many selected roles. It also shows if the capability has been overridden anywhere in the system, which is a great help when you're trying to locate any local modifications.

In the following screenshot, I have selected the capability **mod/forum:rate: Rate posts** and **All** roles. The report that follows shows the values of the capability in the **Student** and the **Teacher** role, and also a forum in a course, where it has been overridden:

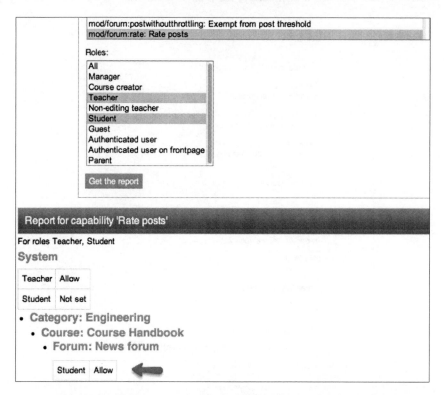

The second tool can be found at **Users | Permissions | Unsupported role assignments**. As the name suggests, it lists any role assignments that are not valid. This usually happens when you upgrade from a previous version of Moodle. If any assignments are listed, you will have to manually modify or remove them.

# Roles management

We have now dealt with the most important tools to use, modify, and create roles. Moodle offers a number of system settings that are important when working extensively with roles.

# Allowing roles assignments and overrides

By default, some roles have the right to allow other roles to assign roles. For instance, a teacher is only allowed to assign **Non-editing teacher** and **Student** roles, whereas the manager is allowed to assign all roles except the **Guest**, the **Authenticated user**, and **Authenticated user on front page** roles (because these are automatically assigned when a user signs in for the first time). There are instances when you either wish to change the default settings, for example, when a teacher assigns roles to other teachers, or when newly created roles have to be managed. To do this, select the **Allow roles assignments** tab in **Users | Permissions | Define Roles**:

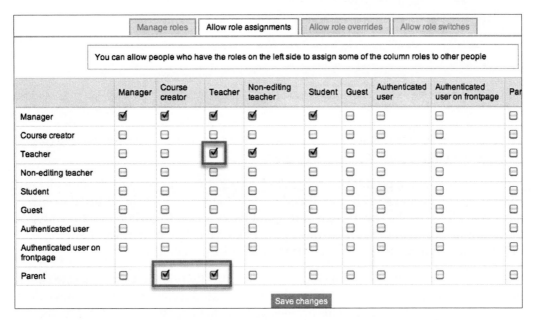

In the preceding screenshot, the modified allowances have been highlighted. The teachers are allowed to assign the **Teacher** role; both the course creators and the teachers are allowed to assign the new **Parent** role.

The identical mechanism exists for role overrides and role switches. They are accessed via the **Allow role overrides** and **Allow role switches** tabs respectively, on the same screen.

# Assigning of default roles

In certain situations, standard roles are assigned. These can be specified in the **User policies** section under **Users | Permissions**:

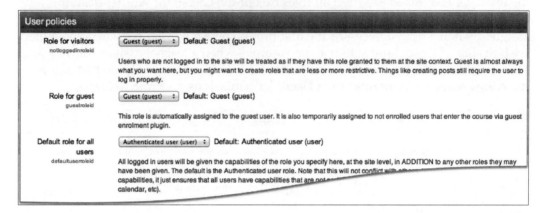

The preceding screenshot shows the assignment of the default role for visitors (users who are not logged in) and the role for guest.

Moodle comes with a predefined role called **Authenticated user**, which is the default role for all logged-in users. It is assigned to *every* logged-in user, in addition to any other roles. The role has been created to grant users access to certain functionality; for example, posting blog entries, managing personal calendar entries, changing profile fields, and so on, even if they are not enrolled in a course.

You can further specify what role is given automatically (via the **Creator's role in new courses** drop-down list) to users who have created a course, but don't have any permissions yet in the course. This applies to restoring courses from backups (see *Chapter 13, Backup and Restore*).

There are three more self-explanatory settings that are not explicitly related to roles—**Auto-login guests**, **Hide user fields**, and **When selecting users, search and display**.

> Changing settings in **User policies** can have a major impact on what new users are allowed to do on your Moodle system, so double-check the default roles before they are applied!

In addition to the default roles in the **User policies** section, it is also possible to specify a default front page role. This can be accessed in **Front page | Front page settings**. To enable logged-in users to participate in activities positioned on the front page, the **Default frontpage role** field can be set, usually to **Student** or **Teacher**. It is also possible to allow logged-in users to participate in these activities by setting an authenticated user role override.

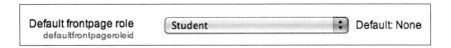

## Moodle role assignment—best practice

Roles can sometimes cause problems in Moodle sites, and you are therefore advised to follow these recommendations:

- Only assign the roles once you have understood them thoroughly
- Never grant a user a role that is beyond his or her competence
- Avoid assigning multiple predefined roles to users if possible
- Avoid system roles as much as possible
- Avoid role assignments that don't make sense
- Keep track of role assignments to ensure maintainability in the future
- Do not change the permissions of predefined roles

# Summary

In this chapter, you have learned what roles are and how they are applied in different contexts. We then covered the modification of existing roles before creating our own custom roles such as Parent, Inspector, or Librarian. Finally, we looked at the management of administrative role-related settings.

Getting your head round the roles concept in Moodle is vital if you wish to add, modify, or remove functionality for a distinct group of users. As always, there is a trade-off between the complexity of such a system and its flexibility. While you can argue about the user-friendliness of the roles system, it has certainly proven to be one of the most powerful concepts in Moodle.

The interconnectedness between courses, users, and roles is crucial. Once this has been set up and configured properly, your Moodle is technically ready to go. However, before that, you probably want to change the look and feel first. This is what the next chapter is all about.

# 7
# Moodle Look and Feel

Your system is now fully operational with users, courses, and roles in place. Now, it is time to change its look and feel. Out goes the standard white Moodle standard theme and in comes a site that is in line with the corporate branding of your organization!

After providing a general overview of Moodle's look and feel elements, we will cover the following subjects:

- **Front page customization**: This includes front page settings, block arrangement, front page roles, backup, restore, and questions. You will also learn how to support personalization through the My Moodle feature, and how to make blocks sticky.
- **Moodle themes**: This includes theme selection, theme types, and theme settings. We will also cover support for mobile devices; that is, cell phones and tablets.
- **Accessibility**: This includes support for Moodle users with different accessibility problems, such as visual impairment and motor difficulties.

 Theme creation is not covered in this book, as it is not the task of an administrator, but of a designer with good CSS skills. Packt Publishing offers *Moodle 1.9 Theme Design: Beginner's Guide*, which is a good read to familiarize yourself with Moodle theme basics.

## Look and feel overview

Moodle can be fully customized in terms of layout, branding, and device support. It must be stressed that certain aspects of changing the look and feel require advanced design skills. While you, as an administrator, will be able to make some adjustments, it will be necessary to get a professional designer involved, especially when it comes to styling.

The two most relevant components for customization are the Moodle front page and Moodle themes. Before we cover these areas, let's try to understand which part is responsible for which element of the look and feel of your site.

In the screenshot on the following page, have a look at the front page of the Moodle site after we have logged in as administrator (designed by, and courtesy of, Synergy Learning). It is not obvious which parts are driven by the Moodle theme and which ones by front page settings. The following table, which looks at the page's elements from top to bottom, sheds some light upon this:

| Element | Settings | Theme | Other |
|---|---|---|---|
| Logo | | X | |
| Logged-in information (location and font) | | X | |
| Language drop-down | | X | X |
| Dockable sidebar | X | X | |
| Pull-down menu | X | | |
| **Navigation** and **Settings** blocks (position) | X | | |
| **Available courses** block (position) | X | | |
| **Available courses** block (content) | | | X |
| **Course categories** and **Calendar** block (position) | X | | |
| **All courses** link in **Course categories** block | X | | |
| Icons, font colors, header, borders, and so on, of all blocks | | X | |
| Show icons to collapse blocks | X | | |
| Show icons to dock blocks | X | X | |
| Footer text | | X | |
| Copyright statement | | X | |
| Number of columns | | X | |

While this list is by no means complete, it hopefully gives you an idea that the look and feel of your site is driven by a number of different elements. It should also give you an idea about elements that can be modified:

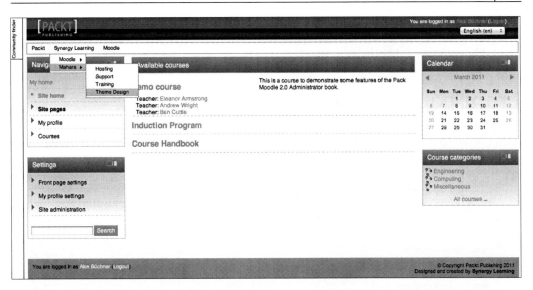

In short, the settings (mostly front page settings as well as a few related parameters) dictate what content users will see before and after they log in. The theme is responsible for the design scheme or branding; that is, the header and footer as well as colors, fonts, icons, and so on, used throughout the site.

# Customizing your front page

Moodle's front page changes after a user has logged in. The content and layout of the page before and after login can be customized. Look at the following screenshot. It is the same site that the preceding screenshot was taken from, but before a user has logged in:

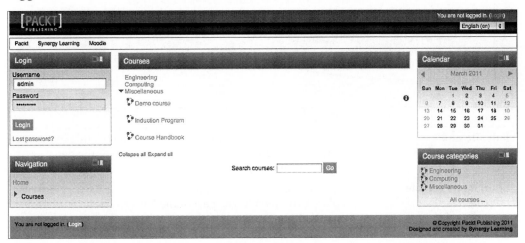

In this particular example, the **Login** block is shown on the left and the **Course categories** and **Courses** are displayed in the center, as opposed to the list of available courses. Additionally, the **Settings** block is not displayed.

# Front page settings

In order to customize the front page (**Front page | Front page settings**), you either have to be logged in as Moodle administrator, or have been granted front page-related permissions in the **Front page** context:

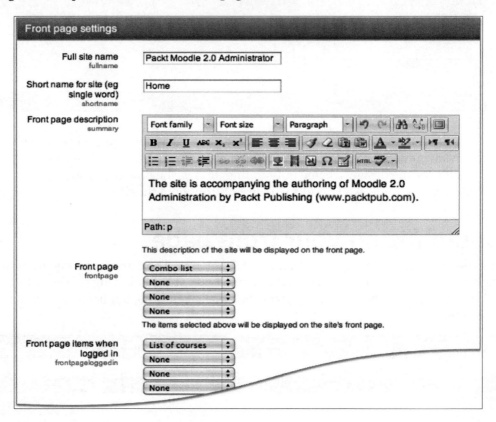

| Setting | Description |
| --- | --- |
| **Full site name** | This is the name that appears in the browser's title bar. It is usually the full name of your organization or the name of the dedicated course or qualification that the site is used for. |
| **Short name for site** | This is the internal name of your site that is used at various places, for instance, as part of the backup name or when networking the site. |

| Setting | Description |
|---|---|
| **Front page description** | This description of the site will be displayed on the front page, on the **Site description** block. The description text is also picked up by the Google search engine spider, if allowed. |
| **Front page** | Moodle can display up to four elements in the center column of the front page, when not logged in: <br><br>• A list of courses <br>• A list of categories <br>• News items <br>• A combo list (**Categories** and **Courses**) <br><br>The order of the elements is the same as the one chosen in the pull-down menus. |
| **Front page items when logged in** | Same as **Front page**, but can be used when logged in. |
| **Maximum category depth** | When course categories are shown, this setting specifies how many levels of the hierarchy are displayed. It is useful to limit this, if your category hierarchy's depth is greater than three or four. |
| **Include a topic section** | If ticked, an additional topic section (just like the topic block in the center column of a course) appears on top of the front page's center column. It can contain any mix of resources or activities available in Moodle. It is very often used to provide information about the site, or to include an image or video. |
| **News items to show** | Number of news items that are displayed. |
| **Comments displayed per page** | This setting dictates how many entries are shown if the **Comments** block is used on the front page. This setting really belongs to the **Comments** block and might be moved in the near future. |
| **Courses per page** | This is a threshold setting that is used when displaying courses within categories. If there are more courses in a category than specified, page navigation will be displayed at the top of the page. Also, when a combo list is used, course names are only displayed if the number is less than the specified threshold. For all other categories, only the number of courses is shown after the category name. |
| **Default front page role** | If logged-in users are allowed to participate in front page activities, a default front page role should be set. The default is **None**. |

The **Front page settings** mainly dictate what is displayed in the center of the page. Now, let's have a look at the blocks at the left and the right.

# Arranging front page blocks

To configure the left and right column areas with blocks, you have turn on editing in the **Front page settings** area of the **Settings** block. Once turned on, you will see the **Add a block** block, which contains all available blocks that can be added to the front page (except the ones that have already been added and only allow a single instance). Some of these are not available in **Courses**, such as **Course/Site description**, **Main menu**, or **Network servers**:

Blocks are added to the front page in exactly the same way as in courses. To change their position, use the **Move** icon. Some blocks have settings that are unique to that block, and which can be accessed through the **Configuration** icon. For example, the **Navigation** block allows you to specify whether the block can be docked and how certain types of content are displayed:

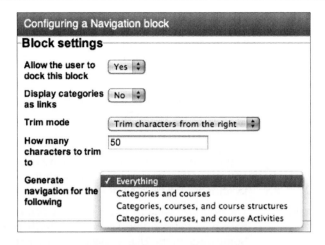

In addition to block-specific settings, every block contains two sets of parameters that control its behavior. These two sections, **Where this block appears** and **On this page**, will be shown for every block:

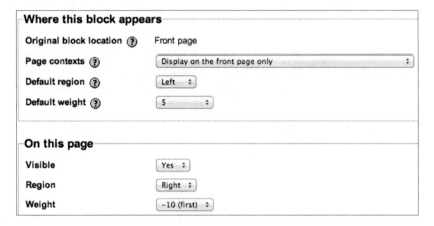

A block, like a role, can be assigned in a context (here, **Front page**) and its properties are inherited and overridden in sub-contexts. The first set of settings specifies where the block will be displayed and what the default properties are. The second set of settings specifies the properties in the current context. The following parameters are available:

| Setting | Description |
|---|---|
| **Original block location** | This shows the context in which the block has been created. This is sometimes referred to as home context. As with roles, pages may inherit blocks from a parent context. |

| Setting | Description |
| --- | --- |
| **Page contexts** (not in all contexts) | This setting dictates on which pages the block will be shown. The following options are available:<br><br>• **Display on front page only**<br>• **Display on the front page and any pages added to the front page**<br>• **Display throughout the site**<br><br>In other contexts, such as **Courses**, other (context-sensitive) options will be shown, depending on the original block location and your current location. |
| **Display on page types** (Unavailable on front page) | The options available depend on the context the block is shown in, for example, **Only user profile pages** and **My home page** in the **User** context, or **Any page**, **Any course page**, and **Any type of course main page** in **Courses**. |
| **Default region (Left, Right)** | Whether the block's position is on the left or on the right. |
| **Default weight (-10...10)** | Think of a block as a balloon: The lighter the block weight, the higher up its position and the heavier the weight, the further down it will be placed. |
| **Visible (Yes, No)** | Whether the block is shown or hidden. |
| **Region (Left, Right)** | Same as **Default region**. On the My Moodle and profile pages, **content** is offered as a third option (see the *My Moodle and Profile pages* section further on). |
| **Weight (-10...10)** | Same principle as **Default weight**. |

In the preceding screenshot, the block is shown in the right-hand column, at the first position. However, when it is displayed on any other page, the block is initially shown on the left and has a weight of -5.

The **Main menu** block allows you to add any installed Moodle resource or activity inside the block. For example, using labels and links to (internal or external) websites, you are able to create a menu-like structure. Another block that has proven popular on the front page is **Online users**, which displays a list of everybody currently logged in to your Moodle site. The **HTML** block lets you add any HTML code, which is useful for any type of content that cannot be displayed using standard Moodle blocks.

If the **Include a topic section** parameter has been selected in the **Front page settings**, you must edit the area and add any installed Moodle activity or resource. This topic section is usually used by organizations to add a welcome message to visitors, often accompanied by a picture or other multimedia content.

Double-check what your site looks like when you are not logged in. Make sure no information is visible that should only accessible to logged-in users.

# Log in from a different website

The purpose of the **Login** block is for users to authenticate themselves by entering their credentials in the form of username and password. It is possible to log in to Moodle from a different website, maybe your organization's home page, effectively avoiding Moodle's front page and **Login** block. To implement this you must add some HTML code on the remote page from which you wish the user to log in:

```
<form class="loginform" name="login" method="post" action="http://www.
mysite.com/login/index.php">
   <p>Username :
     <input size="10" name="username" />
   </p>
   <p>Password :
     <input size="10" name="password" type="password" />
   </p>
   <p>
     <input name="Submit" value="Login" type="submit" />
   </p>
</form>
```

This form will pass the username and password to your Moodle system. You will have to replace www.mysite.com with your URL; this address has to be entered in the **Alternate Login URL** field at **Plugins | Authentication | Manage authentication**.

# Other front page items

The Moodle front page is being treated as a standalone component in Moodle and has therefore been given a top-level menu with a number of features that can all be accessed through the **Front page** item in the **Site administration** section:

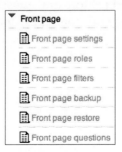

We have already looked at the **Front page settings**; now, let us have a brief look at the other available options. As the front page is treated like a course (internally, it has course ID 1), a number of settings are available, which are identical to their course counterparts.

# Front page roles

The front page has its own context in which roles can be assigned to users. This allows a separate user to develop and maintain the front page without having access to any other elements in Moodle. As the front page is treated as a course, a Teacher role is usually sufficient for this.

We have discussed this feature in detail in the previous chapter, which dealt with the management of roles.

# Front page filters

Any filters that have been activated can be configured at course level. The same applies to the front page. We will discuss filters in detail in *Chapter 9, Moodle Configuration*, when we look at different configuration settings.

# Front page backup and restore

The front page has its own backup and restore facilities to back up and restore any elements of the front page, including any content. The mechanism of performing a backup and restore is the same as for course backups, which is dealt with in *Chapter 13, Backup and Restore*.

Like all other course backups, front page backups are stored in the **User backup** folder of your user file (**System/<your name>/User backup**).

# Front page questions

Since the Moodle front page is treated in the same way as a course, it also has its own question bank, which is used to store any questions used on front-page quizzes. For more information on quizzes, question types, and the question bank, go to the Moodle Docs at docs.moodle.org/en/Quiz.

# Customizing navigation

By default, every user has the main front page, also known as **Site home**, as their top-level page, which is indicated by the **Home** label in the breadcrumb trail. Every user also has a personal page, known as **My home**, but often referred to as **My Moodle**. This page can be customized by the user, and is accessed through the **Navigation** block, can be set.

When you go to **Appearance | Navigation**, you have the option to specify the **Default home page for users**. The options are **Site** (default), **My Moodle** (personal page), and **User preference** (the user can make this choice in **Settings | My profile settings | Make this my default home page**). In the following screenshot, you can see the impact on the breadcrumb trail and **Navigation** block for the settings **My Moodle** (left) and **Site** (right):

Additional navigation settings that specify which courses and categories are shown in the **Navigation** block:

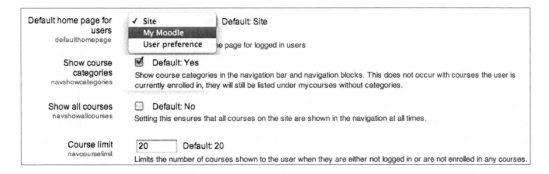

The subject of displaying courses and categories comes up regularly when customizing Moodle sites. The common cause for concern is that the amount of courses seen on the screen is overwhelming and it's difficult for users to navigate through the entire category hierarchy.

[ Only you, as the administrator, will see the long list of all courses and categories. Users will only see the courses they are enrolled in. ]

Bearing this in mind, there are a number of ways the entire category structure can be exposed to users:

- Through the **All courses** link in the **Courses** block, unless the **Hide all courses link** option has been checked in **Plugins | Blocks | Course list**. Here, you can also specify that the admin only will see their courses.

- By selecting **List of categories** or **Combo list** in the front page settings.

- Through the **Courses** listing in the **Navigation** block. This is controlled by the settings in the preceding screenshot.

Which users are shown alongside the course description is related to the way in which courses and categories are presented to the user. By default, this is only users with the Teacher role. You can change this is **Appearance | Course contacts**.

## My Moodle and Profile pages

There are two special pages that users are able to customize themselves. These are the **My Moodle** page and the **Profile** page. This facility is similar to a customizable dashboard. Once logged in, users will have the ability to edit the pages by adding blocks to the respective areas and changing any blocks that have already been added by default. You, as the administrator, have the ability to specify what these default blocks are, where they are positioned, and control how much customization can be carried out.

This two default settings can be found at **Appearance | Default My Moodle page** and **Appearance | Default profile page**, respectively. Once on either page, you have to click on the **Customize this page** button. Any blocks you place on the default pages will appear on users' pages. Interestingly, using the standard **Move** icon, you can place blocks in the center column! It is a shame that the same functionality does not (yet) exist on the front page, or even in courses, by default, as shown in the following screenshot:

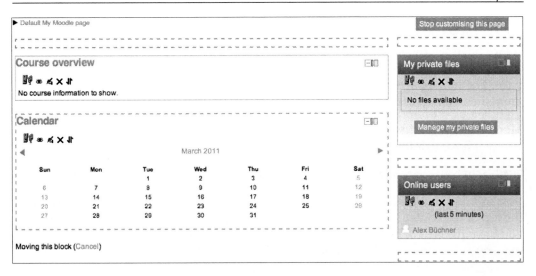

Not only that, you can also make blocks sticky. These are blocks that you wish to display on every page, making them effectively compulsory blocks that cannot be modified or deleted. To facilitate this, the block settings must be extended with the **Select pages** setting that is shown in the properties of any block, on the **Default My Moodle page**:

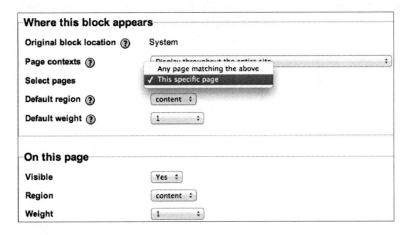

If set to **Any page matching the above,** the block will appear on all those sub-pages and cannot be modified, effectively making the block sticky. The same mechanism applies to the default profile page.

To prevent users from editing their **My Moodle** and **Profile** pages, change the **moodle/my:manageblocks** and **moodle/user:manageownblocks** capabilities in the Authenticated user role.

# Replacing the front page

As we have seen so far, Moodle provides us with a great set of tools to customize the front page. Sometimes though, you might want to replace this with a custom front page. The home page of `www.moodle.org` is a good example of where this has been implemented successfully.

Moodle lets you add a custom script to the front page. To implement this feature, you will have to add the following line to your `config.php` file:

```
$CFG->customfrontpageinclude = "<dirroot>/local/<your front page>";
```

Bear in mind that this will display the output of the `<your front page>` PHP file at the top of the content area, in addition to any elements of the front page. That way you have the best of both worlds—the Moodle elements (disable the ones you don't require) and your custom elements.

# Moodle themes

Moodle provides a flexible skinning mechanism to brand your site according to existing guidelines. As mentioned in the introduction, we only cover theme settings that can be accessed from the Moodle administration menu. For details on how to create Moodle themes, refer to *Moodle 1.9 Theme Design: Beginner's Guide* by Packt Publishing, or contact your Moodle Partner, who will be able to offer you professional theme design services.

## Selecting a Moodle theme

Moodle comes with a number of standard themes, which are selected through **Appearance | Themes | Theme Selector**:

| Device type | Theme | Information |
|---|---|---|
| default | | Select theme |
| legacy | | Select theme |
| mobile | No theme selected | Select theme |
| tablet | No theme selected | Select theme |

You can select up to four themes for your site, each supporting one of the following device types:

- **default**: This is the theme to be used, unless any of the other types are detected. Device detection has to be enabled in the theme settings.

- **legacy**: If you have users on your system who are stuck in the previous millennium; that is, still using Internet Explorer 6, this theme will be used, instead of the default one. Moodle ships with a **Standard (legacy)** theme, which is effectively the **Standard** theme with built-in, non-maintained IE6 support.

- **mobile**: This theme is used when a smartphone is detected.

- **tablet**: This theme is used when a tablet (iPads or Android Honeycomb) is detected.

All modern browsers (Firefox 3.5+ and 4+, Internet Explorer 7/8/9, Safari 5+, and Chrome) are fully supported by Moodle. Internet Explorer 6 and other old browsers are not explicitly supported!

User-created themes also appear in the list of themes to choose from; for example, the Packt theme in the previous screenshot (courtesy of, and designed by, Synergy Learning). There is a database of public Moodle themes at http://www.moodle.org/themes. Alternatively, you can commission a Moodle partner to develop a professional theme for your site.

The **Clear theme caches** button at the top of the screen is relevant if changes have been made to themes but updates have not propagated yet.

Older themes (themes from Moodle 1.9 or previous versions) will not work in Moodle 2. You must only use themes that support the Moodle 2 theme engine.

# Theme types

To understand most theme settings, we need a little bit of background. Like roles, themes are assigned in different contexts, namely Site (**System**), **User**, **Course**, and **Category**. However, two additional areas, that is, Session and Page, are supported by Moodle. These so-called theme types are explained in the following list:

- **Site theme**: If no other theme is selected, this theme is applied throughout the site. This is the default when you first install Moodle.

- **User theme**: If enabled, users are allowed to select their personal theme as part of their profile.

- **Course theme**: If enabled, each editing teacher can specify a course theme in the course settings (**Force theme** parameter in course settings).

- **Category theme**: A theme can be set for each course category (**Force theme** parameter in category settings).

- **Session theme**: If you need to apply a theme temporarily (that is, until you log out), you add the theme parameter to the URL of a course. For example, on our site we would replace `http://.../course/view.php?id=5` with `http://.../course/view.php?id=5&theme=packttheme`.

  There are a number of scenarios where this feature is useful:

  - Theme testing
  - Provision of themes through links instead of Moodle settings (theme gallery or theme switching)
  - Provision of themes for different devices; for example, for PDAs, mobile phones, or game consoles

- **Page theme**: Page themes are set in code and have only been added for completeness.

The following table shows theme priority; where it is displayed, and where the setting is changed. To change the precedence order, modify the `$CFG->themeorder` parameter in `config.php`. The default is set to `array('page', 'course', 'category', 'session', 'user', 'site');`

| Type | Overrides | Displays | Setting Location |
|------|-----------|----------|------------------|
| Site | None | All pages, except course and category, if set. | Theme Selector |
| User | Site | All pages, except course and category, if set. | User profile |
| Course | Site/User/Category/Session | Course | Course settings |
| Category | Site/User/Session | All courses in category, except course, if set. | Category editing |
| Session | Site/User | All pages, except course and category, if set. | `config.php` |
| Page | All | Depends on code. | In code |

There is some trade-off when allowing theme types other than the site theme; while allowing User, Course, Category, and other such themes, additional processing is required that will add overhead to your system and place increased demand on your server. However, not allowing these themes limits the level of customization that can be carried out on your site.

# Theme settings

Armed with all the information up to this point, the theme settings (**Appearance | Themes | Theme settings**) are almost self-explanatory:

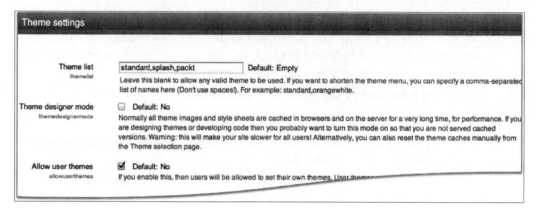

| Setting | Description |
|---|---|
| **Theme list** | To limit the number of available themes, name them in the text box, separated by commas and with no spaces! |
| **Theme designer mode** | Only for theme designers or developers. Effectively turns off theme caching. |
| **Allow user themes** | Users will be able to set their own themes. |
| **Allow course themes** | Editing teachers can set course themes. |
| **Allow category themes** | Enables category themes. |
| **Allow theme changes in the URL** | Enables session themes. |
| **Allow users to hide blocks** | By default, users are allowed to show and hide blocks through the icon at the top-right of each block, which toggles between a plus and minus symbol. This can be turned off if the functionality is not wanted. |
| **Allow blocks to use the dock** | By default, all blocks can be docked in the sidebar through the dock icon. This can be turned off if the functionality is not required. |

| Setting | Description |
|---------|-------------|
| **Custom menu items** | Here, you can add a drop-down menu underneath the header of your page. Each entry represents a menu item in the form of `<Indent><Text>[|<ULR>][|<Tooltip>][|<Language>]`. |
| | `<Indent>` is a series of hyphens; no hyphens represents a top-level menu; one hyphen, a sub-menu; two hyphens, a sub-sub-menu; and so on. `<Text>` is the label of the menu item; the optional `<URL>` is the internal or external link; and `<Tooltip>` is the optional balloon help. |
| | For example, the following **Custom menu items** entry will generate the menu shown in the theme in the first screenshot of this chapter: |

```
Packt|http://www.packtpub.com
Synergy Learning
-Moodle
--Hosting|http://www.synergy-learning.com/moodle/moodle_hosting.php|Hosting
--Support|hhttp://www.synergy-learning.com/moodle/moodle_support.php|Support
--Training|http://www.synergy-learning.com/moodle/moodle_training.php|Training
--Theme Design|http://www.synergy-learning.com/moodle/moodle_themes.php|Themes
-Mahara
--Hosting|http://www.synergy-learning.com/mahara/mahara_hosting.php|Hosting
--Support|hhttp://www.synergy-learning.com/mahara/mahara_support.php|Support
--Training|http://www.synergy-learning.com/mahara/mahara_training.php|Training
--Theme Design|http://www.synergy-learning.com/mahara/mahara_themes.php|Themes
Moodle|http://moodle.org
```

| Setting | Description |
|---------|-------------|
| | Since Moodle 2.1, you can add a language code or a separated list if codes as the last item, which will only be shown if the user has currently selected the listed language, for example: |
| | `English|http://www.synergy-learning.com||en` |
| | `German|http://www.synergy-learning.de||de,de_ kids` |
| **Enable device detection** | Moodle can distinguish between **default** and **legacy** browsers as well as **mobile** and **tablet** devices. If enabled, different themes can be selected for each device type. |
| **Device detection regular expressions** | Unsupported device types can be added, if you know the regular expression (also known as mobile browser ID or user-agent string) that will be sent by the device. |

Now that we have the skill-set, it is time to customize existing themes.

# Customizing themes

As an administrator, you are unlikely to be involved in the creation of a full-blown custom theme as this task requires strong designing skills. However, you will be able to make basic modifications to existing themes.

# Theme customization basics

Moodle uses **Cascading Style Sheets** (CSS) to describe the presentation of each element that is displayed. CSS is used to define different aspects of HTML and XHTML presentation including colors, fonts, layout, and so on. You can find more information about the specification of CSS at www.w3.org/Style/CSS.

To read more on theme basics go to docs.moodle.org/dev/Themes_2.0, where you will find a very well-documented and detailed help section. You might also want to install a number of useful tools when customizing themes such as the popular Firebug or the CSS theme tool block (docs.moodle.org/dev/CSS_theme_tool_block).

At the heart of CSS, are so-called styles; Moodle uses consistent plain English for the naming of styles. For the forum elements displayed in the following screenshot, a few sample styles have been labeled:

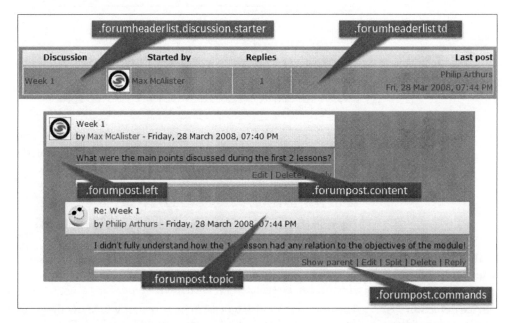

You see that each element of Moodle is represented by a style. In total, there are well over 2,000 (!) styles in Moodle, which gives a designer much freedom.

Moodle themes can be customized through their respective settings in **Appearance | Themes | <Theme name>**. Different themes provide different settings. A good example is the **Formal white** theme, as it contains many different types of parameters:

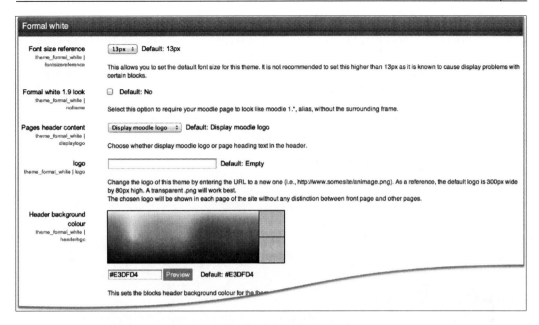

These theme settings include the following elements:

- **Font size**: Default font size is used in themes.

- **Color picker**: Here, the background color for blocks can be selected (foreground and background). Other themes let you specify other styles, such as link color or header color. The color picker offers a preview, which is quite helpful.

- **Logo**: A URL can be specified to replace the one shown in the header. Other themes allow the customization of the tag line, or the background image.

- **Column width**: You can choose the width of the center column, in pixels. Other (usually fixed-width) themes let you specify the width of the left and right hand column separately.

- **Languages menu**: This checkbox indicates whether the languages menu is shown.

- **Footnote**: The footnote text can be fully customized through the standard Moodle editor; that is, images or HTML code can be also added.

- **Custom CSS**: This text box, which has been added to all themes that ship with core Moodle, lets you change any style in the theme. In the following example, the body background has been changed to black with yellow text. Additionally, the **font-size** has been increased to **16px**. These settings are useful for learners that are visually impaired:

| Custom CSS<br>theme_formal_white \| customcss | ```<br>body {<br>    background-color: #000000;<br>    background-image: none;<br>    color=#FFFF00;<br>}<br><br>p {<br>    font-size: 16px;<br>}<br>``` |
|---|---|
| | Default: Empty |

# Accessibility

In most educational settings, accessibility (the ability for users with certain disabilities to access Moodle's functionality), is now a legal requirement. So, it is important to make sure that your system complies with the respective standards. An area has been dedicated to Moodle accessibility in the Moodle Docs, which you can access at docs.moodle.org/en/accessibility. It provides useful links to standards, guidelines, legislation, and also subject-related tools and resources.

# Guaranteeing accessibility through Moodle themes

CSS is Moodle's representation layer that is independent from the content layer, which is represented in XHTML 1.0 Strict. Thus, accessibility can be achieved through the theme itself.

Once you have implemented your accessibility styles, either directly in the theme or through the **Custom CSS**, as shown in the preceding example, Moodle provides links to three external sites, which check the current page for standard compliance. To activate these, go to **Development | Debugging** and check the **Show validator links** box. After saving the changes, links to **Validate HTML**, **Section 508 Check**, and **WCAG 1 (2, 3) Check** will be displayed at the bottom of your page (if supported by your theme).

One popular option is to incorporate accessibility options and offer them in the theme as options. Have a look at the header of the following theme (courtesy of, and designed by, Synergy Learning). It contains a color switcher in the top-right to cater for different visual impairments. Additionally, three different font sizes can be selected:

There is also a useful third-party **Accessibility** block, which lets the user change the font size and background color of his or her Moodle site. It further supports text-to-speech functionality. You can find it in the **Modules and Plugins** section on www.moodle.org. The installation of third-party modules is covered in detail in *Chapter 14, Installing Third-party Add-ons.*

# Accessibility support through the Moodle editor

Moodle is fully compliant with all major accessibility standards. This has been achieved by implementing XHTML 1.0 Strict, which only allows the usage of compliant HTML constructs and the implementation of the Moodle forms library. This guarantees consistency across forms and also supports standard screen readers.

The compliance is only guaranteed for Moodle pages but not for newly-created and uploaded content or any third-party learning resources. We recommend that you encourage the creation of XHTML Strict content if new web content is developed using the built-in TinyMCE editor.

The Moodle interface is accessed through the keyboard only but, at the time of print, not all required functionality can be accessed that way, by default. In order to resolve this shortcoming, you need to install the MDL-21246 patch (`tracker.moodle.org/browse/MDL-21246`). This will add about 20 shortcuts to improve accessibility, such as visual aids. It is expected that this patch will eventually make its way into the Moodle core.

# Screen reader support

A **screen reader** is a form of assistive technology used by blind and partially-sighted users to interpret what is displayed on the screen. Once the information has been located, it can be vocalized using speech synthesis software and audio hardware.

Moodle supports screen-reading devices. This setting has to be enabled separately for each user requiring the assistive mode. This is done in the user's profile, where the **Screen reader** setting has to be changed to **Yes**.

Screen readers can only read text and the ALT tag in images. We therefore recommend that you provide these tags in any images used.

# Summary

After providing a general overview of look and feel elements in Moodle, this chapter covered front page and Moodle themes customization as well as accessibility. We also dealt with supporting mobile devices. Read more on this in *Chapter 15, Moodle Integration via Web Services*, when we cover web services, which allow the usage of your site with dedicated mobile apps.

As mentioned before, the front page in Moodle is a course. This has advantages (you can do everything you can do in a course, and a little bit more), but it also has drawbacks (you can only do what you can do in a course and might feel limited by this). However, some organizations are now using the Moodle front page as their home page. Again, this might or might not work for you.

Also, there has been some criticism about the non-state-of-the-art look and feel of Moodle. The Moodle theme engine is flexible, powerful and has proved you can create a professional look and feel for your site.

Now that your Moodle looks (hopefully) the way you want it to, it is time to enable all the functionalities that you wish to offer your users. These configuration settings are dealt with in the next chapter.

# 8
# Moodle Plugins

Your system is now fully operational and has the look and feel to reflect the branding of your site. As with all complex software, there are a significant number of configuration activities that can be carried out to bring Moodle in line with your organization's needs and requirements.

One of Moodle's many strengths is its pluggable architecture. Moodle supports a wide range of plugins, which will be covered in this chapter. Some will only be dealt with in brief as they are described elsewhere, whereas others are covered in detail:

- **Module plugins**: This covers core functionality available in a course, the front page, My Moodle page, and the user profile pages. They include **Activity modules**, **Blocks**, and **Filters**.
- **Repositories**: Repositories allow incorporating data into Moodle, either from internal sources or from external sites.
- **Portfolios**: These are the opposite of repositories. Portfolios allow exporting content from Moodle to other applications or data storage.
- **Miscellaneous plugins**: These include **Text editors**, **Licences**, **Question types**, **Question behaviours**, and **Plagiarism prevention**.

There are a number of additional plugin types that have been covered in other chapters; namely, **Enrolments** (*Chapter 4, Course Management*), **Authentication** (*Chapter 5, User Management*), **Message outputs** (*Chapter 9, Moodle Configuration*), **Licences** (*Chapter 15, Moodle Integration via Web Services*), and **Web services** (*Chapter 16, Moodle Networking*).

# Plugins—an overview

Moodle plugins are modules that provide some specific, usually ring-fenced, functionality. You can access the plugins area via the **Plugins** menu that is shown in the following screenshot:

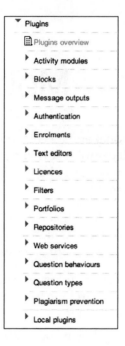

**Plugins overview** displays a list of all installed plugins. The information shown for each plugin includes the **Plugin name**, an internal **Identifier**, its **Source** (Standard or Extension), its **Version** (in date format), its **Availability** (enabled or disabled), a link to the plugin **Settings**, and an option to **Uninstall** the plugin. The table is useful to get a quick overview of what has been installed on your system and what functionality is available.

Some areas contain a significant number of plugins, for instance, **Authentication** and **Portfolios**. Other categories only contain one or two plugins. The expectation is that more plugins will be developed in the future, either as part of the Moodle's core or by third-party developers. This guarantees the extensibility of Moodle without the need to change the system itself. We will be dealing in detail with third-party add-ons in *Chapter 14, Installing Third-party Add-ons*.

 Be careful when modifying settings in any of the plugins. Inappropriate values can cause problems throughout the system.

The last plugin type in the preceding screenshot is labeled **Local plugins**. This is the recommended place for any local customizations. These customizations can be changes to existing functionality or the introduction of new features. For more information about local plugins, check out the `readme.txt` file in the `local` directory in your `dirroot`.

# Module plugins

Moodle distinguishes between three types of module plugins that are used in the courses—the front page (which is treated as a course), the My Moodle page, and the user profile pages:

- **Activities modules** (which also covers resources)
- **Blocks**
- **Filters**

# Activities modules

Navigating to **Plugins | Activity modules | Manage activities** displays the following screen:

| Activity module | Activities | Version | Hide/Show | Delete | Settings |
|---|---|---|---|---|---|
| Assignment | 1 | 2010102600 | 👁 | Delete | Settings |
| Chat | 0 | 2010080302 | 👁 | Delete | Settings |
| Choice | 0 | 2010101300 | 👁 | Delete | |
| Database | 0 | 2011052300 | 👁 | Delete | Settings |
| Feedback | 0 | 2011051600 | ⌣ | Delete | Settings |
| Folder | 0 | 2010101400 | 👁 | Delete | Settings |
| Forum | 7 | 2011052300 | | | Settings |
| Glossary | 0 | 2011052300 | 👁 | Delete | Settings |
| IMS content package | 0 | 2010101400 | 👁 | Delete | Settings |
| Label | 17 | 2010080300 | 👁 | Delete | |
| Lesson | 0 | 2010122200 | 👁 | Delete | Settings |
| Page | 3 | 2010101400 | 👁 | Delete | Settings |
| Quiz | 1 | 2011070100 | 👁 | Delete | Settings |
| File | 21 | 2011022700 | 👁 | Delete | Settings |
| SCORM package | 0 | 2011021402 | 👁 | Delete | Settings |
| Survey | 0 | 2010080300 | 👁 | Delete | |
| URL | 10 | 2010101400 | 👁 | Delete | Settings |
| Wiki | 0 | 2011011001 | 👁 | Delete | |
| Workshop | 0 | 2011061000 | 👁 | Delete | Settings |

The table displays the following information:

| Column | Description |
| --- | --- |
| **Activity module** | Icon and name of the activity/resource as they appear in courses and elsewhere. |
| **Activities** | The number of times the activity module is used in Moodle. When you click on the number, a table, which displays the courses in which the activity module has been used, is shown. |
| **Version** | Version of the activity module (format YYYYMMDDHH). |
| **Hide/Show** | The opened eye indicates that the activity module is available for use, while the closed eye indicates that it is hidden (unavailable). |
| **Delete** | Performs delete action. All activities, except the **Forum** activity, can be deleted. |
| **Settings** | Link to activity module settings (not available for all items). |

Clicking on the **Show/Hide** icon toggles its state; if it is hidden it will be changed to be shown and vice versa. If an activity module is hidden, it will not appear in the **Add an activity** or **Add a resource** drop-down menu in any Moodle course. Hidden activities and resources that are already present in courses are hidden but are still in the system. It means that, once the activity module is visible again, the items will also re-appear in courses.

You can delete any Moodle **Activity module** (except the **Forum** activity). If you delete an activity or resource that has been used anywhere in Moodle, all the already-created activity modules will also be deleted and so will any associated user data! Deleting an activity module cannot be undone; it has to be installed from scratch.

It is highly recommended not to delete any activity modules unless you are 100 percent sure that you will never need them again! If you wish to prevent usage of an activity or resource type, it is better to hide it instead of deleting it.

The **Feedback** activity has been around for some time as a third-party add-on. It is hidden by default because it has been newly introduced in the core of Moodle 2, due to its popularity. You might probably want to make this available for your teachers.

The settings are different for each activity module. For example, the settings for the **Assignment** module only contain three parameters, whereas the settings for the **Quiz** module allow the modification of a wide range of parameters.

The settings for Moodle **Activity modules** are not covered here, as they are mostly self-explanatory and also dealt with in great detail in the Moodle Docs of the respective modules. It is further expected that the activity modules will undergo a major overhaul in the 2.x versions to come, making any current explanations obsolete.

# Configuration of blocks

Navigating to **Plugins | Blocks | Manage blocks** displays a table, as shown in the screenshot that follows. It displays the same type of information as for **Activity modules**. Some blocks allow multiple instances, that is, the block can be used more than once on a page. For example, you can only have one calendar, whereas you can have as many **Remote RSS Feeds** as you wish. You cannot control this behavior, as it is controlled by the block itself.

You can delete any Moodle block. If you delete a block that is used anywhere in Moodle, all the already-created content will also be deleted. Deleting a block cannot be undone; it has to be installed from scratch.

 Do not delete or hide the **Settings** block, as you will not be able to access any system settings anymore! Also, do not delete or hide the **Navigation** block, as users will not be able to access a variety of pages.

Most blocks are shown by default (except the **Feedback** and **Global search** blocks). Some blocks require additional settings to be set elsewhere for the block to function. For example, RSS feeds and tags have to be enabled in **Advanced features**, the **Feedback** activity module has to be shown, or global search has to be enabled (via **Development | Experimental | Experimental settings**).

| Name | Instances | Version | Hide/Show | Delete | Settings |
|------|-----------|---------|-----------|--------|----------|
| Activities | 0 | 2007101509 | 👁 | Delete | |
| Admin bookmarks | 2 | 2007101509 | 👁 | Delete | |
| Blog menu | 0 | 2009071700 | 👁 | Delete | |
| Recent blog entries | 0 | 2009070900 | 👁 | Delete | |
| Blog tags | 0 | 2007101509 | 👁 | Delete | |
| Calendar | 1 | 20071015Q9 | | | |

The parameters of all standard Moodle blocks are explained in the respective Moodle Docs pages.

# Configuration of filters

Filters scan any text that has been entered via the Moodle HTML editor and automatically transform it into different, often more complex, forms. For example, entries or concepts in glossaries are automatically hyperlinked in text, URLs pointing to MP3 or other audio files become embedded, flash-based controls (that offer pause and rewind functionality) appear, uploaded videos are given play controls, and so on.

Moodle ships with 12 filters, which are accessed via **Plugins | Filters | Manage filters**:

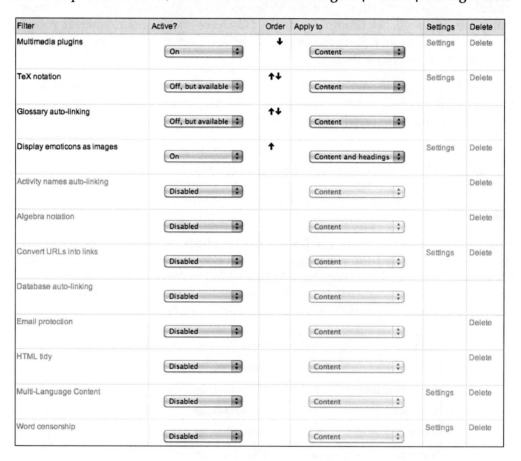

| Filter | Active? | Order | Apply to | Settings | Delete |
|---|---|---|---|---|---|
| Multimedia plugins | On | ↓ | Content | Settings | Delete |
| TeX notation | Off, but available | ↑↓ | Content | Settings | Delete |
| Glossary auto-linking | Off, but available | ↑↓ | Content | | |
| Display emoticons as images | On | ↑ | Content and headings | Settings | Delete |
| Activity names auto-linking | Disabled | | Content | | Delete |
| Algebra notation | Disabled | | Content | | Delete |
| Convert URLs into links | Disabled | | Content | Settings | Delete |
| Database auto-linking | Disabled | | Content | | |
| Email protection | Disabled | | Content | | Delete |
| HTML tidy | Disabled | | Content | | Delete |
| Multi-Language Content | Disabled | | Content | Settings | Delete |
| Word censorship | Disabled | | Content | Settings | Delete |

By default, all filters are disabled. You can enable them by changing the **Active?** status to **On** or **Off, but available**. If the status is set to **On**, it means that the filter is activated throughout the system, but can be de-activated locally. If the status is set to **Off, but available**, it means that the filter is not activated, but can be enabled locally.

In the preceding screenshot, the **Multimedia plugins** and **Display emoticons as images** (smileys) filters have been turned **On** and will be used throughout the system, as they are very popular. The **TeX notation** and **Glossary auto-linking** filters are available, but have to be activated locally. The former is only of use to the users who deal with mathematical or scientific notation and will trigger the **Insert equation** button in the Moodle editor. The **Glossary auto-linking** filter might be used in some courses. It can then be switched off temporarily at activity module level when learners have to appear for an exam.

Additionally, you can change the order in which the filters are applied to text, using the up and down arrows. The filtering mechanism operates on a first-come, first-served basis, that is, if a filter detects a text element that has to be transformed, it will do so before the next filter is applied.

Each filter can be configured to be applied to **Content and headings** or **Content** only, that is, filters will be ignored in names of activity modules. The settings of some filters are described in detail in the Moodle Docs. As with activities and blocks, it is recommended to hide filters if you don't require them on your site.

In addition to the filter-specific settings, Moodle provides a number of settings that are shared among all filters. These settings are accessed via the **Filters | Common filters** menu and are shown in the following screenshot:

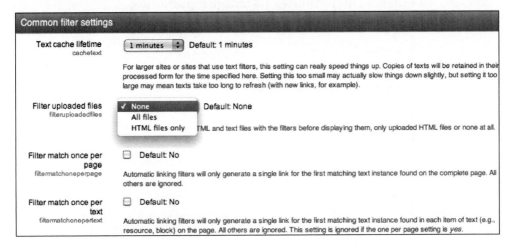

| Setting | Description |
|---------|-------------|
| **Text cache lifetime** | It is the time for which Moodle keeps text to be filtered in a dedicated cache (for more details, see *Chapter 12, Moodle Performance and Optimization*). |
| **Filter uploaded files** | By default, only text entered via the Moodle editor is filtered. If you wish to include uploaded files, you can choose any one from the **HTML files only** and **All files** options. |
| **Filter match once per page** | Enable this setting if the filter should stop analyzing text after it finds a match, that is, only the first occurrence will be transformed. |
| **Filter match once per text** | Enable this setting if the filter should only generate a single link for the first matching text instance found in each item of text on a page. This setting is ignored if the **Filter match once per page** parameter is *enabled*. |

# Moodle repositories

The **File picker** is central to almost all file operations in Moodle. Files can be selected from a wide range of sources known in Moodle as **repositories**. Moodle repositories are accessed via **Plugins | Repositories | Manage repositories**:

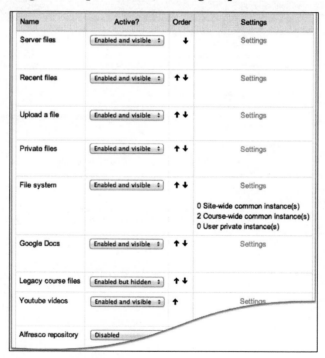

Each repository has one of three states:

- **Enabled and visible**: The repository will be available throughout the system.
- **Enabled but hidden**: Already set up repositories will be available, but no new instances can be created. This only applies to repositories that allow multiple instances (discussed later in this section).
- **Disabled**: The repository is not available in your Moodle system.

The order in which the repositories are listed reflects the order in which the repositories appear in the **File picker**. This can be changed using the up and down arrows. As soon as a repository has been enabled, a **Settings** link will be displayed for almost all repositories. Every repository has a **Repository plugin name** parameter that lets you override its default name. Some repositories also have additional settings, which will be discussed throughout this chapter.

 When you disable a repository plugin, its settings and all of its instances will be removed. Any content that has been added via the plugin will remain, as data is (almost) always copied or streamed from the external source.

Some repository types support multiple instances. The number of existing sitewide, coursewide, and private user instances are displayed under the **Settings** link. These can then be configured in the relevant context, that is, in **Course administration | Repositories** in the course settings, and in **My profile | Repositories** in the user profile page:

| Name | Repository plug-ins | Settings | Delete |
| --- | --- | --- | --- |
| Server files | Server files | | |
| Recent files | Recent files | | |
| Upload a file | Upload a file | | |
| Private files | Private files | | |
| FTP Directory | File system | Settings | Delete |
| Google Docs | Google Docs | | |
| Youtube videos | Youtube videos | | |

### Create a repository instance

- Create "File system" instance
- Create "WebDAV repository" instance

Sitewide instances are created as part of the **Settings** when managing the plugins, for example, the **File system** repository:

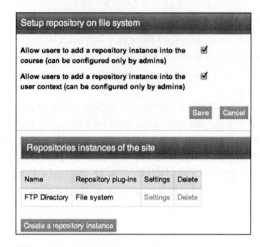

For simplicity, we are distinguishing between internal and external repositories. An **internal repository** is one that accesses internal Moodle files. An **external repository** is located outside Moodle, either on some local media, in another application's data storage, or in the cloud.

# Internal repository plugins

There are a number of internal repository plugins to choose from:

| Name | Description | Settings |
|------|-------------|----------|
| **Server files** | Files on your Moodle system, to which a user has access. Files are arranged in a hierarchy, reflecting Moodle contexts (see *Chapter 2, The Moodle System*). | |
| **Recent files** | Recently used and uploaded files. | **Number of recent files** |
| **Private files** | Personal files of a user, which can be accessed throughout Moodle. | |
| **File system** | Allows access to sub-directories in `$CFG->dataroot/repository`. A directory has to be selected for each instance. Setup and access has been covered in *Chapter 2, The Moodle System*. | **Allow users to add a repository instance into the course** <br><br> **Allow users to add a repository instance into the user context** |
| **Legacy course files** | Access to files after migrating from Moodle 1.9 | |

**Server files**, **Recent files**, and **Private files** are managed by Moodle. The **User quota** parameter can be specified for private files in **Security | Site policies**. The default value is 100 MB. The **File system** plugin has already been described in detail in *Chapter 2, The Moodle System*, when external access to the Moodle filesystem was required; for example, to upload files via FTP.

One area that requires some attention is the **Legacy course files** plugin. In Moodle 1.x, all files were stored in a course files area. They were not linked to a specific activity or resource, nor did personal files, which can be accessed across courses, exist. This caused problems with backups, data security, and data integrity. A new `File API` has been introduced in Moodle 2, which rectifies these shortcomings. An issue arises when updating from Moodle 1.9 to Moodle 2.0. During the migration process, Moodle is able to allot files to activities and resources, but it does not know what to do with unused files or files that have been linked from within certain resources. It stores these in the **Legacy course files** area. Users will have to move those files to the appropriate place manually, that is, their personal files area as well as resources and activities.

 Legacy course files are intended to be a temporary measure. The objective is to discontinue its use once all files have been migrated.

# External repository plugins

External repository plugins will add, that is copy, stream or link, new files or content to your Moodle system. They might be uploaded from your local computer, a USB pen drive, a network drive, or cloud storage such as Dropbox, Box.net, and Amazon S3. Additionally, external applications such as Alfresco, Google Docs, Flickr, Picasa, and YouTube are supported as sources.

It is expected that the number of repository plugins will grow in the near future to access other storage types and applications. The `Repository API` of Moodle makes the development of these add-ons relatively painless for a programmer.

# Data storage repositories

The following repository plugins come as part of core Moodle and act as file or data storage:

| Name | Description | Settings |
| --- | --- | --- |
| **Upload a file** | Manually uploading a file that can be accessed from your local PC or Mac. This will be used a lot by all users. | |
| **WebDAV repository** | Access to a WebDAV server. A repository instance has to be created in the course or user context, where a number of parameters have to be specified: **Name**, **WebDAV type**, **WebDAV server**, **WebDAV path**, **Authentication**, the optional **WebDAV server port**, **WebDAV server user**, and **WebDAV server password** parameters. | **Allow users to add a repository instance into the course**<br><br>**Allow users to add a repository instance into the user context** |
| **Google Docs** | Access to users' documents in Google Docs. Access has to be granted by each user when the plugin is used for the first time. | |
| **Dropbox** | Access to a single Dropbox folder, not one for each user. Click and follow the **Dropbox developers** link under the **Settings** link and click on the **Create an App** button to get access to the two required parameters (**App key and App secret**). | **Dropbox API Key**<br><br>**Dropbox Secret** |
| **Box.net** | Similar to **Dropbox** repository. Follow link on **Settings** page and log on for an API key. | **API key** |
| **Amazon S3** | Access to Amazon S3 storage service. | **Access key**<br><br>**Secret key** |
| **URL Downloader** | Importing a file via a URL link. This can be an internal or external web address. | |

# Application repositories

The following repository plugins that connect to applications come as part of core Moodle:

| Name | Description | Settings |
|------|-------------|----------|
| **Alfresco repository** | Access to Alfresco, a commercial, open source content management system. Both copying and linking are supported. | **Allow users to add a repository instance into the course** |
| | | **Allow users to add a repository instance into the user context** |
| **Flickr** | Access to personal accounts of photo sharing site Flickr. Login required for the first time. | **API key** |
| | | **Secret** |
| **Flickr public** | Access to public area of photo sharing site, Flickr. | **API key** |
| | | **Allow users to add a repository instance into the course** |
| | | **Allow users to add a repository instance into the user context** |
| **Picasa web album** | Access to Picasa web albums. Login required. | |
| **Youtube videos** | Access to YouTube video platform. Videos will be streamed to Moodle, not copied. | |
| **Merlot.org** | Access to MERLOT (Multimedia Education Resource for Learning and Online Teaching). | **License Key** |
| **Wikimedia** | Access to Wikimedia Commons platform. | |

A number of shared settings can be found at **Plugins | Repositories | Common repository** settings. The **Cache expire** setting specifies the amount listings stored locally. The default value of **120** seconds is sufficient unless you have users with erroneous connections.

By default, the **Allow external links** setting is enabled. External links are supported by some repositories, for instance, Alfresco. Legacy course files have been discussed earlier; unless really necessary, it is recommended to leave the **Legacy course files in new courses** checkbox unchecked.

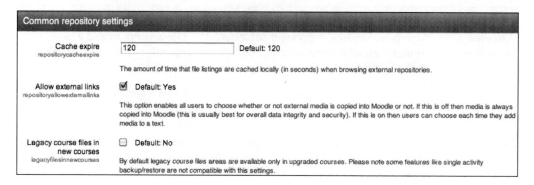

Once the repository setup has been completed, it is best to test out access from a number of contexts (users, site, and course) and also make sure that no users have access to sources they shouldn't have and vice versa.

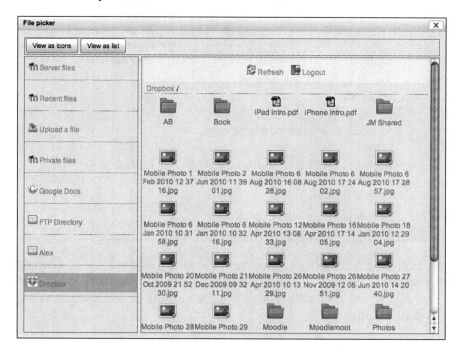

Now that our **File picker** is fully populated and your users are able to get content in to Moodle, let's have a look at how they can achieve the opposite and get content out of Moodle.

 Additional information about all mentioned Moodle repositories can be found at docs.moodle.org/en/Repositories.

# File management

Moodle 2 contains a number of idiosyncrasies when it comes to file management. We covered these in *Chapter 2, The Moodle System*. The two main disadvantages are:

- Due to the fact that files are always copied, it is not possible to use a file in multiple locations (courses) and update all instances at once
- Creating a file pool that can be shared across teachers in the same course is not supported

While these issues are on the roadmap and will be addressed in the near future, in the meantime, you will have to revert to external systems that overcome the existing shortcomings. Two popular candidates are Alfresco and SharePoint.

The **Alfresco** plugin ships as part of Moodle core and supports linking of files. This means that the files are not copied to Moodle, but remain stored in the content management system and only links are provided. The plugin works with all three available editions (Community, Team, and Enterprise).

There is currently a commercial **SharePoint** plugin in development that will also support linking from files. This useful for in particular organizations that already have a SharePoint infrastructure and wish to reuse learning resources that are stored in it.

Two things you have to bear in mind when working with systems that link files instead of copying them:

- Linking of files is not supported throughout: The **Link external** checkbox is only supported by a few features; for example, when adding links inside the HTML editor or when adding images. It will not appear when a teacher is adding resources or activities.
- Moodle won't have control over the content: This is, for instance, relevant when a submission deadline is in place. Moodle can control that the file won't be changed if it is stored in its filesystem. This is not the case for linked files.

# Moodle portfolios

According to Moodle Docs, Moodle portfolios enable data, such as forum posts or assignment submissions, to be exported to external systems.

Moodle portfolios have to be enabled by selecting the **Enable portfolios** parameter in **Advanced features**. Once this has been done, you have access to all available portfolio plugins in **Plugins | Portfolios | Manage portfolios**.

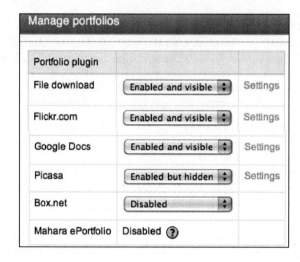

Each portfolio has one of three states:

- **Enabled and visible**: The portfolio will be available throughout the system
- **Enabled but hidden**: Portfolios have to be activated to be used
- **Disabled**: The portfolio is not available in your Moodle system

Once at least one portfolio has been set up, users will see an **Export to portfolio** link or icon at various places in their courses (for instance, assignment submissions, forum posts, and glossary entries). When this link is clicked, they will have to select one of the existing destinations from the **Select destination** drop-down menu. Depending on the chosen portfolio type, additional actions have to be taken, for example, log in to the site, confirm file type, or grant access to the external application.

Export formats that are currently supported are HTML, LEAP2A, images, and text. It is expected that additional formats, such as PDF, will be in added in future.

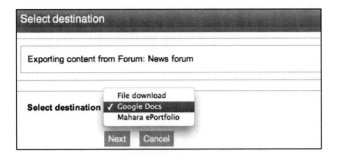

Like repositories, each portfolio plugin has a **Name** setting, where the default plugin label can be changed. Unlike repositories, multiple instances do not exist, nor is it possible to change the order of the plugins.

The following portfolio plugins come as part of core Moodle:

| Name | Description | Settings |
|------|-------------|----------|
| **Box.net** | Follow onscreen instructions to obtain an **API key**. | **API key** |
| | Login to Box.net is required. If successful, users will have to specify whether the created HTML file will be shared and in which folder it has to be placed. | |
| **Google Docs** | Permission has to be granted at first use. An HTML file will be created automatically in the users' **Documents** area. | |
| **File download** | Export formats supported are HTML and LEAP2A (a popular e-portfolio format). | |
| **Flickr.com** | Follow onscreen instructions to obtain an **API key**. | **API key** |
| | Authorization required at first use. | **Secret string** |
| **Mahara ePortfolio** | Disabled by default. Only available if a valid network connection to a Mahara system has been established and the **MNet authentication** plugin has been enabled. *Chapter 16, Moodle Networking* has been dedicated to networking. | **MNet host** **Enable LEAP2A portfolio support** |
| **Picasa** | Access has to be granted when used for the first time. The picture will be placed in the **Drop Box** area of the users' Picasa albums. | |

Users have the ability to select which available portfolios are presented in their **Export to portfolio** list. Under **My profile settings | Portfolios | Configure** in the **Settings** block, they have the option to hide any configured portfolio plugin.

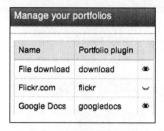

Furthermore, under **My profile settings | Portfolios | Transfer logs**, each user is shown a list of any **Currently queued transfers** and **Previous successful transfers**. The former lists all pending exports, which can either be continued (green button) or cancelled (red button). The latter displays details about all recent transfers:

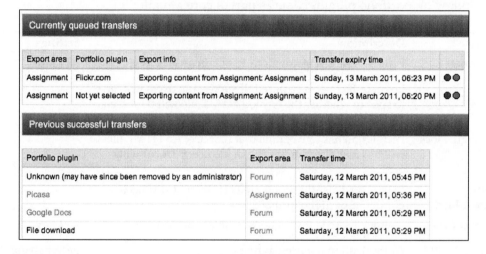

There are a number of settings that apply to all portfolios, which can be accessed under **Plugins | Portfolios | Common portfolio settings**. They include two thresholds for file sizes (**Moderate transfer filesize** and **High transfer filesize**) and two for the number of database records (**Moderate transfer dbsize** and **High transfer dbsize**). If the actual values exceed the threshold values, users will be warned that the export might take some time.

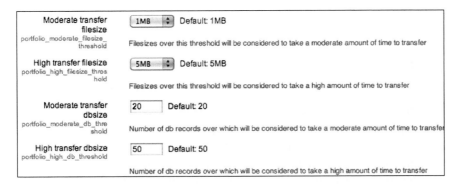

| Moderate transfer filesize<br>portfolio_moderate_filesize_<br>threshold | 1MB | Default: 1MB |
| High transfer filesize<br>portfolio_high_filesize_thres<br>hold | 5MB | Default: 5MB |
| Moderate transfer dbsize<br>portfolio_moderate_db_thre<br>shold | 20 | Default: 20 |
| High transfer dbsize<br>portfolio_high_db_threshold | 50 | Default: 50 |

Additional information about all mentioned Moodle portfolios can be found at docs.moodle.org/en/Portfolios.

# Miscellaneous plugins

There are a number of additional plugin types that are used less frequently than the ones covered. It is expected that more will be added to these categories in the future, either as part of Moodle core or as third-party add-ons.

## Text editors

Moodle uses the **TinyMCE HTML editor** text editor as default for entering HTML text. Additionally, a **Plain text editor** has been implemented for entering any text that does not require formatting. The idea of the **Text editors** plugin area is that additional editors can be installed and utilized throughout Moodle. These can either be replacements for the default editors or editors for entering specialized content.

To get access to the available editors and their settings, go to **Plugins | Text editors | Manage editors**:

| Manage editors | | | |
| --- | --- | --- | --- |
| Available text editors | | | |
| Name | Enable | Up/Down | Settings |
| TinyMCE HTML editor | 👁 | ↓ | Settings |
| Plain text area | 👁 | ↑ | |

Please choose the editor plugins you wish to use and arrange them in recommended order.
Changes in table above are saved automatically.

You can enable/disable each editor, change the order (in which they will be displayed when choosing an editor), and adjust the editor settings through the **Settings** link. For **TinyMCE HTML editor,** the only setting is to select the engine from the **Spell engine** drop-down menu that is used for spell checking.

# Question types and behaviours

Moodle's **Quiz** activity module ships with a number of question types, such as, **Multiple choice, Short answer,** and **Embedded answers**. Moodle has a powerful question engine that supports a range of question behaviours. These are ways in which submitted questions are being dealt with. In true Moodle style, both constructs are handled as plugins and it is possible to add additional **Question types** and **Question behaviours** to the system.

To see the available question types, go to **Plugins | Question types | Manage question types**:

| Question type | No. questions | Version | Requires | Available? | Delete | Settings |
|---|---|---|---|---|---|---|
| Calculated | 0 | 2011051900 | Numerical | 👁 ↑ ↓ | | |
| Calculated multichoice | 0 | 2011051900 | Calculated, Multiple choice | ⌣ ↑ ↓ | Delete | |
| Calculated simple | 0 | 2011051900 | Numerical | 👁 ↑ ↓ | Delete | |
| Description | 0 | 2011051200 | | 👁 ↑ ↓ | Delete | |
| Embedded answers (Cloze) | 0 | 2011051200 | Short answer, Numerical, Multiple choice | 👁 ↑ ↓ | Delete | |
| Essay | 0 | 2011060300 | | 👁 ↑ ↓ | Delete | |
| Matching | 1 | 2011051200 | | 👁 ↑ ↓ | | |
| Missing type | 0 | 2011051200 | | ↑ ↓ | | |
| Multiple choice | 3 | 2011051200 | | | | |

You can only enable/disable each question type, change the order in which they will be displayed when choosing a question, and delete them. The **Settings** column is reserved for third-party types and more sophisticated question types being introduced in future versions of Moodle. When clicking on the number of questions, you will be shown a screen that shows all the courses that contain questions of the respective type.

To see the available question **Behaviour**, go to **Plugins | Question behaviours | Manage question behaviours**:

| Behaviour | No. question attempts | Version | Requires | Available? | Delete |
|---|---|---|---|---|---|
| Adaptive mode | 1 | No database | | 👁 ↑ ↓ | |
| Adaptive mode (no penalties) | 0 | No database | Adaptive mode | 👁 ↑ ↓ | Delete |
| Deferred feedback with CBM | 0 | No database | Deferred feedback | 👁 ↑ ↓ | |
| Deferred feedback | 0 | No database | | 👁 ↑ ↓ | |
| Immediate feedback with CBM | 0 | No database | Immediate feedback, Deferred feedback with CBM | 👁 ↑ ↓ | Delete |
| Immediate feedback | 0 | No database | | 👁 ↑ ↓ | |
| behaviour for information items | 0 | No database | | ↑ ↓ | Delete |
| Interactive with multiple tries | 0 | No database | | 👁 ↑ ↓ | |
| Interactive with multiple tries (credit for earlier tries) | 0 | No database | Interactive with multiple tries | ↑ ↓ | Delete |
| Manually graded | 0 | No database | | 👁 ↑ ↓ | Delete |
| Missing behaviour | 0 | No database | | ↑ ↓ | Delete |

For each behaviour under the **Behaviour** column, the **No. question attempts** and its **Version** are listed. If a type has one or more prerequisites that have to be installed, they will be displayed in the **Requires** column. The **Available?** and **Delete** columns have the same functionality as in the settings for question types.

# Plagiarism prevention

Plagiarism prevention has to be enabled by selecting the **Enable plagiarism plugins** parameter in **Advanced features**. Once this has happened, you have access to any installed plagiarism prevention plugins in **Plugins | Plagiarism prevention | Plagiarism settings**.

At the time of writing, three plugins are available that cater to plagiarism prevention, namely, **Turnitin, Crot,** and **Urkund**:

- **Turnitin**: It appears to be the most popular option among educational organizations, which is why it has been described in more detail later in this section.

- **Crot**: It is an appealing open source alternative (`www.siberiasoft.com`). The Docs page is located at `docs.moodle.org/en/Plagiarism_Prevention_Crot_2.0`.

- **Urkund**: It is another commercial plagiarism prevention tool. You can find details about the Moodle plugin at `docs.moodle.org/en/Plagiarism_Prevention_URKUND`.

The add-ons have to be downloaded from the **Modules and plugins** area at `moodle.` `org` and installed on your Moodle server (see *Chapter 14, Installing Third-party Add-ons*).

A paid subscription is required from `www.turnitin.com`. Once installed and configured, the Turnitin plagiarism prevention functionality will be available as part of the **Assignment** module inside courses.

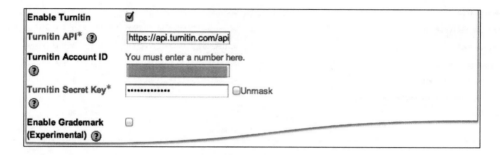

Once you have entered your **Turnitin Account ID** and **Turnitin Secret Key**, you are ready to configure the plugin on the screen shown and the **Turnitin Defaults** tab. It might be best to involve someone who deals with educational and curriculum matters in your organization. More details and further information on these settings can be found at `docs.moodle.org/en/Turnitin_administration`.

# Summary

In this chapter, you have learned how to configure different types of plugins in Moodle. We covered four main types of plugins, namely module plugins, repositories, portfolios, and miscellaneous plugins.

The consistent manner in which plugins have been implemented demonstrates the modular architecture of Moodle and flattens the learning curve when additional modules will be added in the future that have to be administered.

Now, let's move on to the last part of Moodle configuration.

# *9*
# Moodle Configuration

Moodle comes with a multitude of configuration options. In this chapter, we will cover the most important settings, some of which might not be relevant to your organization. We will distinguish between pedagogical and technical configuration:

- **Pedagogical configuration**: These settings are likely to require input from other stakeholders in the organization, as they cover areas that are of an educational (not technical) nature. Areas covered are collaboration, localization, grades and gradebook, and a number of miscellaneous settings.

- **Technical configuration**: These are settings that require some technical knowledge about your infrastructure. Topics dealt with are synchronous communication (instant messaging and video conferencing), asynchronous communication (messaging and RSS feeds), and a number of experimental settings.

There are a number of additional configuration topics, covered in dedicated chapters. These topics include plugins (*Chapter 8, Moodle Plugins*), security (*Chapter 11, Moodle Security and Privacy*), optimization (*Chapter 12, Moodle Performance and Optimization*), and networking (*Chapter 16, Moodle Networking*).

## Collaboration

One of Moodle's many advantages is its built-in support for collaboration among learners and instructors. This ranges from a number of collaborative course activities, such as, **Wiki**, **Glossary**, and **Database**, the ability to run activities in group mode, and the support for groupings. Social networking is the latest buzz on the Internet that conforms with Moodle's pedagogical philosophy of social constructivism. There are three activities in Moodle that have to be configured by the administrator. These activities include blogs, comments, and tags, discussed in the following sections.

# Blogs

Blogs are a means for users to express themselves, either in the form of a learning journal or as a personal account of events. The blogging mechanism provided to users allows for the creation of personal as well as public entries and also posts relating to a course.

As an administrator, you will have to specify the **Blog visibility** in the **Advanced features** menu. The self-explanatory options are:

- **The world can read entries set to be world-accessible**
- **All site users can see all blog entries** (default)
- **Users can see only their own blog**
- **Disable blog system completely**

The choice of option depends on the policy of your organization and how blogs are used as part of the learning process. If blogs are enabled, there are a number of settings available in **Appearance | Blog**:

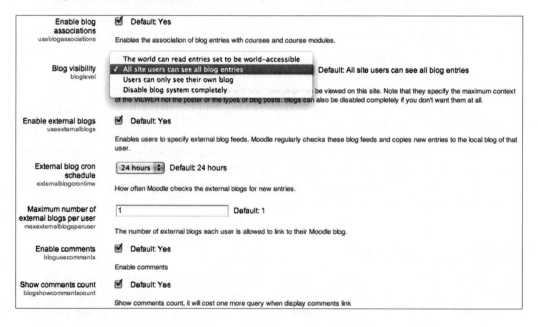

In addition to the **Blog visibility** that has already been covered, there are three groups of blog settings:

If the **Enable blog associations** checkbox is checked, course and activity blogs are available, which allows learners to choose link entries to a course or course module. If it is unchecked, all blog posts are user blog posts. The setting can be overridden locally via the **moodle/blog:associatecourse** and **moodle/blog:associatemodule** role capabilities.

- Moodle supports external blogs, for example, from WordPress or Google's Blogger. If **Enable external blogs** is enabled, users will have the ability to link their blogs via **My profile settings | Blogs | Register an external blog** in the **Settings** block. The entries will be shown as if they have been entered in the Moodle blog but cannot be modified. How often the update is carried out is set in the **External blog cron schedule** parameter (options are **12 hours**, **24 hours**, **2 days**, or **7 days**). You can further specify the number of external blogs each user is allowed to link to their Moodle blog in the **Maximum number of external blogs per user** field.

- A key feature of blogs is the ability for others to provide comments on blog posts; for instance, a teacher can leave private or public feedback on a journal entry. You can also enable the **Enable comments** and the **Show comments count** options.

# Comments

We have just come across comments in blogs. Moodle comes with a generic comments functionality that is independent of the one in the blogging module. It allows the placement of the **Comments** block in any context of the system, for instance, in a course or in an individual activity.

This feature is enabled by default but can be disabled via the **Enable comments** parameter in the **Advanced features** link.

There are a number of areas where additional comments-related settings can be set, for instance, whether they are included in backups or supported by certain activities. You can search for "comments" using the **Search** box to see all of these settings. As always, these settings can be overridden locally via the respective role capabilities.

# Tags

Tagging is the process of describing artefacts or users using key words. These tags are then harnessed for searching, sharing, and other collaborative activities in order to match interests.

As with blogs and comments, tags can be enabled (default setting) and disabled for the entire site. This can be done via the **Enable tags functionality** parameter in the **Advanced features** link.

Users create their own tags that represent their private or educational interests and, depending on the size of their social network (in our case Moodle and any Internet services that can be incorporated), matching will take place. However, as an educational institution, you might want to create a number of sitewide tags that can be used in addition to the user-defined tags. Examples of these global tags are organization-related keywords, topics that your entity is specializing in, campaigns your company is running, or newsworthy topics that are relevant to your institution. To do this, go to **Appearance | Manage tags**:

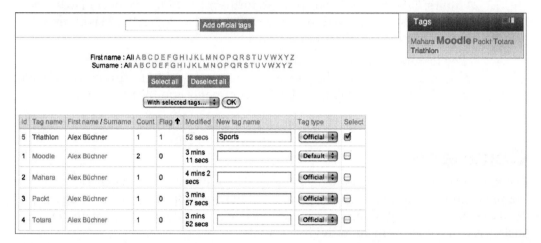

You can add a sitewide tag by entering its name in the textbox at the top and clicking on the **Add official tags** button. All global tags are shown in the list underneath, where, for each tag, the name, creator, usage counter, number of tags that have been flagged as inappropriate, and time since last modified are listed. Tags can further be renamed and their type can be changed (**Official** or **Default**). Additional operations that are available for selected tags are **Reset flag**, **Delete**, **Change tag type**, and **Change tag name**.

It might also be necessary to block a user from certain tagging activities. The two relevant capabilities are **moodle/tag:create** and **moodle/tag:edit**.

Moodle also supports course tags, allowing students to tag courses. This has to be enabled via the **Show course tags** parameter in **Plugins | Blocks | Tags**.

# Localization

Localization is concerned with the adaptation of software so it can be used in different locales. A locale is linked to a region where certain cultural aspects apply, such as, language, formatting of dates and times, calendric representation, and so on.

As Moodle is used throughout the world and given the fact many educational establishments spawn across continents, it is important that localization is fully supported. The key areas in which Moodle can be configured are language-related settings and calendric information.

 If your main language is something other than English, make sure you select this during installation. That way, locale settings as well as role names and descriptions will be localized.

# Languages

Moodle supports over 75 languages, including Latin! To represent the character sets of multiple languages, a standard called Unicode has been adopted; it covers most modern scripts used throughout the world. Moodle also fully supports right-to-left writing systems such as Arabic.

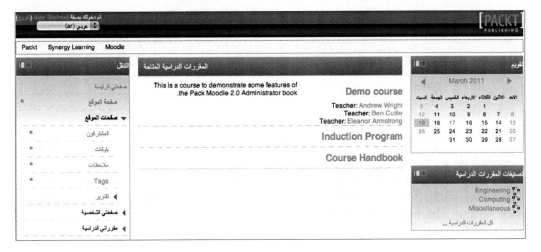

# Language packs

Locales are characterized by standardized two-letter region codes representing a language and optional letters. For example, **pt** represents Portuguese as spoken in **Portugal** whereas **pt_br** represents Brazilian Portuguese. Moodle uses the same representation for its more than 100 available language packs. Some packs of non-standardized languages have made their way into Moodle such as **Deutsch-Kids**, an adopted version targeted at young learners. For these specialized packs, new codes have been made up by their creators, for example, **de_kids**.

In order to support a language, you have to install its language pack, which contains all the terms used in Moodle. Moodle will download any requested language packs from download.moodle.org. Go to **Language | Language packs** to include new packs:

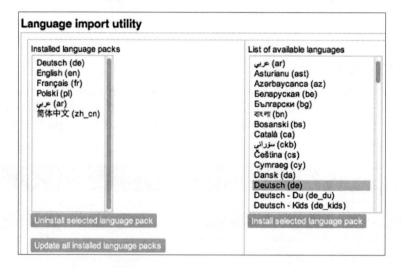

In the preceding screenshot, six language packs, consisting of Arabic, German, English, French, Polish, and Simplified Chinese, have been installed (you see them in the list on the left). To add more language packs, select the locale on the right and click on the **Install selected language pack** button. To reverse this operation, select a language pack in the list on the left and click on the **Uninstall selected language pack** button. The **English (en)** language pack cannot be uninstalled. It is used as a reference language in cases where strings in other languages are not translated.

Once installed, the user can choose a language (if configured) from the language menu, which is usually located in the header, or from within their profile. Bear in mind that only terms and phrases that are part of Moodle will change. Any content created will not be translated, unless the content is configured to make use of the multilingual feature (see the *Language customization* section).

Language packs are kept and maintained at download.moodle.org/langpack/2.x (where x is the current release version number). Some packs are updated more frequently than others; clicking on the **Update all installed language packs** button copies the latest versions to your server.

# Language settings

Moodle offers a number of language settings that you can find at **Language | Language settings**:

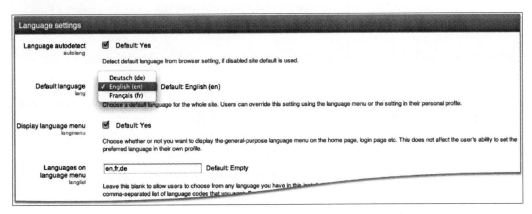

These settings are listed in the following table:

| Settings | Description |
| --- | --- |
| **Language autodetect** | By default, Moodle detects the language from the used web browser locale. If you wish to override this and use the default site language instead, uncheck the checkbox. |
| **Default language** | Allows you to select the language that will be used throughout the site, unless overridden by individual users via the language menu or from their profile. Only those languages appear for which a language pack has been installed and which are shown in the language menu. |

| Settings | Description |
|---|---|
| **Display language menu** | If enabled, the language menu will be displayed on the front page header. The user will always have the ability to change the language in their profile, no matter what the setting is. Some themes do not support this feature. |
| **Languages on language menu** | If left empty, all installed languages appear in the language menu. To narrow down this list, specify a comma-separated list of locale codes. |
| **Cache language menu** | Unless you are adding or removing language packs, it is recommended to leave this setting enabled. It caches the language menu on the front page. |
| **Cache all language strings** | Unless you are modifying a language pack, it is recommended to leave this setting enabled. It caches all language strings rather than loading them dynamically. |
| **Sitewide locale** | The localization operations are internally driven by system locales, which are selected on the basis of the chosen language pack. If you wish to change this (which is hardly ever required), select the sitewide locale in its operating system format, such as en_US.UTF-8. The file has to be installed as part of the operating system. |
| **Excel encoding** | When downloading data in Microsoft Excel format (such as in gradebook reports or logfiles), Moodle uses the Unicode format. Older versions of Excel only support Latin encoding. |

There are two additional language-related settings placed under **Security | Site policies**:

- The **Full name format** drop-down menu allows you choose the format of the full name. If the **Language** option is selected, the decision of how names are displayed is made by the respective current language pack. This way, you can cater to local sensitivities with regard to first names.

- The **Allow extended characters in usernames** parameter removes the limitation of only using alphanumeric characters in usernames.

# Language customization

Each phrase, term, and string used in Moodle is represented in language files, which are tied to certain modules in Moodle (located in the `lang` directory). There are over 16,000 (!) language strings in Moodle, which demonstrates the scale of the system. You have the ability to change any language string in Moodle. You might want to change words or phrases, for example, you may want to change "Grades" to "Marks", "Outcomes" to "Work indicators", "Teacher" to "Instructor", and so on.

To customize a language file, go to **Language | Language customization**, where you will first have to choose a language to be customized. Click on the **Check out strings into translator** button, which will lead to a check-out step; this might take a few seconds. Once this has been done, you can click on the **Continue** button.

> Moodle creates a `local` directory located somewhere inside `$CFG->dataroot`, where it stores your edited phrases. Make sure that you have write access to the `lang` directory to avoid any error messages.

Moodle keeps a separate language file for each module. This separation is beneficial as it frees the underlying code (developed by programmers) from the localization (worked on by translators). However, the disadvantage is that you need to know where (that is, in which PHP module) the respective strings are located. However, Moodle offers a good filter mechanism to simplify the search for strings to be modified.

Let's say you wish to change the term "Guest" to "Visitor". As it is likely that the term "Guest" appears in a number of different modules, it is safe to select all items in the **Show strings of these components** menu.

You further have filter criteria to choose from. The options include **Customized only** for strings that have been changed in previous sessions, **Help only** for balloon help tooltips, and **Modified only** for phrases changed in the current session. The **Only strings containing** parameter requires the word or phrase you are looking for (in our case, **guest**). Internally, Moodle uses string identifiers, which can also be used for searching. To do this, just enter the string identifier in the **String Identifier** textbox.

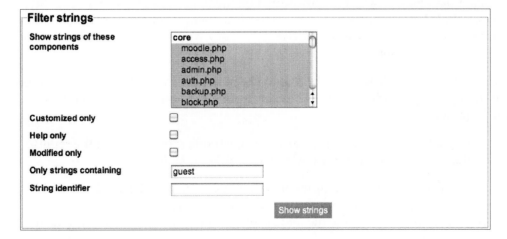

Once the search has been successful, the following information is shown for each string that matches the filter:

| Component | String | Standard text | Local customization |
|---|---|---|---|
| core | guest | Guest | Visitor |
| core | guestdescription | Guests have minimal privileges and usually can not enter text anywhere. | Visitors have minimal privileges and usually can not enter text anywhere. |
| core | guestskey | Allow guests who have the key | Allow visitors who have the key |
| core | guestsno | Do not allow guests in | Do not allow visitors in |
| core | guestsnotallowed | Sorry, '{$a}' does not allow guests to enter. | Sorry, '{$a}' does not allow visitors to enter. |
| | | ⓘ string contains a placeholder | |

| Item | Description |
|---|---|
| **Component** | System component to which the string belongs. This also includes third-party add-ons. |
| **String** | String identifier (mainly used by programmers). |
| **Standard text** | String text or phrases in English. If the language chosen is other than English, the translated version is displayed underneath. |
| **Local customization** | This is where you can override the current text. |

You might have spotted the **$a** parameter in the fifth phrase from the top. This is a so-called placeholder, which is substituted on the fly; in this instance, with name of a course. These have to be included in the local customization. Some placeholders will contain a parameter, such as $a->id or $a->query. You should keep them as they are to avoid any problems.

Make sure that you click on the **Save and check in strings into files** button to reflect the changes on your Moodle site. These changes will be maintained when your site is updated.

You can grant a user access to the **Language customization** menu via the **report/customlang:edit** and **report/customlang:view** role capabilities.

There is also a setting in **Development | Debugging** called **Show origin of languages strings**, which is useful when you customize a language pack. If this setting is enabled, it shows the file and string identifier besides each string as the output on screen.

If you wish to contribute to a language pack or want to create a new one, go to the Moodle languages portal at `lang.moodle.org`. On this site, you will find information on how to utilize the AMOS tool and the AMOS Moodle block (for more details, see `docs.moodle.org/en/AMOS`).

If you have users who deal with multi-language content, it is recommended to turn on the **Multi-Language Content** filter in **Plugins | Filters | Manage filters**. The **Multi-Language Content** filter supports the `<span lang="xx" class="multilang">` tag by default; the older `<lang>` tag can be enabled as well, in the settings of the filter. Your designers and content creators might want to make use of this feature, especially when dealing with language-related content.

One more thing about content: sometimes, it is necessary to replace a string, for example, a URL that has changed, throughout your site. There is a script located at `your-moodle-domain.com/admin/replace.php` that performs the replacement. It performs a search–and–replace for text throughout the whole database. Be careful, though, as this operation affects your entire Moodle system and may be irreversible! It is recommended to put your system in maintenance mode and create a sitewide backup before making use of this script.

# Calendric information

Different cultures represent calendric information—date, times, and time zones—in different formats.

 Locales have to be installed for non-English calendars to work properly. On Unix systems, check with the `locale -a` locale.

# Calendars

Moodle formats date and time according to the set locale for Gregorian calendars (others are currently not supported). A few additional settings are changeable at **Appearance | Calendar**. These settings are shown in the following screenshot (only fields relevant to localization are shown):

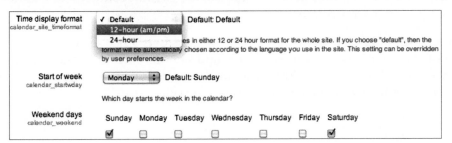

Times are displayed according to the selected locale, which can be overridden by a 12-hour or a 24-hour clock. Different countries have a different start day for the week, for instance, in North America, the week starts from Sunday whereas in Europe it starts from Monday. Users can override both settings in their **Calendar** preferences.

Not all countries use the default values of **Saturday** and **Sunday** as the weekend days. For example, in Islamic countries, the weekend is on Friday and Saturday whereas Sunday is a normal working day. This can be specified in the **Weekend days** parameter.

## Time zones

Moodle supports systems that span across time zones. This happens in three scenarios:

- In countries which cover more than a single time zone
- Sites which have learners from multiple countries/time zones
- Where the server is hosted outside the time zone of the organization, for example, with an Internet Service Provider

To modify the default time zone parameters, go to **Location | Location settings**:

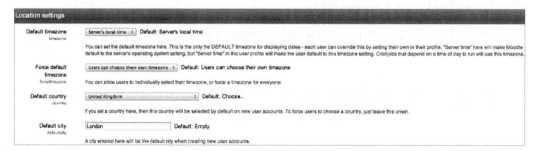

The value selected in the **Default timezone** parameter is used throughout the system. The default value is **Server's local time**, which might not reflect your local time. Each learner can change this setting in his or her user profile, unless it is forced to a particular time. Displayed times, for example, for an assignment deadline, are adjusted to the selected time zone. If specified, the **Default country** and **Default city** are used for new user accounts.

Every so often, rules in certain time zones (there are over 2,000 separate ones!) change, for instance, the adjustment of daylight savings time. In this case, you should update these settings via **Location | Update timezones**. New versions of Moodle always contain the latest version of the time zone rules.

# Grades and gradebook settings

The gradebook is one of the most important constructs of any virtual-learning environment, and Moodle is no exception. A **gradebook** is a container holding grades for all learners in Moodle. The flexibility and customizability of the Moodle gradebook results in a very high degree of complexity. As a consequence, there are a huge number of administrator settings at your disposal that affect the way teachers use grades throughout the system.

The majority of settings are tightly linked to the gradebook and the related reports dealt with by teachers at course level. A sitewide agreement on default values and global settings for grades should be in place for your organization.

Additionally, the inline help for each setting is very comprehensive, as is the accompanying area in the Moodle Docs at `docs.moodle.org/en/Gradebook`, which contains a number of pages dedicated to administrators. We briefly describe each section (submenu) in the **Grades** area in the **Site administration** section and highlight some key parameters, which are listed as follows:

- **General settings**: These are parameters that influence the gradebook and grades in general. A setting that is turned off by default and is required often is **Enable publishing** (the ability to publish results via external URLs). Another setting that is changed frequently is the **Navigation method**, in which most users prefer the **Tabs** option as it is consistent with the rest of Moodle.

- **Grade category settings**: Grades are organized into categories and, here, you set the relevant settings.

- **Grade item settings**: These are settings that impact individual grades and grade items.

- **Scales**: Here, you can specify sitewide scales that are used for grading and rating. The global scales are often linked to qualifications that are offered by your organization. Most sites remove the provided scale **Separate and Connected ways of knowing** as it doesn't map to their learning environment.

    Each scale comprises of a name, the scale itself (a list of comma-separated items) and an optional description. Scales can be uploaded indirectly via the **Outcomes** menu at course level.

- **Outcomes**: Outcomes are used by most vocational and some academic curricula to specify the expected competencies or goals of a subject being taught. Outcomes have to be enabled in the **Advanced features** link.

    You can either add global (standard) outcomes one-by-one or create a CSV file and upload it in batch mode from the **Outcome** menu at course level (select the **Import as standard outcome** option).

Each outcome comprises of a full name, a short name, a scale and an optional description. The import file supports the following values in its header: `outcome_name`, `outcome_shortname`, `outcome_description`, `scale_name`, `scale_items`, and `scale_description`.

- **Letters**: A lot of education systems use a system of letters (A, A-, B+, …, F) to grade items. Here, you specify which percentage range corresponds to which grading letter.

- **Report settings**: Moodle comes with a number of predefined gradebook reports. The respective settings determine appearance and content of the reports. If additional user-defined reports (plugins) are installed on your system, this list is likely to have a separate configuration page for each report type (a good tutorial on how to create your own custom reports can be found at `docs.moodle.org/en/Development:Gradebook_Report_Tutorial`). The different types of reports are:

  - **Grader report**: These settings include whether to show calculations and show or hide icons, column averages, and so on. Teachers can override most settings in **My report preferences** tab.

  - **Overview report**: Two settings that determines whether ranking information is shown and how to deal with totals that contains hidden grades, respectively.

  - **User report**: It shows the settings that determine whether ranking information is shown and how to deal with hidden items.

We only touched upon the customization options of the gradebook. Some Moodle Partners run courses that are dedicated to the management of usage of the gradebook and any related functionalities.

# Miscellaneous pedagogical settings

There are a number of remaining settings and parameters that might have to be configured on your system, depending on whether the functionalities will be used by your teachers and learners. These settings are:

- **Conditional access**: This is a feature often required by course authors and teachers. By default, this is not activated; it has to be turned on in **Advanced features | Enable conditional access**.

- **Completion tracking**: This is needed in courses if progress of learners has to be tracked. Again, this feature is disabled by default and has to be turned on in **Advanced features | Enable completion tracking**.

- **Other settings**: Other course-related settings are **Course default settings** (**Courses | Course default settings**) as discussed in *Chapter 4, Course Management* and *Chapter 8, Moodle Plugins*.

# Communication

Communication is a key feature in Moodle as it enhances the learning experience of all users involved. Moodle supports synchronous and asynchronous communication, which have to be configured by the administrator.

# Synchronous communication

We cover two types of synchronous communication in Moodle: instant messaging and video conferencing, both of which are discussed in the following sections.

## Instant messaging

Moodle's on-board facility for instant messaging is the **Chat** activity that is used in courses or the front page. The module works out of the box, without configuration, using the **Ajax method** (default) or **Normal method**. However, it creates significant load on the server on large installations or when chat rooms are used intensively.

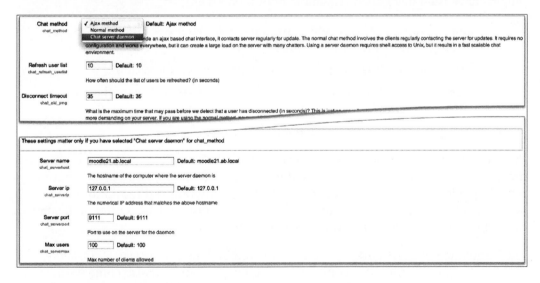

To rectify this, the activity supports a chat server daemon, which has to be configured. The setting up of the daemon takes place in **Plugins | Activity modules | Chat**.

To make use of a chat server daemon, you will have to change the **Chat method** to—you guessed it!—**Chat server daemon**. The daemon, usually called `chatd`, has to run in the background on your Unix system (it does not work on Windows servers). This might either be a PHP script or an executable. The **Refresh user list** (interval for updating user list) and **Disconnect timeout** (time without connection after which a user is treated as disconnected) parameters are common for both chat methods and might have to be adjusted if you experience connection issues.

The chat server daemon-specific settings require a **Server name**, the **Server IP** address, and the **Server port** that is used by `chatd`. These can be on the same system as Moodle (as shown in the preceding screenshot) or, for better performance, on a separate or dedicated server. The **Max users** parameter specifies the maximum number of users who can use a chat simultaneously.

An alternative method to the chat daemon is the use of a stream for updating conversations in the normal chat method. However, Apache has to be configured to support this update method.

# Video conferencing

One often-requested synchronous feature that is absent from Moodle core is video conferencing. However, there are number of external systems for which Moodle plugins have been developed. The most popular ones are:

- **Adobe Connect**: It is an enterprise web conferencing solution for online meetings, e-Learning, and webinars
- **BigBlueButton**: It is an open source web conferencing system
- **OpenMeetings**: It is an open source, browser-based software that allows you to instantly set up a conference
- **WizIQ**: It is a commercial virtual classroom system

Providing video conferencing to your teachers and learners has one major technical drawback—depending on what types of tools are used (audio, whiteboard sharing, recording, video) and what quality is chosen (sampling rate and resolution), the facility can be very bandwidth-hungry. This is why most providers offer dedicated hosting services in addition to local installation options.

The installation of third-party add-ons is covered in detail in *Chapter 14, Installing Third-party Add-ons*. All video conferencing systems mentioned also come with comprehensive configuration and usage instructions. The following screenshot is of the configuration screen of the Adobe Connect Pro add-on for Moodle:

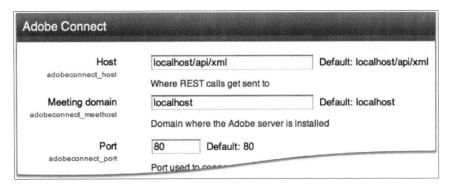

# Asynchronous communication

There are two types of asynchronous communication options available in Moodle—messaging and RSS feeds.

# Messaging configuration

Moodle comes with a flexible messaging facility that can be seen as a basic multichannel communication system. It supports input plugins (*providers*), which send messages, and output plugins (*processors*), which receive messages. Currently, only messages from other Moodle users and notifications from activities can be received, but it is expected that this will change in the future, with third-party plugins supporting external applications.

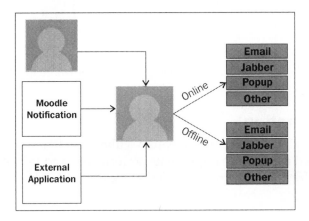

Messaging has to be turned on by checking the **Enable messaging system** checkbox in **Advanced features**.

Each user has the ability (via **My profile settings | Messaging**) to configure how to receive messages, depending whether they are online or offline. For each notification type (such as, subscribed forums, posts, or feedback notifications), the following so-called message outputs can be selected, once they have been enabled and configured:

- **Popup notification**: This uses the built-in messages tool and does not require any customization.

- **Email**: The message will be forwarded to an e-mail address.

- **Jabber message**: Jabber is an instant messaging protocol that is used by a number of popular clients, such as Google Talk and Apple's iChat. Other applications (for example, Facebook) provide an interface to Jabber.

- **Other**: It is expected that additional channels, for example, Twitter, Google+, or SMS, will be added in the future, most likely as third-party plugins.

**Email** and **Jabber message** (and any additionally installed notification methods) have to be configured before they are available to users in your Moodle system. This configuration takes place in **Plugins | Message outputs | Manage message outputs**:

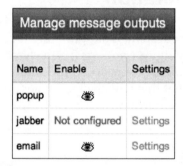

| Manage message outputs | | |
| --- | --- | --- |
| Name | Enable | Settings |
| popup | 👁 | |
| jabber | Not configured | Settings |
| email | 👁 | Settings |

From this screen, you also launch the settings screen for the respective message output via the respective **Settings** link:

## Email configuration

Like instant messaging, Moodle e-mail works without configuration, using its internal PHP-based method. To improve its performance and to make use of your existing e-mail infrastructure, you have to configure an SMTP host:

| SMTP hosts<br>smtphosts | relay.your-organisation.com | Default: Empty |
| | Give the full name of one or more local SMTP servers that Moodle should use to send mail (eg 'mail.a.com' or 'mail.a.com;mail.b.com'). To specify a non-default port (i.e other than port 25), you can use the [server]:[port] syntax (eg 'mail.a.com:587'. If you leave it blank, Moodle will use the PHP default method of sending mail. | |
| SMTP username<br>smtpuser | mail@your-organisation.com | Default: Empty |
| | If you have specified an SMTP server above, and the server requires authentication, then enter the username and password here. | |
| SMTP password<br>smtppass | ••••••••••••• | ☐ Unmask |
| | If you have specified an SMTP server above, and the server requires authentication, then enter the username and password here. | |
| SMTP session limit<br>smtpmaxbulk | 1 | Default: 1 |
| | Maximum number of messages sent per SMTP session. Grouping messages may speed up the each email. | |

| Setting | Description |
| --- | --- |
| **SMTP hosts** | Name or IP address of the SMTP server. If multiple servers exist, they have to be separated by a semicolon ( ; ). Standard port syntax is supported. |
| **SMTP username** | Self-explanatory. |
| **SMTP password** | Self-explanatory. |
| **SMTP session limit** | Number of messages (groups) sent per SMTP session. |
| **No-reply address** | The "From" address for a user when a notification is sent from an activity; for example, a forum. |
| **Hour to send digest emails** | Users can receive their messages bundled in so-called digests. This setting specifies at what hour of the day the e-mails will be processed. |
| **Character set** | Character set to be used for sending e-mails. |
| **Allow user to select character set** | Whether users are allowed to override the default setting in their user profile. |
| **Newline character in mail** | Different mail servers treat and convert newline characters differently. Change this only if you experience problems with line spacing. |

If you experience issues sending e-mails, check the **Debug email sending** checkbox under **Development | Debugging**. This will display detailed information when sending emails via SMTP.

# Jabber configuration

You require access to a Jabber host to be able to use this feature. You can either set up your own XMPP server or use a commercial host; for example, Google Talk. The Jabber configuration settings are shown in the following screenshot:

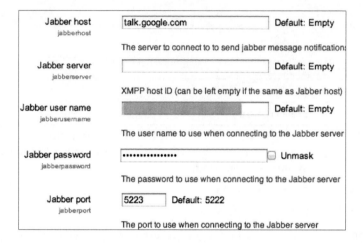

Once the self-explanatory fields in the Jabber configuration screen have been set up, each user will have the ability to specify their Jabber ID in **My profile settings | Messaging**.

# Default message outputs

Once your message outputs have been configured, each user has the ability to set preferences for any notification types they have permissions to receive and each configured message output. This takes place in **My profile settings | Messaging**. As the administrator, you should specify default values for these settings. Additionally, you can decide which settings non-administrator users cannot change:

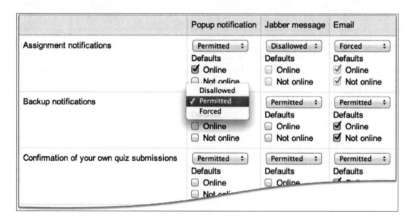

For each notification type, you can individually specify for each message output (**Popup notification**, **Jabber message** and **Email**) whether the default settings are:

- **Disallowed**: If selected, the functionality is deactivated
- **Permitted** (default): If selected, users can change settings in their profile
- **Forced**: If selected, values are frozen and cannot be modified locally

The values under **Defaults** are **Online** (when logged in to Moodle) and **Not online** (when not logged in).

In the preceding screenshot, users will receive an e-mail about **Assignment notifications**, whether or not they are online. They cannot change this setting so can avoid claims that they were unaware of any deadlines. When they are online, they will receive a pop-up message. This setting can be overridden in their profile message settings. Jabber has been disallowed for this notification type.

# Support contact

A topic related to asynchronous communication is users of your Moodle system seeking assistance. Under **Server | Support contact**, Moodle lets you specify a **Support name**, a **Support email** address, and a **Support page**.

The contact details are displayed at various places throughout Moodle, for instance, during self-registration. There is no support block you can put in the front page, but you can easily mimic this using a (sticky) **HTML** block.

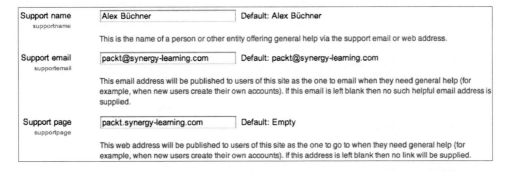

There is a great third-party add-on called **Help Desk block**. Unfortunately, it has not been updated to Moodle 2 yet. Keep an eye on its status, as I am sure that this will be updated soon.

## RSS feeds configuration

RSS (**Really Simple Syndication**) feeds have to be enabled via the **Enable RSS feeds** setting in **Advanced features**. Moodle supports the consumption as well as the production of RSS feeds!

The RSS consumption takes place in the **Remote RSS Feeds** block and can be configured in **Plugins | Blocks | RSS client**. The parameters available are **Entries per feed** (number of atoms loaded and displayed) and **Timeout** (amount of time before the feed expires in cache).

The RSS production can take place from within a number of activities, namely, **Blog, Database, Forum**, and **Glossary**. Each module has a setting, **Enable RSS feeds**, in their respective plugin settings. For security and privacy, each RSS feed URL contains an automatically-created token for the user. If there is a suspicion that this has been compromised, users can reset this in **My profile settings | Security keys**.

# Experimental settings

Moodle is a very dynamic software that evolves and improves constantly. Some functionality is still in the experimental stage, but is sufficiently mature to be included in a shipped version. These features are located under **Development | Experimental | Experimental settings**.

The list changes over time. Some features have passed quality assurance and moved to the set of core features (for instance, AJAX support resided in the experimental section for almost two full versions) while others will be included over time. At present, the following three settings are available:

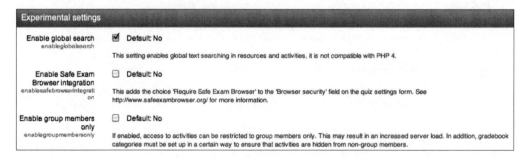

| Setting | Description |
|---------|-------------|
| **Enable global search** | The default search functionality is restricted to a course. To enable global searching that takes into account set permissions of the user carrying out the search, check this checkbox. |
| **Enable Safe Exam Browser integration** | This will be dealt with in *Chapter 11, Moodle Security and Privacy*. |
| **Enable group members only** | If enabled, the **Available for group members only** setting will appear in the advanced section of the **Common module settings** of all core activities and resources. |

It is needless to say that any functionality in the experimental section should be used with caution and that potential problems are possible to be encountered.

# Summary

In this chapter, you have learned how to configure relevant system settings that are not dealt with in a dedicated chapter. We covered pedagogical configuration, dealing with collaboration, localization, grades and gradebook, and a number of miscellaneous settings. We then moved on to the more technical configuration, which mainly focused on synchronous and asynchronous communication as well as some experimental settings.

The abundance of features available via the **Site administration** section can initially be overwhelming, but you will get to terms with them relatively quickly. Also, expect this number to increase with every new version of Moodle.

This concludes Part II of the book that dealt with Moodle configuration and we are now ready to move on to all aspects of Moodle maintenance.

# 10
# Moodle Reporting

Moodle collects usage data from all activities taking place from the time a user logs in until he or she logs out. This data can be utilized for a range of reporting activities that will be dealt with in this chapter. After an overview, you will learn about four reporting techniques:

- **Moodle's reporting facilities**: This includes activity reporting and user tracking as well some basic statistics
- **Report generation**: This covers some powerful add-ons to create user-defined reports
- **Data analysis**: This includes web log analyzers and live data trackers such as Google Analytics
- **Miscellaneous reports**: This covers a number of additional reports provided by Moodle

## Reporting overview

Moodle records a detailed log of each action performed by a user. Each record (or hit) contains data about:

- Who did (user)
- What (action)
- When (date and time)
- Where (IP address)

Given this trail of information, it is possible to perform two reporting tasks using Moodle's on-board facilities; namely, reporting and statistics.

*Reporting* is mainly concerned with summary information of users' activities. For instance, the number of views of a learning resource in a particular course. Ideally, reports allow some interaction to drill down to more specific information, usually via filters. This is useful if you need to locate data about an individual, an activity, or a course. For example, a pupil insists that he or she has submitted an assignment, which cannot be located; the tracking log will be able to shed light on this.

Moodle offers a *Statistics* mode, which provides a graphical summary about the number of hits in courses and the entire site.

Bear in mind that most information you retrieve as part of data reporting is also available to teachers at course level. While teachers use this information mainly in a pedagogical context (to monitor progress and to measure performance), your role as administrator requires you to view this data in a sitewide context. Furthermore, you are the one who will be approached if any problems occur; for example, if a student claims to have submitted an assignment that is not on the system, or a teacher is not able to log in from home. Additionally, the local course view provides activity reports that are more targeted from a teacher's perspective and, if activated, also some basic statistics.

# Moodle's reporting facilities

A report presents the content of the Moodle log in some sort of uniform format. Different reports make use of the same log. The sitewide logs can be accessed via **Reports | Logs**. At the top of the page, you have the ability to drill down to the data via filters:

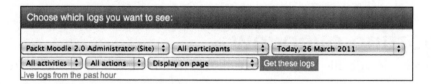

The following seven filters are available:

| Field | Description |
| --- | --- |
| Courses | Select a specific course or the entire Moodle site. |
| Groups | Select a specific group or **All groups** — only displayed if group mode is enabled in the selected (filtered) course. |
| Participants | Select a specific user or **All participants**. |
| Date | Specify a particular day or all days of activity. Unfortunately, it is not possible to specify date ranges. |

| Field | Description |
|---|---|
| Activities | Select whether to run a report of **All activities** or **Site errors**. |
| Actions | You can choose from **All actions**, **View**, **Add**, **Update**, **Delete**, and **All changes** options. |
| Display | Specify how to display the report on a page (in your web browser); in an Excel spreadsheet, in ODS format, or in a text file. |

Once you have selected a course and clicked on the **Get these logs** button, the content in each drop-down menu changes in a context-sensitive manner. For example, the participants menu contains all the names of users who have a role in the course and the activities menu is populated with all activities and resources. If you watch the breadcrumb trail, you can see what happens internally. Moodle temporarily redirects the reporting tool inside the selected course where the course log viewer is called, which is identical in appearance.

Once you have selected your filtering criteria, a report is displayed as follows:

Displaying 113 records

Page: 1 2 (Next)

| Time | IP address | Full name | Action | Information |
|---|---|---|---|---|
| Sat 26 March 2011, 04:28 PM | 192.168.56.1 | Alex Büchner | course report log | Demo course |
| Sat 26 March 2011, 04:27 PM | 192.168.56.1 | Eleanor Armstrong | forum view forum | A forum |
| Sat 26 March 2011, 04:27 PM | 192.168.56.1 | Eleanor Armstrong | forum add discussion | Log Test |
| Sat 26 March 2011, 04:27 PM | 192.168.56.1 | Eleanor Armstrong | forum view forum | A forum |
| Sat 26 March 2011, 04:27 PM | 192.168.56.1 | Eleanor Armstrong | resource view | A file |
| Sat 26 March 2011, 04:27 PM | 192.168.56.1 | Eleanor Armstrong | course view | Demo course |
| Sat 26 March 2011, 04:26 PM | 192.168.56.1 | Alex Büchner | user view | Eleanor Armstrong |
| Sat 26 March 2011, 04:25 PM | 192.168.56.1 | Alex Büchner | course report log | Demo course |
| Sat 26 March 2011, 04:25 PM | 192.168.56.1 | Alex Büchner | course report log | Demo course |
| Sat 26 March 2011, 04:25 PM | 192.168.56.1 | Alex Büchner | assignment view | Assignment |
| Sat 26 March 2011, 04:24 PM | 192.168.56.1 | Alex Büchner | user view | Eleanor Armstrong |

The header displays the number of records that are being displayed. In this case, all usage data from the **Demo course** has been selected, which returns 113 hits. This tabular information is displayed in reverse order of user's access date and time; that is, the last hit is displayed first. The columns of the table represent the following information:

| Field | Description |
| --- | --- |
| Time | Date and time of the hit. |
| IP Address | The (unresolved) IP address; this is useful to see from where the user accessed the page (for example, from home or within the organization). |
| Full Name | Name of the user – if a particular user is selected, the same value will be displayed in each row. |
| Action | Short description of what the user has been doing – this is very useful to see what resources are being accessed, or to check whether an individual has viewed the resource he or she claims to have read. |
| Information | More details on the action. |

When you click on the IP address in the log, a new window will open that displays the location of the user as a pin on the world map (this is not the case for local or private IP addresses), as shown in the following screenshot. The default database used is called NetGeo, which is not maintained anymore and often provides incorrect positions. You can improve this shortcoming by either installing the GeoIP City binary data file (both commercial and free versions are available) or by specifying a Google Maps API key. Both settings are found in the **IP address lookup** section under **Location | Location settings**.

# Live logs

Moodle provides a live view of activities in the last hour, as you can see in the following screenshot. It is a prepared report that shows activities that took place in the previous 60 minutes and is updated automatically every 60 seconds. It can be accessed from the **Live logs from the past hour** link found on the **Reports | Live logs** page.

This is useful if you have changed the configuration, for instance a supported authentication or enrolment mechanism, and want to monitor that it is working properly. Alternatively, you can just sit back and watch what is happening on your site.

Note that the first entry in the live log is the one for you, as you are looking at it!

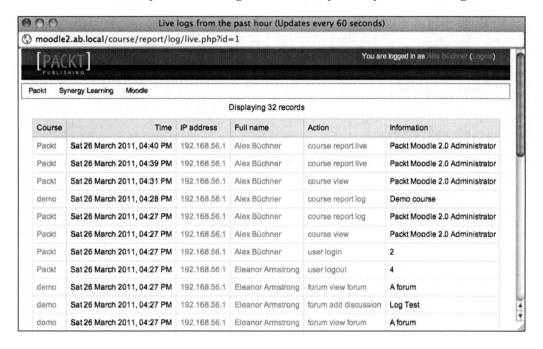

# Error reports

When selecting **Site errors** from the activities drop-down menu, all errors (mainly failed logins that have occurred) are displayed. For example, the report that is shown in the following screenshot displays all invalid logins:

| Course | Time | IP address | Full name | Action | Information |
|--------|------|-----------|-----------|--------|-------------|
| Packt | Sat 26 March 2011, 04:44 PM | 192.168.56.1 | | login error | admin |
| Packt | Sat 26 March 2011, 04:44 PM | 192.168.56.1 | | login error | acraig |
| Packt | Sat 26 March 2011, 04:43 PM | 192.168.56.1 | Guest user | login error | aileen |
| Packt | Sat 26 March 2011, 07:17 AM | 192.168.56.1 | | login error | admin |
| Packt | Sat 26 March 2011, 07:07 AM | 192.168.56.1 | | login error | admin |
| Packt | Sat 26 March 2011, 07:05 AM | 192.168.56.1 | | login error | admin |

It is a good practice to check the error logs on a regular basis to identify problems on your site and potential unauthorized access attempts. These reports can also be set up to be sent by e-mail to the site administrator (see *Chapter 11, Moodle Security and Privacy*).

# Export of logs

Unlike other applications (such as web servers), Moodle does not save its log information in text files but stores it in the Moodle database (in the `mdl_log` table). This allows the exporting of data (via Moodle or phpMyAdmin) for more detailed analysis in third-party applications.

In order to make further use of the information, export the data in either a comma-separated text file or an Excel or ODS spreadsheet by selecting the **Display filter** accordingly. This will show the same information as shown in Moodle, but it will be possible to massage and analyze the data further or run a valid spreadsheet operation against it:

|   | A | B | C | D | E | F |
|---|---|---|---|---|---|---|
| 1 | Saved at:26 March 2011, 04:48 PM | | | | | |
| 2 | | | | | | |
| 3 | Course | Time | IP address | Course full name | Action | Information |
| 4 | Packt | 2011 March 26 16:48 | 192.168.56 | Alex Büchner | course report log | Packt Moodle 2.0 Administrator |
| 5 | Packt | 2011 March 26 16:45 | 192.168.56 | Alex Büchner | course report log | Packt Moodle 2.0 Administrator |
| 6 | Packt | 2011 March 26 16:45 | 192.168.56 | Alex Büchner | course report log | Packt Moodle 2.0 Administrator |
| 7 | Packt | 2011 March 26 16:45 | 192.168.56 | Alex Büchner | course view | Packt Moodle 2.0 Administrator |
| 8 | Packt | 2011 March 26 16:45 | 192.168.56 | Alex Büchner | user login | |
| 9 | Packt | 2011 March 26 16:44 | 192.168.56.1 | | login error | admin |
| 10 | Packt | 2011 March 26 16:44 | 192.168.56.1 | | login error | acraig |
| 11 | Packt | 2011 March 26 16:44 | 192.168.56 | Alex Büchner | user logout | |
| 12 | Packt | 2011 March 26 16:43 | 192.168.56 | Alex Büchner | course report log | Packt Moodle 2.0 Administrator |
| 13 | Packt | 2011 March 26 16:43 | 192.168.56 | Alex Büchner | course report log | Packt Moodle 2.0 Administrator |
| 14 | Packt | 2011 March 26 16:43 | 192.168.56 | Alex Büchner | course view | Packt Moodle 2.0 Administrator |
| 15 | Packt | 2011 March 26 16:43 | 192.168.56 | Alex Büchner | user login | |
| 16 | Packt | 2011 March 26 16:43 | 192.168.56 | Guest user | login error | aileen |
| 17 | Packt | 2011 March 26 16:43 | 192.168.56 | Guest user | course view | Packt Moodle 2.0 Administrator |
| 18 | Packt | 2011 March 26 16:43 | 192.168.56 | Guest user | user login | |
| 19 | Packt | 2011 March 26 16:43 | 192.168.56 | Alex Büchner | user logout | |
| 20 | Packt | 2011 March 26 16:41 | 192.168.56 | Alex Büchner | course report log | Packt Moodle 2.0 Administrator |
| 21 | Packt | 2011 March 26 16:41 | 192.168.56 | Alex Büchner | course report log | Packt Moodle 2.0 Administrator |
| 22 | Packt | 2011 March 26 16:40 | 192.168.56 | Alex Büchner | course report live | Packt Moodle 2.0 Administrator |
| 23 | Packt | 2011 March 26 16:39 | 192.168.56 | Alex Büchner | course report live | Packt Moodle 2.0 Administrator |
| 24 | Packt | 2011 March 26 16:31 | 192.168.56 | Alex Büchner | course view | Packt Moodle 2.0 Administrator |
| 25 | demo | 2011 March 26 16:28 | 192.168.56 | Alex Büchner | course report log | Demo course |
| 26 | Packt | 2011 March 26 16:27 | 192.168.56 | Alex Büchner | course report log | Packt Moodle 2.0 Administrator |
| 27 | Packt | 2011 March 26 16:27 | 192.168.56 | Alex Büchner | course view | Packt Moodle 2.0 Administrator |

For example, the preceding data can be presented in a spreadsheet with the introduction of an additional column to calculate how much time a user has spent on a particular activity.

# Course and user reports

Moodle supports reporting at course and user level. This feature can be utilized by teachers to monitor progress of students for particular activities, or it could be used by managers to view the access patterns of their staff. Given the sensitivity of such data and the policies in your organization, the access to some operations can be deactivated via roles and capabilities.

The reports Moodle provides via **Courses | Reports** in the **Navigation** block are:

| Report | Description | Capability |
|---|---|---|
| **Course completion** | Progress report listing students versus criteria matrix (course completion has to be enabled). | **coursereport/ completion:view** |
| **Logs** | Same as sitewide logs, but with the courses menu frozen to the current course. | **coursereport/ log:view** |
| **Activity report** | Shows number of views, related blog entries, and last access for each activity and resource in the current course. | **coursereport/ outline:view** |

| Report | Description | Capability |
|---|---|---|
| **Participation report** | For a selected activity module or resource and time period, all actions by user are shown. | **coursereport/ participation:view** |
| **Activity completion** | A matrix showing users versus activities and their completion status. | **coursereport/ progress:view** |
| **Statistics** | View course statistics report (see the *Statistics* section ). | **coursereport/ stats:view** |

The types of reports Moodle provides via the **Activity reports** section in the user profile are shown in the following table. Access to the menu can be controlled via the **moodle/user:viewuseractivitiesreport** capability but not access to individual reports.

| Report | Description |
|---|---|
| **Outline report** | Lists each topic or week and displays a summary of activity modules for each item. It displays the title of the resource (hyperlinked), the number of views, the last access, and the time since the last access. |
| **Complete report** | Displays same information as in the **Outline report,** just in a different format. |
| **Today's logs** | Same as site logs but only for today's data of the current user; supplemented by an hour-by-hour graph. |
| **All logs** | Same as site logs but only for the current user; supplemented by a day-by-day graph. |
| **Statistics** | View course statistics report for that user (see the *Statistics* section ). |
| **Grade** | User report of the gradebook for the current user. |

An example report is shown in the following screenshot, where today's hits for the user **Donna Kennedy** are displayed for the **Packt** course:

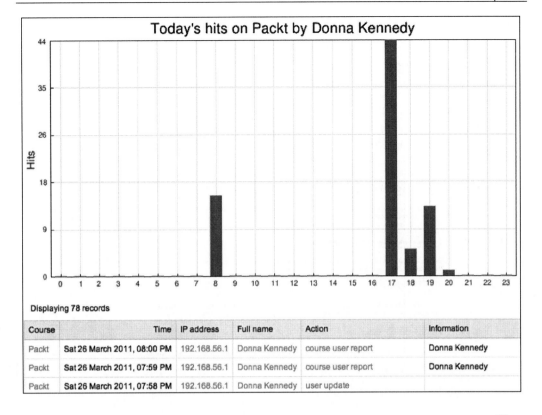

Displaying 78 records

| Course | Time | IP address | Full name | Action | Information |
|--------|------|-----------|-----------|--------|-------------|
| Packt | Sat 26 March 2011, 08:00 PM | 192.168.56.1 | Donna Kennedy | course user report | Donna Kennedy |
| Packt | Sat 26 March 2011, 07:59 PM | 192.168.56.1 | Donna Kennedy | course user report | Donna Kennedy |
| Packt | Sat 26 March 2011, 07:58 PM | 192.168.56.1 | Donna Kennedy | user update | |

 The GD PHP extension has to be installed for bar charts to be shown.

As mentioned before, teachers in a course have full access to the same information to monitor progress and track performance. However, you, as the administrator, are often approached with claims, problems, or any other anomalies. To shed light on these, you will have to revert to the preceding logging data.

Statistics information has been mentioned a few times in course reports, which we will cover next.

# Statistics

Moodle has a built-in statistics module, which you can reach via **Reports | Statistics**. By default, the component is disabled; this has to be changed first (**Enable statistics** in **Advanced features**), along with some settings.

# Statistics settings

The **Statistics** module is deactivated by default due to the fact that the component is very resource-hungry both in terms of disk space usage and, more importantly, memory usage.

 Use the **Statistics** module only if you really require the information and can accept some potentially significant performance reduction.

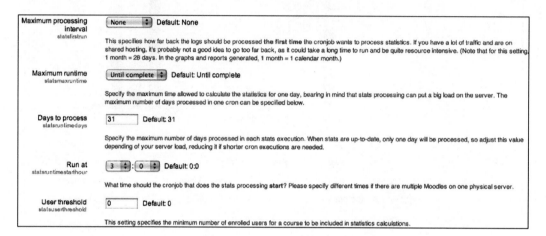

The statistics settings are located in **Server | Statistics**. The following parameters are available:

| Setting | Description |
| --- | --- |
| **Maximum processing interval** | After enabling the **Statistics** module, Moodle utilizes the logs described here to derive statistical information. Here, you need to specify the time Moodle should go back by, to gather the stats. Be aware that this is quite a resource-intensive operation. |
| **Maximum runtime** | You can limit the time for which the statistics gathering process is allowed to run; this is another mechanism to avoid too much burden on the system. |
| **Days to process** | Number of days that will be processed in each statistics execution. |
| **Run at** | Time at which the statistics processing should start. It is highly recommended that this does not clash with the site backup as both operations are potentially very resource-intensive. |
| **User threshold** | Here, the statistics module can be instructed to ignore courses with less than a certain number of enrolled users. |

Now, let us have a look what statistics actually look like.

# Statistics view

Once you have selected the **Course**, the **Report type** (views, post, logins, or all), and the **Time period**, a graph and some tabular information is displayed. Basically, the data shown represents the number of "hits" on a certain day, broken down by roles:

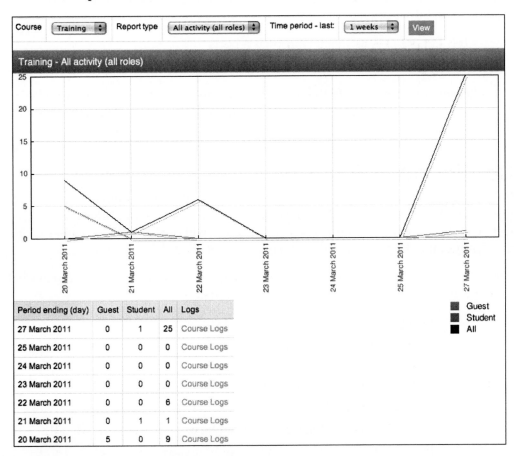

| Period ending (day) | Guest | Student | All | Logs |
|---|---|---|---|---|
| 27 March 2011 | 0 | 1 | 25 | Course Logs |
| 25 March 2011 | 0 | 0 | 0 | Course Logs |
| 24 March 2011 | 0 | 0 | 0 | Course Logs |
| 23 March 2011 | 0 | 0 | 0 | Course Logs |
| 22 March 2011 | 0 | 0 | 6 | Course Logs |
| 21 March 2011 | 0 | 1 | 1 | Course Logs |
| 20 March 2011 | 5 | 0 | 9 | Course Logs |

If no data is displayed, you might have to readjust your statistics settings. Also, while the statistics gathering is in progress, a message might be displayed stating that the module is in catch-up mode. If this is the case, you have to wait until the processing has been completed.

I don't know about you, but I find this information unsatisfactory. Given the burden the module places on our system and the amount of data available, this seems to be a very simplistic – some would say useless – way to display statistics.

To rectify the situation, let us look at report generation and alternative techniques that make use of external data analysis tools.

# Report generation

Moodle comes with a number of pre-defined reports that are based on the log information stored. While this is sufficient for certain activities, there are two drawbacks to this approach:

- It is not possible to create your own reports
- Additional data stored in the database is not taken into account

The following two tools rectify this situation. Currently, neither is part of Moodle core, but it is expected that one of them, or a variation thereof, is likely to be added in the near future.

# Configurable Reports

**Configurable Reports** is a third-party add-on for Moodle, which will appear as a block once it has been installed. It can be downloaded from the **Modules and plugins** section on the **Download** menu at moodle.org. We will deal with the installation of the **Configurable Reports** module in *Chapter 14, Installing Third-party Add-ons*.

Anyone who has been given permission can create new reports at site or course level. **Configurable Reports** supports five types of reports:

- **Courses report**: Reports using course data
- **Categories report**: Reports using category data plus optional embedded course reports
- **Users report**: Reports using user data and their course activities
- **Timeline report**: Reports across time for courses, users, and their activities
- **SQL report**: Any valid SQL statement can be used to query the Moodle database

Depending on what type of report has been chosen, different selection criteria (fields, conditions, ordering, and calculations) are offered. Additionally, filters for drill-down can be specified, the layout can be created, and permissions for who is allowed to run the report can be set. Furthermore, the report builder has the ability to plot different types of graphs. A sample report that shows information about users and their time dedication to courses, which can be filtered by city, is shown in the following screenshot:

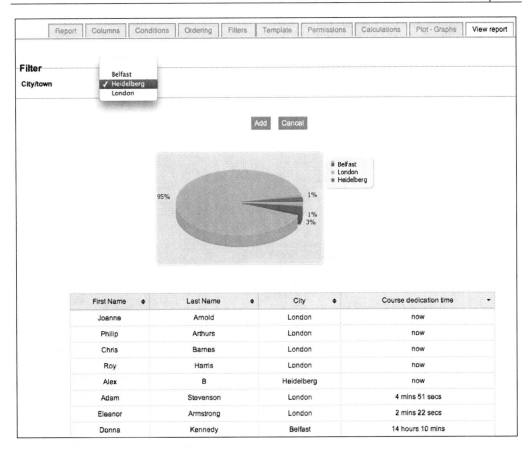

Further information about the **Configurable Reports** module can be found at its Moodle Docs page at `docs.moodle.org/en/blocks/configurable_reports`. One feature this add-on is missing is the ability to schedule reports to be created automatically and e-mailed to specific users. The next tool adds, among other interesting features, this option to the mix.

# Totara report generation

An alternative to **Configurable Reports** is the report generator that comes as part of Totara (`www.totaralms.com`). **Totara** is an open source, subscription-based custom distribution of Moodle, designed for the corporate and public sector. It provides additional functionality such as competency management, individual learning plans, organizational mappings, program management user dashboards, and a powerful report generator.

A report that lists details about users, their competencies, organization, position, proficiency level, and completion date is shown in the following screenshot. It also shows nicely the Moodle-style filters:

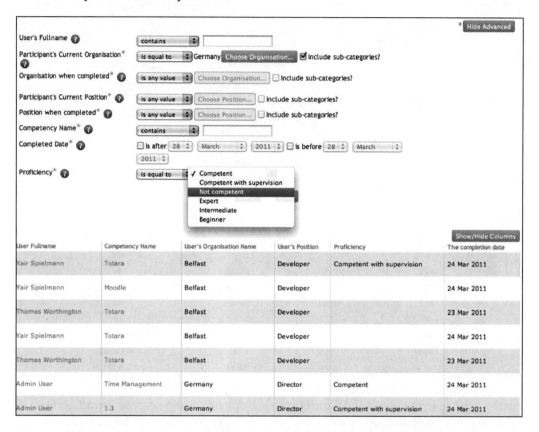

In addition to pre-defined embedded reports; such as report of learning based on competencies or the team members of a manager, the team builder lets you create new reports based on a number of sources; for example, competency evidence, courses, face-to-face sessions, site logs, SCORM, and many more. For each report, **Columns** (including summary information and sorting), **Filters** (search options), **Content control** (contextual information), and **Access** (which role is allowed to view the report in which context) can be specified.

Reports can be exported to CSV, Excel, ODF, and Google Fusion tables. Furthermore, reports can be scheduled for execution by each user, who will then receive a report by e-mail.

For more information about Totara and its powerful reporting capability, contact a Totara Partner.

It has to be noted that there are two more alternative Moodle distributions that target the commercial sector. ELIS (a community edition for Moodle 1.9) is available in the **Modules and Plugins** section at moodle.org and Joule can be found at www.moodlerooms.com/lms-solutions/joule. Both provide comprehensive reporting solutions for the underlying Moodle systems.

# Data analysis

If these described reporting facilities do not satisfy your hunger for usage data, you might consider using *external web analysis tools* such as Web Log Analyzers. You can also utilize a *live data tracking system*, such as Google Analytics, that can be embedded in your Moodle site.

# Web Log Analyzers

Web servers, such as Apache and Microsoft IIS, keep textual logfiles that keep track of every hit on a web site. The fields and their formats can be customized so each logfile will look potentially different. The following two lines are from our Moodle test site (IP addresses have been replaced and server directories shortened):

```
123.45.67.89 - - [26/Mar/2010:08:15:30 +0000] "GET .../synergy-
learning/packt/httpdocs/course/view.php?id=3 HTTP/1.0" 404 1045 "-"
"-"
123.45.67.89 - - [26/Mar/2010:08:15:30 +0000] "GET .../synergy-
learning/packt/httpdocs/mod/quiz/view.php?id=12 HTTP/1.0" 404 2180 "-"
"-"
```

As you can see, these files are not meant to be read by human beings. Instead, web log analysis software exists, which can read and interpret these files. Open source examples are AWStats, Webalizer, and munin; a popular commercial product is WebTrends.

These tools produce detailed statistics that look at the logfiles from every possible angle. The problem when using Web Log Analyzers with Moodle is that it is database-driven, which requires parameterized URLs (the ?id=12 part). You will have to configure the software you use to reflect these parameters; for example, at course level.

# Google Analytics

Google Analytics is a free service (`google.com/analytics/`) that tracks any traffic to your site. You have to sign up for an account before using this service, which offers an abundance of statistics about visitors, traffic sources, content, and user-defined goals. You can find a detailed list of features at `www.google.com/analytics/features.html`.

Once set up, you will be able to see powerful analytics of your Moodle site, as shown in the following screenshot:

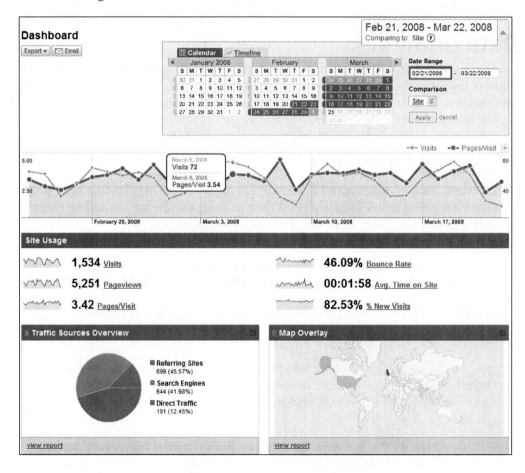

All you have to do is add the following piece of code into the `footer.html` file of your theme before the `</body>` tag:

```
<script type="text/javascript">
var gaJsHost = (("https:" == document.location.protocol) ? "https://
ssl." : "http://www.");
```

```
document.write(unescape("%3Cscript src='" + gaJsHost + "google-
analytics.com/ga.js' type='text/javascript'%3E%3C/script%3E"));
</script>
<script type="text/javascript">
var pageTracker = _gat._getTracker("UA-XXXXXX-X");
pageTracker._initData();
pageTracker._trackPageview();
</script>
```

You need to update the xxxxxx-x in the preceding sample with your own Google Analytics account number. While it is possible to add the code in the `header.html` file, it is not recommended to do so, as it has an impact on the perceived performance of your system.

# Miscellaneous reports

Moodle ships with a number of additional reports, which assist the administrator in monitoring certain activities that take place. Some are only described briefly; for others, references to dedicated chapters are given. All reports are accessible via the **Reports** menu. These reports are listed as follows:

- **Comments**: A table is shown containing the **Author** and **Content** of any comment left on the system. You have the ability to delete any of the comments. For more information on this topic, see the *Collaboration* section in *Chapter 9, Moodle Configuration*.

- **Backups**: For each automated backup, the **Course**, **Time taken**, **Status** (OK, **Skipped**, **Unfinished**, or **Error**), and time of the **Next backup** are listed. For more information on backups, see *Chapter 13, Backup and Restore*.

- **Config changes**: This table shows any changes made to any settings in the **Site administration** section. For each modification, the **Date**, **First name/ Surname**, **Plugin**, **Setting**, **New value**, and **Original value** are shown.

  This is a great tool when something has gone wrong on your site, as you can go back and check what has been changed recently. This report is also useful when you have to support a site administered by another user (see the following screenshot).

  Additional information about these config values is provided in the *Appendix, Configuration Settings*.

| Config changes | | | | | |
|---|---|---|---|---|---|
| **Page:** 1 2 3 4 5 6 7 8 9 10 11 12 13 14 15 16 17 18 ...29 (Next) | | | | | |
| Date ↑ | First name / Surname | Plugin | Setting | New value | Original value |
| Sunday, 27 March 2011, 08:56 AM | Admin User | core | statsruntimestarthour | 9 | 3 |
| Sunday, 27 March 2011, 08:56 AM | Admin User | core | statsfirstrun | all | none |
| Sunday, 27 March 2011, 08:56 AM | Admin User | core | statsruntimestarthour | 3 | 0 |
| Saturday, 26 March 2011, 05:00 PM | Admin User | moodlecourse | showreports | 1 | 0 |
| Saturday, 26 March 2011, 05:00 PM | Admin User | quiz | review | 71760879 | 1073741823 |

- **Course overview**: This report shows some basic statistics about courses. The options for a period to be selected are:
    - ° **Most active courses** — number of hits per course
    - ° **Most active courses (weighted)** — based on activities per user
    - ° **Most participatory courses (enrolments)**
    - ° **Most participatory courses (views/posts)**

    In each report, a table is shown and also a graph visualizing the course data (PHP GD extension has to be installed).

- **Question instances**: This report shows the **Context** (usually course) and **Total, Visible**, and **Hidden** instances in which questions of a selected type or all types are used.

- **Security overview**: A list of some key issues that can compromise the security of your system, listed under the **Issue** column, with links to the relevant settings, its **Status (OK, Information, Warning, Critical)** and a **Description**. We will cover this report in *Chapter 11, Moodle Security and Privacy*.

- **Spam cleaner**: If your system has self-registration activated, and user profiles have been created by spammers, this report will list and clean all compromised profiles according to the provided key words. We will cover this in *Chapter 11, Moodle Security and Privacy*.

# Summary

In this chapter, you have learned how to report on user activities using Moodle's internal reporting facilities, to use report generation alternatives, as well as external web analytics tools. We have also dealt with a number of miscellaneous reports provided by Moodle.

Early on, we mentioned a student who insisted that he or she has submitted an assignment that cannot be located. The student will approach the teacher who will then use the course logs to identify the file. If this remains unsuccessful the teacher will contact you as the administrator to shed some more light on the issue. You can then use the sitewide logs for the user, in case the file has been uploaded in a different course. This escalation is typical in scenarios when problems arise that cannot be resolved at course level.

One concern about reporting on user activities is the preservation of the users' privacy and protection of associated data stored. The next chapter will cover these aspects.

# 11
# Moodle Security and Privacy

Moodle, like any other web application, has the potential to be misused. Moodle has dedicated an entire administration section to security settings, using which you can fine-tune its safety. After an overview of Moodle security, you will learn about the following topics:

- **Security notifications**: We will learn how to set up a number of notification mechanisms that warn you about potential security issues and look at the built-in security report.

- **User security**: We will look at access to Moodle (self-registration, guest access, protection of user details, and course contacts), Moodle passwords, security in roles, and spam prevention.

- **Data and content security**: We will deal with potential issues in content created within Moodle, and visibility of content. You will learn how to set up a site policy and how to configure the antivirus scanner.

- **System security**: We will discuss configuration settings (location of the dataroot directory and the cron process), HTTPS, IP blocker, Module security, and Safe Exam Browser integration.

We'll conclude the chapter with information on privacy and data protection concerns.

Packt Publishing has a dedicated title on *Moodle Security* in its portfolio at www.packtpub.com/install-and-configure-moodle-in-the-most-secure-way/ book. While it covers Moodle 1.9, the majority of topics are relevant to Moodle 2, too.

# Security—an overview

Moodle takes security extremely seriously and any potential issues are given highest priority. Fixed vulnerabilities often trigger the release of minor versions, which emphasizes the importance of the subject.

The security of a system is as good as its weakest link. Moodle relies on significant software, hardware, and network infrastructure; security can potentially be compromised in a number of areas. As the focus of this book is on Moodle and the administration thereof, we only cover security elements of Moodle per se. The following areas are not dealt with, and it is necessary to consult the respective documentation on security issues:

- **Software**: As described in *Chapter 2, The Moodle System*, Moodle's key components comprise of a web server (usually Apache or Microsoft IIS), a database server (for example, MySQL, MS SQL Server, or Oracle), and a programming language (PHP). Additional PHP and operating system extensions are required, for instance, to support multiple locales or networking.

- **Hardware**: Moodle runs on (physical or virtual) servers that have to be physically hosted. There is ongoing debate about the safety and security of such systems, which is reflected by ever-extending precautions by data centers.

- **Network**: Any system that is part of a network is potentially vulnerable. Configuration of firewalls, proxy servers, and routers as well as general network security are key aspects in protecting your system from any attacks.

A number of these topics are covered in docs.moodle.org/en/Security.

One rule that applies to all elements is that the latest software updates should be installed regularly. Updating Moodle was covered in *Chapter 1, Moodle Installation*.

With the increasing complexity and growing popularity of Moodle, it is imperative that you make sure all possible measures are taken to prevent any security issues. Let's get started.

# Security notifications

Moodle has set up a dedicated site that you can find at security.moodle.org, dealing with security issues. If you register your Moodle site, which is highly recommended, your e-mail address will automatically be added to the security alerts mailing list. To set this up, go to **Registration** and click on the **Register with Moodle. org (MOOCH)** button.

# Moodle notifications

When you click on the **Notifications** link in the **Site administration** section, Moodle will display any potential issues with your site. This link is also used to initiate installed Moodle updates and add-ons (see *Chapter 14, Installing Third-party Add-ons*).

Some sample messages are displayed in the following screenshot; the first issue would clearly fall into the security category:

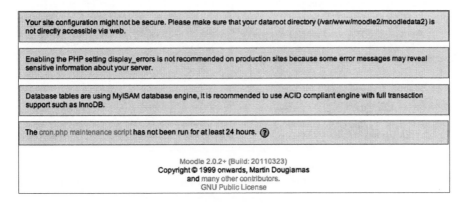

Moodle monitors failed login attempts in its logfile, as described in *Chapter 10, Moodle Reporting*. Repeated login failures can indicate that unauthorized users are trying to get access to your system. In addition to checking your log files regularly, you should consider monitoring these activities by configuring the settings at **Security | Notifications**:

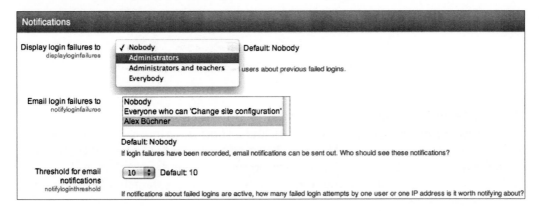

You can specify who will see a message displayed on screen and who will be e-mailed about login failures. You can further set the number of failed logins from the same IP address that will trigger these notifications.

While this is not foolproof, it can potentially highlight some problems within your system, and it is recommended that you activate it. Another benefit of getting these notifications e-mailed to you is the "customer care" aspect of being able to get back to legitimate users who have felt frustrated when trying to get into your site.

# Security report

Another mechanism we already touched upon in *Chapter 10, Moodle Reporting* is the security report (**Reports | Security overview**):

| Security overview | | |
|---|---|---|
| **Issue** | **Status** | **Description** |
| Register globals | OK | Register globals are disabled. |
| Insecure dataroot | OK | Dataroot directory must not be accessible via the web. |
| Displaying of PHP errors | Warning | The PHP setting to display errors is enabled. It is recommended that this is disabled. |
| No authentication | OK | No authentication plugin is disabled. |
| Allow EMBED and OBJECT | OK | Unlimited object embedding is not allowed. |
| Enabled .swf media filter | Critical | Flash media filter is enabled - this is very dangerous for the majority of servers. |
| Open user profiles | OK | Login is required before viewing user profiles. |
| Open to Google | OK | Search engine access is not enabled. |
| Password policy | Warning | Password policy not set. |
| Password salt | OK | Password salt is OK. |
| Email change confirmation | OK | Confirmation of change of email address in user profile. |
| Writable config.php | OK | config.php can not be modified by PHP scripts. |
| XSS trusted users | Warning | RISK_XSS - found 24 users that have to be trusted. |
| Administrators | OK | Found 2 server administrator(s). |
| Backup of user data | Warning | Found 1 roles, 0 overrides and 2 users with the ability to backup user data. |
| Default role for all users | OK | Default role for all users definition is OK. |
| Guest role | OK | Guest role definition is OK. |
| Frontpage role | Information | Frontpage role is not set. |

The report shows a number of potential key security issues, their status (**OK**, **Information**, **Warning**, and **Critical**), and a short description (as shown in the preceding screenshot). When you click on the issue name, you will be re-directed to a page that provides more information about the problem and, if available, also a further link to the settings page where you can rectify the situation (here, **Manage filters**):

The **Security overview** report is a good starting point to identify some potential issues. However, it does not replace a full security audit, penetration test, or health check, as offered by some Moodle Partners.

# User security

The key to the security of your system lies in making sure that users only have access to their privileged areas in Moodle. In this section, we will be dealing with access to Moodle, passwords, security in roles, and spam prevention.

# Access to Moodle

Users can access Moodle in different ways and it is important to configure access mechanisms correctly.

# Self-registration

Self-registration is a great feature, which reduces the workload of the administrator significantly. However, it poses a potential risk that unwanted users may create an account either manually or automatically. To reduce this risk, two pairs of settings are located in the **Common settings** section under **Plugins | Authentication | Manage authentication**:

- Allowed and denied e-mail domains
- ReCAPTCHA private and public keys

The settings have been described in detail in *Chapter 5, User Management*.

# Guest access

Moodle provides a feature called guest access to users who do not wish to register with a site. While this is very useful for some public sites (such as `moodle.org`), it is unwanted in most educational and commercial settings. To deactivate guest access, go to the **Common settings** section under **Plugins | Authentication | Manage authentication** and change the **Guest login button** setting from **Show** to **Hide**.

A second setting that relates to guest access is located in **Users | Permissions | User Policies**, where you will find the **Auto-login guests** checkbox. Turn this on only if you want to log in visitors automatically when entering a course with guest access.

If you allow guest access as an authentication method, you can specify inside courses if guest access is available as an enrolment mechanism and also specify a guest access password. We dealt with this in *Chapter 4, Course Management*.

# Protection of user details

Identity theft is a common problem on the Internet, and Moodle is no exception. To avoid the possibility of fraudsters gathering details about authenticated users, a number of settings are located in **Security | Site Policies**:

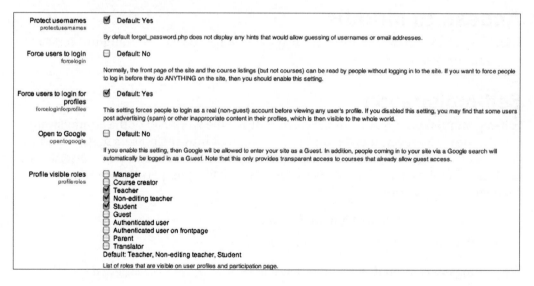

| Setting | Description |
|---|---|
| **Protect usernames** | If a user cannot remember his/her username or password Moodle provides a **Forgotten password** screen. By default, the message displayed reads: **If you supplied a correct username or email address then an email should have been sent to you**. If the protection is turned off, however, the message reads as **An email should have been sent to your address at \*\*\*\*\*\*@<domain name>** which could allow the guessing of a username. |
| **Force users to login** | By default, the front page of Moodle is visible to everyone, even if he/she is not logged in to the site. If you wish to force users to log in before they see the front page, change this parameter. |
| **Force users to login for profiles** | When set to **Yes** (default setting) users will have to log in with an authentic account before they can access the profile pages of other users. |
| **Open to Google** | Moodle can be configured to allow Google to crawl through courses with guest access and add the content to its search engine database. This functionality is turned off by default. |
| **Profile visible roles** | Any role selected will be visible on user profiles and participation pages. |

At the bottom of the **Site policies** screen, you have the ability to activate **Email change confirmation**. If set to **Yes**, users will be sent an e-mail to confirm that their change of e-mail address in their profile is genuine.

# Course contacts

When courses are displayed on the front page, users that are not logged on to the system can see a description and the names of the course managers of each course by clicking on it. By default, these are the teachers of the course. To change the names that are displayed for each course, go to **Appearance | Course contacts** and select the roles to be displayed:

To hide names completely, deselect all roles. As a result, no names will appear when course descriptions are shown.

# Moodle passwords

Moodle offers a password policy feature that applies to manual accounts and which can be configured in **Security | Site policies**, as shown in the following screenshot:

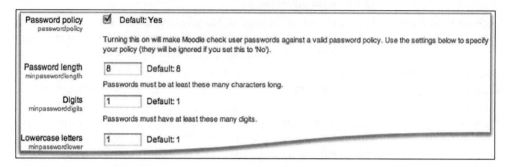

The following self-explanatory constraints for passwords are available:

- **Password length** ($\geq 0$)
- **Digits** (0...9)
- **Lowercase letters** (a...z)
- **Uppercase letters** (A...Z)
- **Non-alphanumeric characters** (such as $\$\%\&*$)
- **Consecutive identical characters** ($\geq 0$)
- **Group enrolment key policy** (whether the specified password policy rules should apply to group enrolment key or not)

Moodle's site policy does not provide a password expiry parameter. However, if you use an LDAP server, this limitation can be overcome by specifying an expiry duration.

 It is highly recommended to use a strong password (long, complex, and random) for the Moodle administrator account even if the password policy is deactivated.

Moodle stores passwords in an encrypted form using a so-called MD5 hash. To improve the security of the passwords further, Moodle supports password salting, which is activated by default. You should not deactivate this measure as it will be easier for hackers to gain unwanted access to your site. Password salting adds a random string to the MD5 hash—the longer the string, the harder it is to crack the password.

The password salt for each Moodle site is stored as an entry in the `config.php` file:

```
$CFG->passwordsaltmain = 'a long random string added as salt';
```

The salt cannot be accessed via the Moodle interface for security reasons. It is recommended that you also store the salt somewhere else, in case it gets lost or you have to migrate your site.

If you need to change the salt, you have to retain the old salt, which is supported for up to 20 changes:

```
$CFG->passwordsaltalt1 = 'first long random string added as salt';
$CFG->passwordsaltalt2 = 'second long random string added as salt';
$CFG->passwordsaltmain = 'current long random string added as salt';
```

If you ever lose your admin password and have no means of recovering it, you are able to manually override the **password** field in the **mdl_user** table in the SQL database. Because the passwords are stored MD5 hash encrypted, you will have to replace the current value with an encrypted password. For example, to set the password to `newpassword`, you need to use the following SQL statement:

```
UPDATE mdl_user
    SET password = md5('newpassword')
    WHERE username = 'admin';
```

If your database does not support the `md5` function, you will have to set `password` to the actual MD5 hash tag. For example, this would be `5e9d11a14ad1c8dd77e98ef9b53fd1ba` for `newpassword`. Use one of many available online generators to find out the tag.

The first time you log in to Moodle, the salt will be added and the new encrypted password will be stored in the database. More information on password salting in Moodle can be found at `docs.moodle.org/en/Password_salting`.

# Security in roles

Moodle allows the creation of custom roles such as Parent, Teaching Assistant, Secretary, Inspector, and Librarian. However, the flexibility of this powerful mechanism comes with a price in the form of a potential security risk.

Moodle displays the risks associated with each capability, that is, the risks that each capability can potentially raise. To recapitulate from *Chapter 6, Managing Permissions: Roles and Capabilities*, the five risk types are explained in the table that follows:

| Risk | Icon | Description |
| --- | --- | --- |
| Configuration | ▲ | Users can change site configuration and behavior. |
| XSS | ▲ | Users can add files and texts that allow cross-site scripting (potentially malicious scripts that are embedded in web pages and executed on the user's computer). |
| Privacy | ▲ | Users can gain access to private information of other users. |
| Spam | ▲ | Users can send spam to site users or others. |
| Data loss | ▲ | Users can destroy large amounts of content or information. |

Because risks are only displayed to indicate what potential damage a capability can cause, you are responsible for the role definitions and contexts in which the roles are applied. Make use of the capability report and system permission checker, as we discussed in *Chapter 6, Managing Permissions: Roles and Capabilities*.

It is highly recommended to minimize the number of global role assignments as they are applicable throughout the entire site, including the front page and all the courses.

The **Authenticated user** role is assigned to everybody who is logged in to your site. It does not conflict with any other roles and guarantees that certain operations can be carried out outside courses. Make sure that you don't change the scope of this role unless you really have to, as any changes to this role will apply to every authenticated user on the system.

Default roles for different user types are assigned in **Users | Permissions | User Policies**. We dealt with these settings in detail in *Chapter 6, Managing Permissions: Roles and Capabilities*. Make sure that these settings are set correctly, especially for the guest and visitor-related roles.

# Spam prevention

If Moodle is not configured correctly, it allows spammers to insert content into user profiles of accounts created via self-registration. This type of attack is known as **profile spam**. To prevent this, make sure that the following settings are set correctly (which they are by default):

- Only use e-mail based self-registration if it is really necessary. No self-registration, no spam!

- Keep the **Force users to login for profiles** parameter enabled in your site policies (see the *Protection of user details* section). That way, you can prevent anonymous visitors and search engines from seeing user profiles.

- Make sure that the **Profiles for enrolled user only** parameter remains enabled.

Also be aware that legit users can be the cause of spam. Make sure that no user has any unnecessary capabilities in their roles that allow for this (see *Spam* risk in the *Security in roles* section). You might even consider the creation of a Spammer role that allows access to activities such as forums but prevents content from being posted.

If your site has been the victim of spam, make use of **Reports | Spam cleaner**. You can either let Moodle **Auto-detect common spam patterns** (the list makes for some interesting reading!) or search for your own keywords:

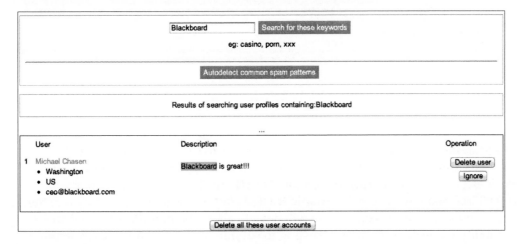

Any user profiles where the **Description** field contains any of the listed keywords are shown. You then have the option to delete the user accounts. For more information on spam prevention in Moodle, go to docs.moodle.org/en/Reducing_spam_in_Moodle.

If you are interested how spam is fought on moodle.org, have a look at the blog post at interestingshizzle.com/2011/08/fighting-spam-at-moodle-org.

# Data and content security

Content can potentially contain malicious elements. It further needs to be protected from unauthorized access. In this section, we shall deal with the security of data and content.

## Content created within Moodle

Users are able to create content in Moodle either by using the resource editor or by uploading files. A number of settings are available to prevent misuse.

HTML allows the embedding of code that uses explicit <EMBED> and <OBJECT> tags. This mechanism has recently gained popularity with sites such as YouTube, Prezi, Voki, and Google Maps, providing code to be embedded for their users. Potentially, malicious code can be put in the embedded script, which is why its support is deactivated by default. To activate it, go to **Security | Site policies** and locate the **Allow EMBED and OBJECT tags** parameter.

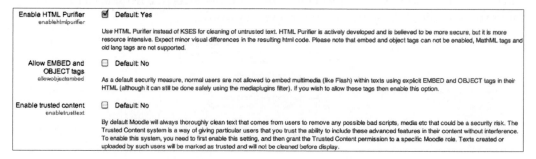

The Moodle editor uses a mechanism called KSES to remove any unwanted HTML elements and attributes. Moodle supports a more secure version called **HTML Purifier**. It is possible to turn the **Enable HTML Purifier** filter off for users you trust. First, you have to set the **Enable trusted content** parameter, as shown in the preceding screenshot. Second, you will have to allow the **moodle/site:trustcontent** capability for each user you are trusting to submit JavaScript and other potentially malicious code.

The multimedia plugin supports a number of audio and video formats. Shockwave files can contain code that could cause problems on users' local machines. To avoid the usage of SWF files, it is recommended that the **Flash animation** parameter in **Plugins | Filters | Multimedia plugins** is turned off.

Moodle also comes with a **Word censorship** filter (**Plugins | Filters | Manage filters**). However, it does recognise expressions within words, which doesn't make it that useful, as it would mark valid terms such as sextant, sparse and altitude.. You can either enter additional words and phrases in the **Settings** of the filter or edit the `badwords` language string in `filter_censor.php` (careful, this list is far from G-rated).

# Visibility of content

Blogging, tagging, and commenting are social networking tools that are popular in Web 2.0 environments. Blog entries, tags, and comments are harnessed for searching, sharing, and other collaborative activities in order to match interests. The potential issue is that the content is visible to users who should not be able to share or view entries. Moodle has catered for this by providing a number of settings, which we already have dealt with in the *Collaboration* section in *Chapter 9, Moodle Configuration*. Here is a list of areas where the respective functionalities need to be turned on and off:

- **Appearance | Blog | Blog visibility**
- **Appearance | Blog | Enable comments**
- **Advanced features | Enable tags functionality**

If you deactivate any of the mechanisms, tags, comments, and blog entries already on the system are kept and will re-appear when the functionality is turned on again; In other words, there is no risk of data loss when turning the functionality off and then back on.

You might also consider creating a dedicated role on your system, for example, a Blogger role utilizing the **moodle/blog:create** capability. This will limit blogging to specific users only—those who have been assigned the new role. You can find more details on a Blogger role in the Moodle Docs at `docs.moodle.org/en/ Blogger_role`.

# Site policy

Users who have access to Moodle are sometimes as much a threat as unauthorized users. If you have a site policy that all users (not just learners) must see and agree to before using Moodle for the first time, you will have some ammunition when taking action against a user who has misused your system. The document, often referred to as an Acceptable Use Policy, should aim to adhere to the LARK principle—Legal, Appropriate, Responsible, and Kind.

You can specify the URL address of the text in **Security | Site policies**, which includes a **Site policy URL** and a **Site policy URL for guests** entry. You will have to specify a URL that contains the policy text, which should be an HTML document. The file is often at a publicly accessible URL, for example, the policy already available on your main website.

Once the site policy address has been specified, it has to be confirmed by each user the first time they log in to Moodle. If the policy is in any other format than HTML or plain text, only a link will be provided to the selected file. It is therefore not recommended to use PDFs or Word files.

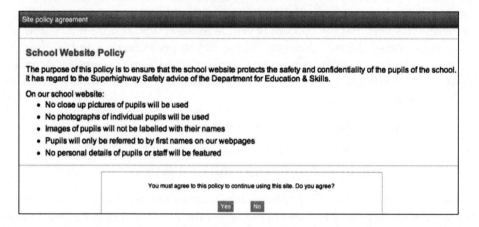

While the site policy does not prevent any misuse, it introduces a psychological barrier and also protects your organization in case legal action needs to be taken. Site policies allow users to understand the expectations of how to most effectively and appropriately use a site. While it often has a legal undertone to dealing with bad users, it can also teach new users about the social expectations of those using the site.

# Antivirus

Moodle supports scanning of uploaded files for viruses using **Clam AntiVirus (ClamAV)**, which is an open source antivirus toolkit for Unix, designed especially for systems such as Moodle. See `www.clamav.org` for details, downloads for different operating systems, and how to keep the virus definition database up-to-date. You need to install ClamAV on your system. Once installed, the scanner is configured at **Security | Anti-Virus**:

| Anti-Virus | |
|---|---|
| **Use clam AV on uploaded files** <br> runclamavonupload | ☑ Default: No <br><br> When enabled, clam AV will be used to scan all uploaded files. |
| **clam AV path** <br> pathtoclam | /usr/bin/clamdscan    Default: Empty <br><br> Path to clam AV. Probably something like /usr/bin/clamscan or /usr/bin/clamdscan. You need this in order for clam AV to run. |
| **Quarantine directory** <br> quarantinedir | Default: Empty <br><br> If you want clam AV to move infected files to a quarantine directory, enter it here. It must be writable by the webserver. If you leave this blank, or if you enter a directory that doesn't exist or isn't writable, infected files will be deleted. Do not include a trailing slash. |
| **On clam AV failure** <br> clamfailureonupload | Treat files as OK ▾   Default: Treat files as OK <br><br> If you have configured clam to scan uploaded files, but it is configured incorrectly or fails to run for some unknown reason, how should it behave? If you choose 'Treat files like viruses', they'll be moved into the quarantine area, or deleted. If you choose 'Treat files as OK', the files will be moved to the destination directory like normal. Either way, admins will be alerted that clam has failed. If you choose 'Treat files like viruses' and for some reason clam fails to run (usually because you have entered an invalid pathtoclam), ALL files that are uploaded will be moved to the given quarantine area, or deleted. Be careful with this setting. |

| Setting | Description |
|---|---|
| **Use clam AV on uploaded files** | Turn ClamAV on or off. |
| **clam AV path** | Location of ClamAV on your system. Typical default paths are provided. |
| **Quarantine directory** | By default, any infected files are deleted. If you wish to keep them, specify a writeable directory that is then used to quarantine the files instead. |
| **On clam AV failure** | If, for whatever reason, ClamAV fails to run or scan files, you as the administrator will be alerted. Additionally, you can change the default setting **Treat files as OK** (the scanner is ignored) to **Treat files like viruses** (all files are deleted or moved to the quarantine directory if the scanner fails). |

There are two limitations of ClamAV:

- ClamAV does not exist for Windows servers. You will need to install a Windows-based virus scanner to provide this functionality and monitor any quarantined files separately.

- ClamAV will have an impact on the performance of your system. This only becomes an issue if the file upload facility is used plentifully. You might have to add more RAM to your server if this is the case.

# System security

In this section, we are dealing with configuration settings, login via secure HTTP, IP blocker, module security, and Safe Exam Browser integration.

# Configuration security

There are a number of general configuration settings that potentially have an impact on the security of your system.

## Accessibility of dataroot

In the **Notifications** screenshot at the beginning of the chapter, you must have probably spotted the warning that the dataroot directory is directly accessible via the Internet. Moodle requires additional space on a server to store uploaded files, such as, course documents and user pictures. The directory is called dataroot and must not be accessible via the Web. If this directory is accessible directly, unauthorized users can get access to content.

To prevent this, move your dataroot directory outside the web directory and modify config.php accordingly, by changing the $CFG->dataroot entry.

In externally-hosted environments, it is often not possible to locate the directory outside the web directory. If this is the case, create a file called .htaccess in the data directory and add a line containing deny from all.

## Cron process

We already described the cron process in *Chapter 1, Moodle Installation*. It is a script that runs regularly to perform certain operations, such as, sending notifications, processing statistics, cleaning up temporary files, and so on. Scripts that run at operating-system level can potentially contain malicious code.

It is possible to run the script via a web browser by simply typing in the URL, which is <your Moodle site>/admin/cron.php. To prevent this, two mutually exclusive settings are located in **Security | Site policies**:

If you only allow the cron process to be executed from the command line, running the script via a web browser will be disabled and a message will be displayed saying **Sorry, internet access to this page has been disabled by the administrator**. The cron process can still be executed automatically if set up correctly.

If the **Cron password for remote access** parameter is set, Moodle requires that executing the cron script via a web browser requires the provision of a password in the form of a parameter, such as, `<your Moodle site>/admin/cron.php?password=yourpassword`. If the password is not provided or is incorrect, an error message, the same as before, is displayed.

# HTTP security

Moodle offers HTTPS support, which runs HTTP requests over SSL (a more secure, but significantly slower, socket layer). The login of every system is a potential vulnerability and it is possible to enable the **Use HTTPS for logins** parameter, which is activated in **Security | HTTP security**.

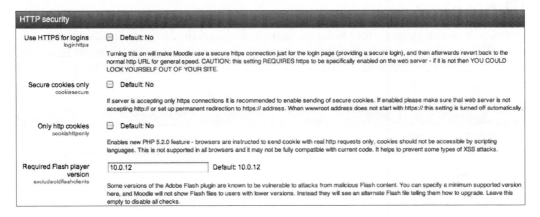

HTTPS encrypts the username and password before they are transferred from a user's browser to the server that hosts Moodle. HTTPS has to be enabled on your web server and you will have to purchase or generate an SSL certificate. Every web server has a different method for enabling HTTPS, so you will have to consult the documentation of your server.

 If you turn on HTTPS for logins without the relevant system components installed, you will lock yourself out of your own system!

HTTPS is only used for the login procedure itself; once a user has logged in, Moodle reverts to HTTP. It is possible to run your entire Moodle system via HTTPS by changing the `$CFG->wwwroot` variable in the `config.php` file to the new secure URL. However, be aware that using HTTPS across the whole site will cause increased CPU load on your web server and is therefore not recommended. If this becomes an issue, you can get HTTPS/SSL accelerator cards that offload the encryption from the main CPU.

Web servers can be configured so they only accept HTTPS URLs. If this is the case on your system, it is recommended to enable the **Secure cookies only** parameter. Moodle already supports a new feature that instructs web browsers to send cookies only with real requests, which prevents some cross-scripting attacks. However, the **Only http cookies** feature is not supported by all web browsers.

Adobe Flash player has caused some serious security concerns, especially the vulnerabilities in older versions. You can specify a minimum **Required Flash player version** that has to be installed on the user's browser before executing any Flash content.

# IP blocker

Users will access your system from stationary and mobile devices. The one thing they all have in common is that they will access your site via an IP address. You have the ability to limit that access by specifying a whitelist and a blacklist in **Security | IP blocker**:

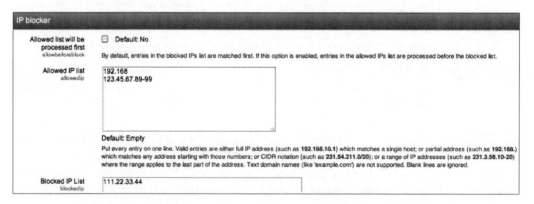

The whitelist (**Allowed IP list**) can contain IP addresses in a number of formats (full IP address, partial address, ranges of IPs, and the CDIR notation). The same applies to the blacklist (**Blocked IP list**). By default, the blacklist has priority over the whitelist. If you wish to reverse this, select **Allowed list will be processed first**.

As an example, you might want to add `10.*.*.*` to your whitelist and blacklist a particular IP, say `10.123.45.67`, that was trying to guess your admin password multiple times.

# Module security

The objective of the **Module security** feature is to restrict the usage of Moodle activities and resources in courses. If activated in **Security | Module security**, a separate **Restrict activity modules?** frame appears in the settings of certain courses.

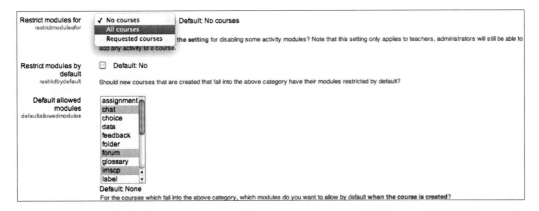

You can choose whether modules can be restricted for **No courses**, **All courses**, or **Requested courses**. The other two default settings specify whether modules are restricted by default, and which ones are selected.

This feature is useful if you wish to limit access to a certain module to particular courses. For instance, you might have a license for a video conferencing system that comes with a Moodle **Activity** module. However, due to cost implications, you do not want this module to be used in all courses. To facilitate this, select the module, as in the preceding screenshot, and only activate it in the course(s) where it should be used. Teachers will not see the selection in the course settings, but the module will appear in the list of available activities.

# Safe Exam Browser integration

Safe Exam Browser is a system that regulates the access to any utilities like system functions, other websites, and applications and prevents unauthorized resources being used during an exam (`www.safeexambrowser.org`). The software has to be installed on the computer on which the exam is to be carried on and is freely available to download for Windows and Mac OS X.

The system integration with Moodle is currently at an experimental stage and has to be activated in **Development | Experimental | Experimental Settings**. Once activated, the **Require Safe Exam Browser** choice will appear in the **Browser security** section of the settings of the **Quiz** activity.

# Moodle privacy

Some of Moodle's default functionality might infringe legislative privacy or data protection regulations in the country you operate Moodle in or the rules of the organization for which the VLE is run. As different organizations are obliged to follow different guidelines, for example, FERPA in the United States, we are only able to point you in the direction of some of the most common issues, and how to resolve them in Moodle.

The key issue is to protect personal information in educational records. Examples of such data are: personal details, grades, usage data (as described in *Chapter 10, Moodle Reporting*), and notes by teachers about students.

# Information stored about users

Some regulations prescribe what information about users is allowed to be stored, with or without their consent:

- **Logfiles**: You cannot prevent Moodle from keeping a track of any user activities, but you have the ability to prevent reports from accessing this data. We have listed all the relevant capabilities for roles in the *Course and user reports* section in *Chapter 10, Moodle Reporting*.

- **Notes about users**: Moodle contains a tool that allows users with teacher rights to take notes about students. Other users with teaching rights can potentially see these notes. If this facility is not in conformance with your regulations, go to **Advanced features** and uncheck the **Enable notes** parameter.

If there is any other information about users that it is prohibited to store, you are most likely to find a capability in the roles setting to achieve this.

# Information available to other users

Moodle is usually very open about what users can see about each other. While this might be in line with the philosophy of social constructivism, it might not conform to the regulations you have to abide by:

- **Online users**: The **Online users** block displays the name of all users who have been active on the system in the last 5 (default setting) minutes. You can disable this block by hiding it in **Plugins | Blocks | Manage blocks**.

- **User profile information**: The user profile is visible to other users on the system. You can limit what information is shown to non-teachers and non-administrators by selecting **Hide user fields** in **Users | Permissions | User policies**. This also includes two fields providing information about **First access** and **Last access**.

- **Courses a user is enrolled to**: Same as above, by selecting the **My courses** field.

- **Revealing e-mail addresses**: When searching for users or enrolling them into courses, their e-mail address is shown. To replace this, go to **Users | Permissions | User policies** and select **ID number** for the **When selecting users, search and display** parameter instead. It is not recommended to use the **Username** option for security reasons.

- **Grades**: Grades of students in a course can be seen and edited by teachers. Moodle supports the export of grades, which can be prohibited using a number of `gradeexport` capabilities. It is further possible to publish grades so they can be viewed via a public URL without access to Moodle. This might be useful for external examiners, but can cause issues with your privacy regulations and is therefore turned off by default (see **Enable publishing** in **Grades | General settings** and various `gradeexport` capabilities).

- **Backups**: Teachers have the ability to take course backups, which also contain user information. We are going to deal with limiting backups in *Chapter 13, Backup and Restore*.

If there is any other information that it is prohibited for other users to see, you are most likely to find a capability in the roles setting to achieve this.

# Summary

In this chapter, you have learned how to protect your Moodle system from misuse and how to protect users' privacy. However, it is important to stress that Moodle security is only a single variable in the overall equation. Make sure that all other underlying software, infrastructure, and hardware components are set up correctly as well.

Most Moodle systems run on the LAMP platform, which has proven to be very secure if configured correctly. Moodle developers are very conscious that security is vital when dealing with personal user data such as grades. Hence, the topic has been given highest priority. However, there is no guarantee that your system is 100 percent protected against misuse. New hacking techniques will emerge and users will continue to be careless with their credentials (you have all seen the post-it notes under the keyboard). So, make sure the security patches and updates on your entire system, not just Moodle, are always up-to-date and keep educating your users about the dangers. Also consider undergoing a regular security audit or health check as offered by some Moodle Partners.

Now that you system is secure, let's make sure that it performs to its full potential.

# 12
# Moodle Performance and Optimization

The performance of web-based systems is a critical issue and it is a key responsibility of the administrator to configure, monitor, and fine-tune the virtual learning environment for maximum speed. While Moodle has the potential to scale to thousands of simultaneous users, good performance management is required to guarantee adequate scalability.

After providing an overview, we will cover the following topics which are most related to Moodle performance and optimization:

- **Moodle content**: We will look at how content creation, content volume, different content types, and various filter settings can have an impact on the performance of your Moodle system.
- **Moodle system settings**: A range of system-related performance settings are dealt with. These include:
    - Caching
    - Session handling
    - Memory management (cron, course backups, and search)
    - Module settings (gradebook, chat, and forum)
    - Miscellaneous settings (logfiles, system paths, front page courses and roles)

We will conclude the chapter with a section on performance profiling and monitoring.

# Performance and optimization—an overview

LAMP software in general and Moodle in particular have very distinct application layers consisting of the operating system, web server, database server, and the application developed in a programming language. Each layer has its own idiosyncrasies when it comes to optimization. We will mainly focus on the application layer, which is the focus of this book.

The following areas are not dealt with in detail in any of the following pages, and it is necessary to refer the respective documentation on performance and optimization issues:

- **Operating system performance**: The choice of operating system and its configuration will have a major impact on how Moodle will perform. In principle, Linux or any other Unix derivative performs better than any other operating system. PHP applications such as Moodle run significantly slower in a Windows environment than on Linux. Some aspects of this have been covered in *Chapter 1, Moodle Installation*.

- **Database performance**: The database is a core element of Moodle but also a major bottleneck as it requires disk access, which is slower than memory access. Many books and conferences have been dedicated to database optimization with indexing, caching, buffering, querying, and connection handling as the main candidates. The two optimizations that have a significant impact on your database performance are enabling query caching and the increase of buffer sizes. You might also want to consider running the database on a separate dedicated server or a cluster.

  There is also much debate about what database is best suited for Moodle. While the open source camp is divided between MySQL and PostgreSQL, corporate advocates are split between MS SQL Server and Oracle. Whatever may be your choice of system, a well set up and tuned database will always perform better than one that is used with its out of the box settings.

- **Web server performance**: Each web server offers an array of optimization settings that include memory handling, caching, process management, and other minor tweaks.

- **PHP performance**: There are a number of ways in which PHP can be forced to execute code significantly faster. The key is the usage of a PHP accelerator (such as eAccelerator, XCache, Zend, or APC) in combination with good memory management and caching techniques. There are some very good discussions and performance comparisons on PHP accelerators in the *Hardware and Performance* forums on moodle.org.

- **Hardware performance**: We have already covered some aspects of this in *Chapter 1, Moodle Installation*, where we mentioned that there is no one-size-fits-all approach when it comes to the ideal hardware setup. For single-server systems the key is RAM—the more, the better; simple as that. Once the system size increases, it is inevitable to use multiple servers, ideally in a load-balanced environment.

An additional layer of complexity is added when your system is run in a virtualized environment. This might be running Moodle on Windows in a virtualized environment or even running Linux virtualized machines on Windows Hyper-V. While all the above criteria apply, some elements can be changed on the fly. For example, during exam week, you might consider increasing the memory available for Moodle, while during the summer break, you can reduce the number of servers to carry out maintenance. More sophisticated setups let you specify load and usage thresholds, which trigger the allocation of resources automatically.

For each area mentioned, benchmark and stress tests are available that will help you to gauge what performance bottlenecks are present and, after optimization has been carried out, if they have been reduced. There are also add-ons available for most web browsers that display information on how long it takes to load pages, thus offering some indicative performance measurements.

An entire area has been dedicated to performance and optimization in the Moodle Docs. You find most of the relevant information as well as links to related sites at `docs.moodle.org/en/Performance`.

One thing you should bear in mind is that Moodle performance cannot be seen without taking Moodle security into account, and vice versa. Very often, improving security comes at a price in terms of performance reduction; for example, running your site over HTTPS.

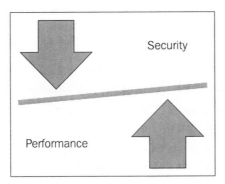

# Moodle content

The content that is created and uploaded by your course creators or front page designers will have an impact on the performance of your system. While you cannot dictate what learning sources are added to Moodle, the following pointers can provide explanations if certain aspects within courses behave sluggishly, or users on slower internet connections experience difficulties in accessing learning materials.

## Content creation

Moodle is significantly slower when run in editing mode. Unless you are editing or any other user is modifying any content, it is recommended to turn editing off as this will put less strain on the system.

Some content is created quicker in a separate stand alone application such as web development tools, word processors, or SCORM editors, as opposed to the built-in Moodle tools.

## Content volume

The amount of content within a course can cause problems for student access. While each resource and activity is accessed individually, there are pedagogical limits on the number of learning objects that should be stored in a course. Furthermore, a course with hundreds of large resources is less likely to provide a good learning experience than a number of courses broken down in more manageable chunks. It will also slow down backing up and importing of courses.

## Content types

Moodle supports a large number of content types such as office document, graphics, animation, audio, and video. In principal, there exists a trade-off between size, quality, and functionality. There are a number of precautions that can be taken for each of the following types:

- **Office documents**: The following precautions can be taken:
    - Save office files as PDF files (which are much smaller in size) unless editing is required
    - Encourage the use of online repositories, such as **Google Docs** and **Dropbox**, which put less strain on your server
    - Scan text using OCR recognition and not as images

- **Graphics**: The following precautions can be taken:
    - ○ Reduce the image resolution, especially when pictures have been taken with digital cameras
    - ○ Reduce image color depth
    - ○ Use a compression format
    - ○ When using Microsoft Word, insert images in text documents as metafiles (using the **Paste Special** command)
    - ○ Use formats that are supported directly by web browsers (usually, JPG and PNG)

- **Audio files**: The following precautions can be taken:
    - ○ Reduce the sample rate (especially for spoken content)
    - ○ Mono recording is often sufficient for spoken content
    - ○ Use a compression format such as MP3

- **Animations and video**: The following precautions can be taken:
    - ○ Keep animation quality, dimension, and sample rate to a minimum
    - ○ Use Flash or HTML5 for better performance
    - ○ Stream video (from external sources such as `www.teachertube.com`) if possible

These are just a few recommendations that will help to reduce the stress on your system. The more informed your course content creators are, the less resources will be taken up by the content per se. While the usage of different types of textual and multimedia resources should be encouraged, it is important to introduce a culture of how these content types are streamlined as much as possible.

# Moodle filter settings

When we looked at filters in *Chapter 8, Moodle Plugins,* we put an emphasis on functionality. Now, let's look at them again, highlighting some performance issues. The following is a list ordered by priority when setting up filters in **Plugins | Filters | Manage filters**:

1. Activate all filters needed by course creators, but not more. Having too many Moodle filters active has effects on server load, especially on lower-end systems. The number of active filters will increase the time it takes to scan each page as filters are applied sequentially, not in parallel.

2. Configure as many active filters as possible using the **Off, but available** setting. They can then be activated locally at course or activity level.

3. Place the filters used most often (usually, **Multimedia plugins**) at the top of the list, as filters are applied on a first-come, first-served basis.

Caching is applied to pages that use text filters, that is, copies of text are kept in memory. This is discussed in the *Caching* section. Additionally, only enable the **Filter uploaded files** parameter, if required, in **Common filter settings**. Also, enable the **Filter match once per page** and **Filter match once per text** parameters if the resulting behavior is acceptable.

A bigger problem than content complexity is scalability, which is caused by concurrent users of the system. We will be spending the rest of the chapter on this issue.

# Moodle system settings

Moodle offers a wide range of system-related performance settings that are set at various places in the **Site administration** menu.

# Caching

Caching stores frequently accessed data in a temporary storage, and expedites its access using the cached copy as opposed to re-fetched (from disk) or re-computed (in memory) data. It has proven to be one of the most efficient performance optimization techniques and Moodle is no exception.

Moodle has some basic built-in caching and manages memory allocation and compression automatically. Additionally, you might consider installing a caching system such as eAccelerator, APC or memcached. Please refer to the respective documentation on how to set these up.

The principal trade-off in caching is between refreshing the cache too often (small values), which slows down the server and refreshing it not often enough (larger values), which potentially means values are not updated on time. There are a number of caching-related settings:

- **Language caching**: We have already dealt with localization in great detail in *Chapter 9, Moodle Configuration*. In addition, to keep the number of languages to a minimum, language caching should be utilized.

  Language packs are cached to speed up the retrieval of language strings. You find the **Cache language menu** and **Cache all language strings** parameters in **Languages | Language settings**. Unless you are modifying a language pack, it is highly recommended to leave this setting enabled. It caches all language strings rather than loading them dynamically.

- **Filter caching**: Caching is applied to pages that use text filters, that is, copies of text are kept in memory. Go to **Plugins | Filters | Common filter settings** and set the **Text cache lifetime** parameter to **1 minutes** or **30 seconds**.

- **Theme caching**: Moodle caches the images and style-sheets of themes either locally in the web browser or on the server. Unless you are designing or modifying a theme, the **Theme designer mode** setting in **Appearance | Themes | Theme settings** should remain disabled.

  You can clear the theme cache using the **Clear theme caches** button in **Appearance | Themes | Theme selector**.

- **Javascript caching**: Moodle makes use of JavaScript and AJAX. The **Cache Javascript** setting in **Appearance | AJAX and Javascript** should be kept on unless you are a developer.

- **RSS caching**: RSS feeds are cached locally. You can modify the time after which the cache will be refreshed by changing the **Timeout** parameter in **Plugins | Blocks | RSS clients**.

- **Network caching**: Moodle uses cURL to fetch data from remote sites. The **cURL cache TTL** setting can be modified in **Server | Performance**. The larger the time-to-live value is kept in the cache, the better the performance. For more details on networking, see *Chapter 16, Moodle Networking*.

- **Repository caching**: When browsing external repositories such as **Google Docs** or **File system**, the file listing is kept in a local cache. The amount of time the listing is kept can be changed via the **Cache expire** parameter in **Plugins | Repositories | Common repository settings**.

You can purge all these caches in a single operation by pressing the **Purge all caches** button under **Development | Purge all caches**. Effectively, this clears out all directories in $CFG->dataroot/cache. While this feature is more relevant to developers, it is a recommended step after installing updates or when your system is behaving oddly.

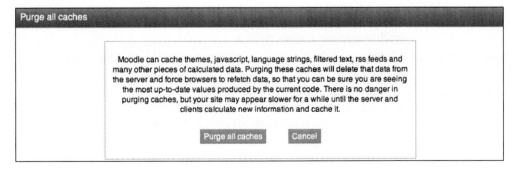

# Session handling

A session is initiated for each user who authenticates against Moodle. This also applies to guests. There are a number of relevant settings, which can be found under **Server | Session handling**:

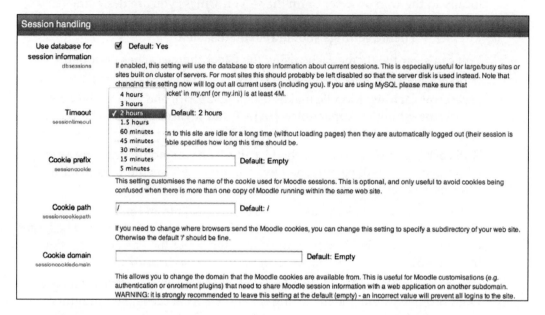

| Setting | Description |
|---|---|
| **Use database for session information** | By default, session information is stored in the filesystem. On larger installations or systems that make use of a clustered environment, it is recommended to store the information in the Moodle database instead. |
| **Timeout** | The duration for which a session is kept open when there hasn't been any activity. |
| **Cookie prefix** | This setting is only relevant if you run more than a single Moodle instance on the same web server and try to open instances of both in the same web browser. If this is the case, give the cookie a name on each site to avoid any conflicts. |
| **Cookie path** | Only change the location where cookies are stored if there is a requirement in your environment. |
| **Cookie domain** | If your Moodle system shares its cookie space with another application, you can modify the domain they both use. Be careful with this setting as it can prevent users from logging in if not specified correctly! |

Moodle manages sessions and cookies very well. However, when problems occur, it is sometimes necessary to intervene manually. This should be done locally in the web browser if a specific user experiences issues (clear cache and cookies) or on the server if the problem affects multiple users. The latter is done by clearing out the `mdl_sessions` table if sessions are stored in the database or by emptying the `$CFG->dataroot/sessions` directory if sessions are stored in files. Bear in mind that all logged in users will be logged out.

# Memory management

Moodle's memory management has proven to be very efficient. However, there are scenarios where extra memory is required to execute complex PHP scripts. You can change this using the **Extra PHP memory limit** setting in **Server | Performance**. The parameter has an impact on the following three modules:

## Cron optimization

We have already covered this as part of the installation, but it is worth re-iterating that the method by which you call the Moodle cron job can have a significant impact on the performance of the system, especially on larger installations.

If the `cron.php` script is invoked over HTTP (either using `wget` or `curl`), more memory is used than calling directly via the `php -f` command.

If you run more than one instance of Moodle on the same server, it is recommended to run the cron processes in batch mode to avoid simultaneous executions.

It is expected that the existing cron mechanism in Moodle will be replaced in a future version with a more sophisticated scheduler to avoid conflicts and to optimize performance.

## Course backups

As you will learn in the next chapter, course backups have a negative impact on the performance during their execution, especially on larger systems. If possible, schedule the backup procedure when the load on the overall system is low. If you turn off sitewide course backups and use a system-level backup instead, you avoid the performance problems, but you lose the ability to recover individual items. A compromise is to include only important data and leave out less relevant information such as logfiles. All this will be dealt with in *Chapter 13, Backup and Restore*.

# Search settings

By default, searches only apply within courses. Moodle supports global text searching in resources and activities, which is still in the experimental stage. You can activate it under **Development | Experimental | Experimental settings**.

Once you enable the **Enable global search** parameter, any searches spawn across courses and fully consider access rights. Global searches are computationally significantly more expensive, which is why the extra memory is needed.

# Module settings

A number of Moodle modules offer settings that have an impact on the performance of your Moodle system.

# Gradebook optimization

Due to the complexity of the gradebook, there are a number of settings in the **Grades** menu that will have an impact on performance. In general, when more aggregation and other calculations have to be carried out, the population of the gradebook data store becomes slower. For example, enabling the **Aggregate including subcategories** parameter in **Grades | Grade category settings** will add some minor overhead to the calculation of grades.

A second gradebook-related area that has an impact on performance is the gradebook history, which forces Moodle to keep track of any changes in grades. Go to **Server | Cleanup** and you will see two gradebook history settings at the bottom:

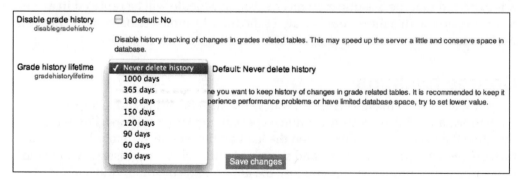

The gradebook history is turned on by default and values are kept for ever. You can either turn the facility completely off, or limit the number of days you wish to keep grade entries.

# Chat optimization

By default, Moodle chat uses the **AJAX method**, which, like the **Normal method**, contacts all participating clients on a regular basis. The upside of both approaches is that they require no configuration and work on any system, the downside being that they have a significant performance impact on the server, especially when the chat activity is used regularly. A solution is to use the **Chat server daemon**, which ensures a scalable chat environment. However, the daemon—a small system-level program that runs in the background—has to be installed on the operating system level and only works on Unix (check your administration guide for how to do this).

To change the chat method that Moodle uses and configure a number of performance parameters go to **Plugins | Activity modules | Chat**. We have dealt with these in the *Synchronous communication* section in *Chapter 9, Moodle Configuration*.

The following table lists the settings that are performance-related and the context (that is, the chat method used) in which they apply:

|  | AJAX method | Normal method | Chat server daemon |
|---|---|---|---|
| **Refresh user list** | √ | √ | √ |
| **Disconnect timeout** | √ | √ | √ |
| **Refresh room** |  | √ |  |
| **Update method** |  | √ |  |
| **Max users** |  |  | √ |

# Forums

On systems with very large forums, tracking unread posts can slow down the activity. Though the impact is rather minor, the tracking can be turned off in **Plugins | Activity modules | Forum** where you will find the **Track unread posts** parameter.

# Miscellaneous settings

Finally, we will deal with a number of performance-related settings that do not belong to any category described so far.

# Large logfiles

In *Chapter 10, Moodle Reporting*, we looked at Moodle reporting and statistics. Keeping track of user behavior can potentially have a negative impact on your server.

All monitoring facilities require a logfile, which is populated in the background. In **Server | Cleanup**, you will see a **Keep logs for** parameter where you specify the number of days for which user data is kept. Here, you can also turn off login access of guests (**Log guest access**).

If you have enabled the statistics functionality, be aware that it is likely to have a profound impact on the performance of your system whenever the statistical information is updated. Go back to the *Statistics settings* section in *Chapter 10, Moodle Reporting* (**Server | Statistics**) and make sure that the configuration is set such that it has minimum impact on the server.

## System paths

An operation Moodle performs regularly is listing directories. The operation can either be run using Moodle's internal routine coded in PHP or, alternatively, by a native version of the function provided by the host operating system. The latter approach is significantly faster as it reduces the load on your server, but is only supported in Unix environments.

You can specify the path for the du command in **Server | System paths**. On most systems the location of the executable is /usr/bin/du. If this does not work, run the which du command on the Unix shell to find out where the program is located. Once specified correctly, this will accelerate displaying directory content, especially, if the directories contain a lot of files.

## Front page courses

The front page is likely to be accessed frequently by all users. On sites with a large number of courses, displaying all of them every time the front page is called, is unlikely to be a pleasant user experience. You can limit the **Maximum number of courses in combo list** in **Server | Performance**.

## Roles

We dedicated an entire chapter to roles management. Its powerful flexibility comes at a price, which is some minor performance drop if a lot of lookups are required in the context hierarchy (avoid global roles) and if the override mechanism is applied frequently.

There is also a performance-related setting **Don't return all default role users** in **Users | Permissions | User policies**. If you experience speed problems in courses with large number of users, enable this option and monitor the performance. We will be dealing with this in a later section.

# Moodle performance profiling and monitoring

When you set up your Moodle system, you will be able to take some initial precautions to optimize the performance of your VLE. However, the real test is when Moodle is in full operation, that is, when the system is under load.

## Built-in profiling

Moodle provides some basic profiling information that you turn on under **Development | Debugging**, where you have to enable the **Performance info** parameter. This will display information about execution time, RAM usage, number of files in use, CPU usage and load, session size, as well as various filter and caching measures (less information will be shown on a Windows-based installation). The data will be displayed in the footer of Moodle as long as it is supported by the theme in use (for instance, **Standard White**).

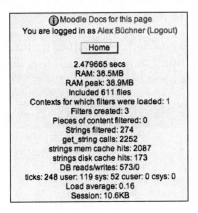

```
ⓘ Moodle Docs for this page
You are logged in as Alex Büchner (Logout)

              [ Home ]

           2.479665 secs
           RAM: 38.5MB
         RAM peak: 38.9MB
          Included 611 files
Contexts for which filters were loaded: 1
          Filters created: 3
   Pieces of content filtered: 0
        Strings filtered: 274
       get_string calls: 2252
   strings mem cache hits: 2087
   strings disk cache hits: 173
      DB reads/writes: 573/0
ticks: 248 user: 119 sys: 52 cuser: 0 csys: 0
       Load average: 0.16
         Session: 10.6KB
```

Moodle further supports profiling at PHP level. While this is mainly targeted at developers it may be helpful for administrators to identify bottlenecks in their system. The internal profiling is built on top of XHProf, which is a hierarchical profiler written by Facebook. It allows the profiling of PHP pages at relatively little performance cost. First of all you have to make sure that XHProf is working on your server:

1. Install XHProf PHP extension.

2. Add the following to your `php.ini` file:

   ```
   [xhprof]
   extension=xhprof.so
   xhprof.output_dir="/var/tmp/xhprof"
   ```

3. Restart Apache.

Once this has been successful (check with the `php -m` command that the `xhprof` extension is listed) you will see a new menu item under the **Development** menu called **Profiling**:

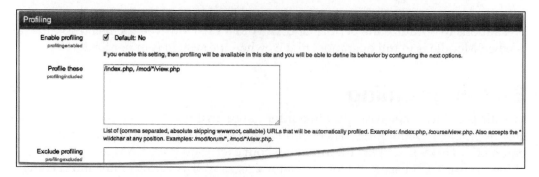

The profiler can be configured to run automatically (set the **Automatic profiling frequency** to any value except 0 and specify URLs in the **Profile these** field) or manually. The latter can be **Selective** (you will have to initiate the profiling) or **Continuous** (once started, you will have to stop it).

As soon as profiling has been enabled, yet another menu item called **Profiling runs** will appear under the **Development** menu, which lists the summary information about all the profile runs that have been executed:

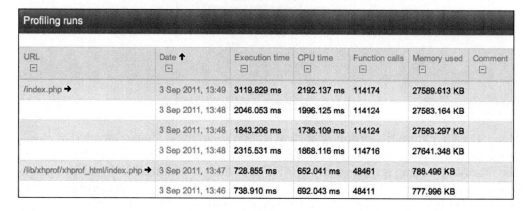

| URL | Date ↑ | Execution time | CPU time | Function calls | Memory used | Comment |
|---|---|---|---|---|---|---|
| /index.php ➜ | 3 Sep 2011, 13:49 | 3119.829 ms | 2192.137 ms | 114174 | 27589.613 KB | |
| | 3 Sep 2011, 13:48 | 2046.053 ms | 1996.125 ms | 114124 | 27583.164 KB | |
| | 3 Sep 2011, 13:48 | 1843.206 ms | 1736.109 ms | 114124 | 27583.297 KB | |
| | 3 Sep 2011, 13:48 | 2315.531 ms | 1868.116 ms | 114716 | 27641.348 KB | |
| /lib/xhprof/xhprof_html/index.php ➜ | 3 Sep 2011, 13:47 | 728.855 ms | 652.041 ms | 48461 | 788.496 KB | |
| | 3 Sep 2011, 13:46 | 738.910 ms | 692.043 ms | 48411 | 777.996 KB | |

When you click on the **URL** or the **Date** of a single run, you can mark the run as reference and provide a comment. You can also view profiling details, where execution times and memory usage of each function call are shown in tabular form.

From the table in the preceding screenshot, you can view a call graph. However, this requires dot to be installed (part of the Linux graphviz package) and the **Path to dot** (usually, /usr/bin/dot) specified in **Server | System paths**. The result (as shown in the following screenshot) is a scary looking graph showing the order, dependencies, and details of each function call.

The general strategy with profiling is to identify the functions that take longest to execute, make tweaks to your setup, and see if the time has been reduced. The difficulty is to make sure that the test runs take place under the same or at least very similar conditions.

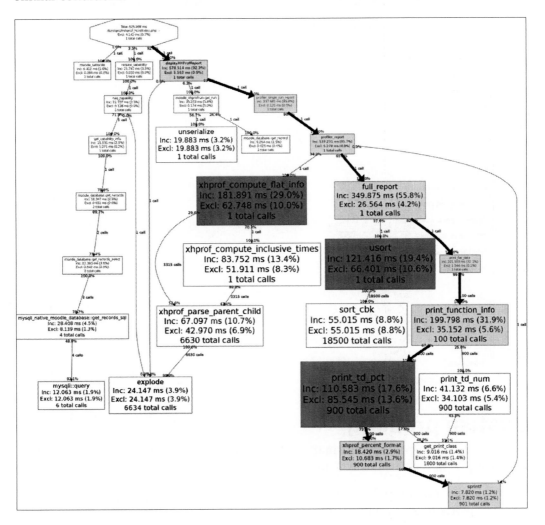

Moodle further comes with a nifty script that lets you generate random course data. That way, you can simulate having hundreds of courses with various levels and types of activities. You will have to call the script manually at `<yoursite>/admin/generator.php`. As you can see from the message that is displayed at the top of in the following screenshot, this script is only for test sites and not for production environments:

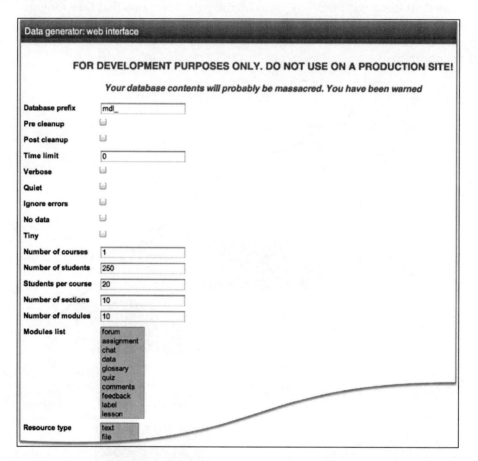

# System profiling

In addition to the profiling information that Moodle provides, you can gather more data using a combination of system-level tools:

- Run a monitor to know what your system is doing (for example, Cacti, an open source graphing tool).

- Run an alerts and notification monitor (for instance, Nagios).

- Use a performance measuring suite where you simulate different loads of your system (Apache JMeter is supported by Moodle).

- Test your network speed (using the `iperf` command).

- Check your disk usage statistics (using the `iostat` command).

- See what processes are doing (using `strace`).

All the mentioned systems and tools are for Linux only and you will find help in their respective documentation.

Now that you have been armed with a number of profiling and monitoring tools, you can change settings as described throughout the chapter and see what impact, positive or negative, they have on the performance of your Moodle system.

# Summary

In this chapter, you have learned how to optimize and monitor Moodle's performance.

As you have probably gathered from the content, system and application optimization is not always straightforward. It depends on a range of circumstances such as the system Moodle is running on, the hardware that is utilized, the network, the number of concurrent users logged in to the system, the types of activities that are carried out, and so on. While the basic optimization is usually straightforward, fine-tuning can become a bit of an art in itself. A lot of trial and error (that is, profiling) will be required to achieve the ideal setup for your Moodle system.

Some Moodle Partners offer health checks that include performance checkups. It is worth investigating this option, if your system runs sluggishly.

Now that your system should perform to its maximum potential, let's make sure that you have a professional backup and recovery strategy in place, which is covered in the next chapter.

# 13
# Backup and Restore

Your hosted Moodle will contain a lot of very important data such as coursework, assignments, grades, and all administrative data, for example users, cohorts, and roles. Therefore, it is vital that you have a good backup strategy in place.

Moodle itself supports two types of backups:

- **Course-level backups**: Course backups are usually run on an ad hoc basis, and only save the selected course. You will learn to create course backups, restore courses, and copy course content using the related course import facility.

- **Site-level backups**: Site backup saves all courses and their related data to a specified location at regular intervals. You will learn how to set this up and recover data from it.

Both mechanisms will be covered in detail before we look at *system-level backups*, which include Moodle backups (covering the Moodle software itself as well as the data stored in it) and snapshot creation (full system images).

We will conclude the chapter with two applications that make use of the backup and restore facilities, namely year-end procedure and course templates.

## Course-level backup and restore

We will first have a look at the backup procedure before going into detail of how to recover data during the restore operation.

# Course backup

To back up a course it is best if you are inside that course, where you will have to click on the **Backup** link in the **Course administration** section. Alternatively, you can back up courses from within course categories. Go to **Courses | Add/edit courses** in the **Site administration** section and click on the category in which the course to be backed up resides. Click on the **Backup** icon (by default, a yellow box), which directs you to the same screen as using the **Backup** link inside a course.

The backup procedure comprises of a number of steps, which are described in the following sections. You can navigate backwards to any step via the process links at the top of the screen or by using the navigation buttons at the bottom.

# Initial settings

There are a number of settings (as shown in the following screenshot), which dictate how the backup will be performed and what type of information will be included:

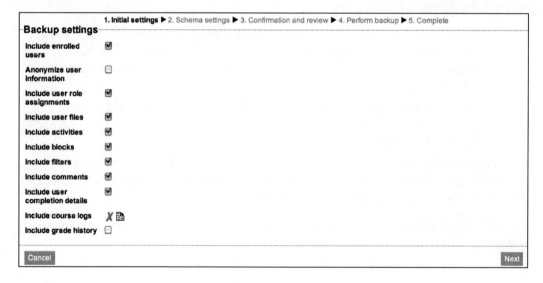

Some settings are only available if other settings have been activated. This is described in the following table:

| Setting | Description | Prerequisite |
| --- | --- | --- |
| **Include enrolled users** | Records can be included in the backup of users who are enrolled in the course. | None |
| **Anonymize user information** | User data (username, first name, last name and e-mail address) will be substituted by aliases. For example, "Jonny Walker" might become "anonfirstname69 anonlastname69" | **Include enrolled users** |
| **Include role assignments** | Whether assigned roles (including locally assigned and overridden roles) should be included. | **Include enrolled users** |
| **Include user files** | Specify whether user files should be included. This includes all student submissions for assignments and other file uploads. | **Include enrolled users** and **Anonymize user information** |
| **Include activities** | Whether course activities are being shown for selection on the next screen. | None |
| **Include blocks** | Whether blocks placed in the course and their settings (location, weight, and so on) should be included. | None |
| **Include filters** | Whether locally used filters should be included. | None |
| **Include comments** | Whether user comments should be included. | **Include enrolled users** |
| **Include user completion details** | If enabled, course completion and progress tracking information will be backed up. | **Include enrolled users** |
| **Include course logs** | Specify whether the logfiles should be included in the archive. Beware that logfiles can enlarge the backup files significantly. | **Include enrolled users** |
| **Include grade history** | Moodle keeps a history of grade changes. Specify whether it should be included in the backup. | **Include enrolled users** |

# Backup Default Values

By default, all options are available for selection to the users who have the appropriate permissions in the course context. If you wish to either change the default values and/or lock certain settings (such as **Include course logs** in the previous screenshot), go to **Courses | Backups | General backup defaults**:

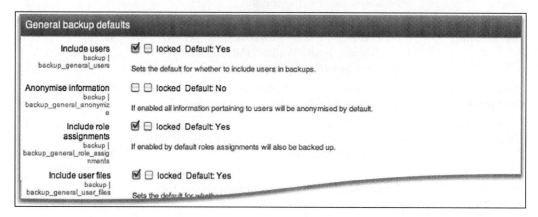

For every single setting, there are two checkboxes. The first indicates whether the setting is enabled or not, whereas the second indicates whether it is locked or not.

## Content-only backup versus full-course backup

There are usually two types of course backups you are likely to perform:

- Content-only backups
- Full-course backups

If you wish to pass a course on to another user or make it available for download, a content-only backup is the best option. As the name suggests, it only contains content that can be passed on to another person without transferring any information about users, roles, grades, and so on. To perform a content-only backup, you will have to disable the **Include enrolled users** option. You can see from the preceding table that this option is a prerequisite for most other backup options. When you publish courses on a community hub (see *Chapter 15, Moodle Integration via Web Services*), you will also create a content-only backup.

By default, users with teaching rights can only perform content-only backups. This can be changed via the `moodle/backup:userinfo` capability, but this should be done with care.

If you wish to back up a course for potential recovery purposes, you should create a full-course backup, which includes user data (for example, forum posts), course data, and the user information. To do this, you leave all the settings at their default values, except **Include grade history**.

If you wish to back up the log information of the course as well, the **Include course logs** setting has to be enabled. Bear in mind that logs can be extremely large and often exceed multiple gigabytes.

Whether you choose to create a content-only or a full-course backup, Moodle will automatically include the configuration of a course. However, you might experience problems with content created by third-party add-ons. If you encounter any issues, you will have to exclude these items from the backup. Ideally, you should report the issue on the tracker so that the maintainer of the module can fix any shortcomings, and the contributed module can be included in your backup again.

## Schema settings

All learning resources and activities are shown in the order in which they appear in the course. This also includes orphaned content, that is, resources and activities that have been placed in a topic that is not shown in the course. If the **Include activities** parameter has been deactivated in the previous screenshot, only resources are available for inclusion. By default, all available elements are selected. If you wish to exclude any individual items, you will have to deselect them. Additionally, you can exclude/include all items of a topic by deselecting/selecting the topic name itself. For instance, in the following screenshot, **Topic 2**, **Topic 3**, and **Topic 4** and the **A video** resource have been excluded from the backup. Moodle's backup routine also supports hidden learning objects, also known as orphaned activities.

Moodle distinguishes between *course content* and *user data*. For example, in a forum activity, the forum description and all settings are classified as course content whereas all topics, posts, and replies to a forum are classified as user data. If the **Include enrolled users** setting has been left activated on the initial setup screen, user data can be included/excluded for each selected activity and resource:

1. Initial settings ▶ **2. Schema settings** ▶ 3. Confirmation and review ▶ 4. Perform backup ▶ 5. Complete

**Include:**

| | | | |
|---|---|---|---|
| General | ☑ | User data | ☑ |
| News forum | ☑ | - | ☑ |
| Questionnaire ? | ☑ | - | ☐ |
| Topic 1 | ☑ | User data | ☑ |
| A forum | ☑ | - | ☑ |
| A file | ☑ | - | ☑ |
| A video | ☐ | - | ☑ |
| Assignment | ☑ | - | ☑ |
| Topic 2 | ☐ | User data | ☑ |
| Topic 3 | ☐ | User data | ☑ |
| Topic 4 | ☐ | User data | ☑ |
| Hidden section | ☑ | User data | ☑ |
| Hidden file | ☑ | - | ☑ |

# Confirmation and review

The third screen lets you choose the backup filename and review the items to be included in the archive.

The default value in the **Filename** field is `backup-<type>-<format>-<course short name>-<year><month><day>-<hour><minute>[-nu].mbz`.

Currently `<type>`is always set to `moodle2` and the only value supported for `<format>` at the moment is `course`. This is likely to change in future versions. The optional `-nu` parameter stands for 'no users':

1. Initial settings ▶ 2. Schema settings ▶ **3. Confirmation and review** ▶ 4. Perform backup ▶ 5. Complete

**Filename**

Filename*    backup-moodle2-course-demo-20110413-1335.mb

**Backup settings**

| | |
|---|---|
| Include enrolled users | ✓ |
| Anonymize user information | ✗ |
| Include user role assignments | ✓ |
| Include user files | ✓ |
| Include activities | ✓ |
| Include blocks | ✓ |
| Include filters | ✓ |
| Include comments | ✓ |
| Include user completion details | ✓ |
| Include course logs | ✗ |
| Include grade history | ✗ |

**Included items:**

| | | | |
|---|---|---|---|
| General | ✓ | User data | ✓ |
| News forum | ✓ | - | ✓ |
| Questionnaire ? | ✓ | - | ✗ |
| Topic 1 | ✓ | User data | ✓ |
| A forum | ✓ | - | ✓ |
| A file | ✓ | - | ✓ |
| A video | ✗ | - | ✗ 🔒 |
| Assignment | ✓ | - | ✓ |

The **Backup settings** section shows which items have been selected and deselected on the initial settings screen. The **Included items** section indicates with a green tick all resources and activities that will be included as well as any user data that will be part of the course backup. A red cross means that the item has been deselected, whereas a red cross followed by a lock indicates that it wasn't possible to select the item as a prerequisite has not been fulfilled.

# Finalizing backup

Once you click on the **Perform backup** button, the Moodle course archive will be created.

The actual archive file is saved in the **Course backup area**. This can take a few minutes depending on the amount of course content. If the **Anonymize user data** setting has been chosen at the beginning, the backup file will be placed in the **User private backup area**.

After completion, a brief status message is shown. You will have to take appropriate actions, if this contains any errors or warnings.

Moodle creates a bespoke file format for backups, known as the Moodle backup format, using the .mbz extension. A Moodle backup file is a compressed zip file consisting of an XML file (which describes the content of the file) and the actual user, course, and log data.

Backups sometimes fail on large courses. The cause is usually that the backup process runs out of time or memory. This usually happens on commercial web hosts that are not dedicated to Moodle. If this happens, increase the max_execution_time value in your php.ini file.

# Course restore

To restore an entire course or parts thereof, use the **Restore** link within a course or in the course category screen. You will be directed to the area (as shown in the following screenshot) where both course backups and private, that is, anonymized, backups are stored. Additionally, you can import backup files via the file picker:

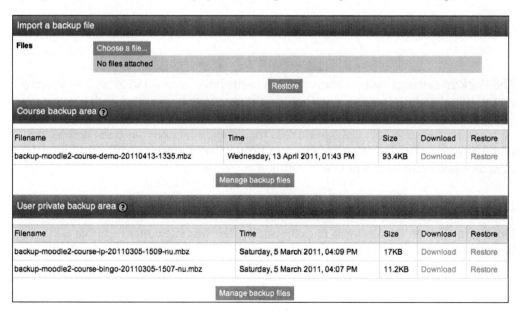

In the preceding screenshot, a single course is present in the **Course backup area**, called `backup-moodle2-course-demo-20110413-1335.mbz`. From its name, we can conclude that the course called `"demo"` was backed up on April 13, 2011 at 13:35.

> Backups from Moodle version 1.9 can be recovered in Moodle 2.1 and 2.2 However, user data is currently not supported. This is planned for version 2.3. In the meantime, you will have to restore the courses to a 1.9 system, upgrade this to version 2.x, and then create a new backup of the course.

Click on the **Restore** link beside a backup file to kick off the recovery process. Like the backup, the restore procedure goes through a number of steps. The first screen displays information about the course backup (**Type**, **Format**, **Mode**, **Date taken**, **Moodle version**, **Backup version**, and **URL of backup**), **Backup settings** (identical to the initial settings in the backup), and **Course details**. Once you have confirmed this screen, you will have to specify the destination to which to recover the backup:

# Restore destination

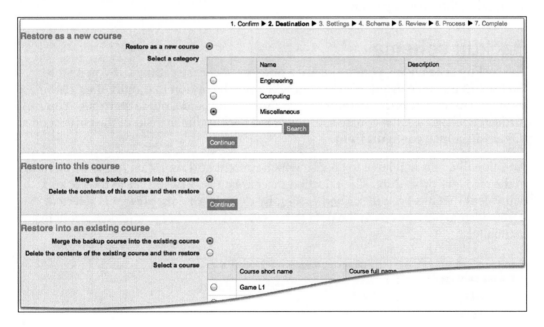

If you wish to restore to a new course, you will have to select a category in which the new course will be created. If the number of categories exceeds 20, you will have to use the provided search facility. Alternatively, you can choose the current course as destination (**Restore into this course**). You can either combine the current course content with the backup (**Merge the backup course into this course**) or replace it (**Delete the contents of this course and then restore**). If you choose the merging option and an activity or resource with the same name exists, both will be kept and not be overridden. The third option is to restore the course into another existing course, which you will have to select. The same options (merge and replace) exist as for restoring the backup in the current course. Make sure that you click on the correct **Continue** button before you proceed.

# Restore settings

The restore settings screen shows all available options that have been selected during the backup process (see the *Initial Settings* section). As before, the choices made here dictate which types of data will be recovered and which type of content will be offered for further selection. Also, most options have prerequisites, which are identical to their backup counterparts.

# Backup schema

The backup schema lets you to specify a number of course settings. If you restore the backup into an existing course, you will have the option to modify the existing settings. These are **Course name**, **Course short name**, and **Course startdate**. You can further choose to use the course settings of the backup file instead of the current ones (**Override course configuration**).

Additionally, you will have to choose which content and user data has to be included in the recovery procedure. The selection mechanism is very similar to the backup equivalent that has been described earlier. By default, all data present is selected. If you wish to narrow down the data to be restored you will have to deselect items manually:

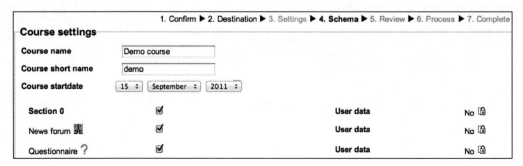

# Finalizing restore

Once you have confirmed the **Schema** screen by clicking on the **Perform restore** button, any selected data will be recovered to the chosen destination. After completion, a brief summary message is shown.

If you see a topic heading labeled **"Orphaned activities"** in your recovered courses, go to the course settings and increase the number of topics.

If you cancel a restore operation halfway, a course called **"Course restoration in progress"** might be displayed. It is usually safe to delete this course.

# Course import

It is sometimes necessary to copy data from one course to another. To achieve this, Moodle provides the import course data feature. However, unlike the backup function, it will not import user data, such as assignment submissions or forum posts. It will only import the structure of activities, blocks, and filters. For example, you might want to import a single quiz from one course to another.

Teachers are allowed to import content only from courses for which they have editing rights; as administrator this restriction does not apply. This mechanism bypasses the requirement for a backup and restore procedure, if you want to copy course content from one course to another and do not require the user data.

First, click on the **Import** link from the **Course administration** section. As shown in the following screenshot, you will have to select a course from which you wish to import content. If the list exceeds 20 courses (or whatever has been specified in the **Courses per page** field under **Front page | Front page settings**), you will have to use the provided search facility. You can also select the current course. That way, you can duplicate activities:

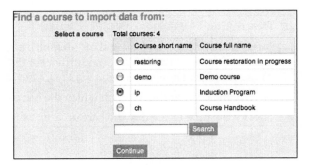

Next, you will have to choose whether you want the import activities (and resources), blocks, and/or filters, as shown in the following screenshot:

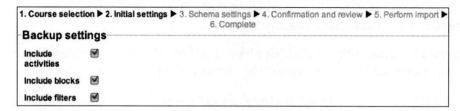

For activities, the familiar selection screen will be shown next. If you chose either filters or blocks, all their content and settings will be copied, that is, no selection is possible.

As usual, a **Confirmation and review** screen has to be confirmed by clicking on the **Perform import** button, before the copying starts, and a concluding summary message is displayed.

# Site-level backups

So far, we have covered how to back up a single course. The site-level backup performs the same operation for every course on the system, including hidden courses and the front page, which is also a course (the name of the front page backup uses the site name).

# Backup settings

To schedule site backups go to **Courses | Backups | Automated backup setup**. You will see a number of settings:

| Setting | Description |
| --- | --- |
| Active | Turns automatic backup on and off (default). Make sure that your backup is activated! You can further set the backup mode to **Manual**, which allows execution via the CLI (discussed later). |
| Schedule | Specify the days of the week on which the backup has to run. |
| Execute at | Specify the time of the day the backup is executed. |

| Setting | Description |
| --- | --- |
| **Automated backup storage** | By default, all backups are stored in the **Course backup area** of each course. If you wish to keep all the backups at the same location you have to select **Specified directory for automated backups**. It is also possible to save the backups in both locations (**Course backup area** and **specified directory**). This will take up twice the storage. For the latter two options you will have to specify the **Save to** value. |
| **Save to** | Specify the full (absolute) path to the directory and make sure that the access rights are set to writable. |
| **Keep** | Specify the number of backups to be kept. Beware that a large number will have an impact on disk usage. Older versions will be deleted automatically. |

The remainder of the settings page covers **Automated backup settings** that specify which elements will be included in the backup. These are identical to the initial backup settings, except the anonymize option, which has been excluded.

For the backup to start automatically at the specified time, the cron process has to be set up correctly, which is already covered in *Chapter 2, The Moodle System*. Alternatively, you can initiate the backup process via the CLI. The command execution from the shell or for inclusion in scripts is as follows:

```
sudo -u <apache_user>/usr/bin/php admin/cli/automated_backups.php
```

The script has to be run as Apache user, usually `www-data`. In the preceding command, it is executed from the main Moodle application directory. The script executes the same script that is called by the cron process.

The recovery of courses is identical to restoring data from course-level backup archives.

# Backup reports and notifications

The backups usually run during the night. As a Moodle administrator, it is your duty to ensure that the backup execution has been successful. For this purpose, Moodle provides a backup report, which you can find under **Reports | Backups**.

| Last execution log | | | | |
| --- | --- | --- | --- | --- |
| Course | Time taken | | Status | Next backup |
| Packt Moodle 2.0 Administrator | 14 Apr, 18:30 - | 14 Apr, 18:30 | OK | 15 Apr, 18:30 |
| Course Handbook | 14 Apr, 18:30 - | 14 Apr, 18:30 | OK | 15 Apr, 18:30 |
| Demo course | 14 Apr, 18:30 - | 14 Apr, 18:30 | OK | 15 Apr, 18:30 |
| Induction Program | 14 Apr, 18:30 - | 14 Apr, 18:30 | OK | 15 Apr, 18:30 |
| Course restoration in progress | 14 Apr, 18:30 - | 14 Apr, 18:30 | OK | 15 Apr, 18:30 |

The report provides details for each course being backed up; namely, the **Time taken** (start and end time), the **Status** (**OK** or **ERROR**), and the **Next backup** (the date and time of the next backup).

Courses in which there hasn't been any activity for 30 days; that is, no changes have been made to the course content and no users have using the course, are excluded from the automated backup and the status is shown as **SKIPPED**.

As a Moodle administrator, you will receive an e-mail after the execution of the scheduled site-level backup has been completed. It provides details about the total number of courses backed up and a breakdown of how many course backups were OK, had an error, are unfinished, and were skipped. Make sure that your e-mail settings have been configured properly (see *Chapter 9, Moodle Configuration*). It is highly recommended to check the content of this e-mail every day.

# Backup strategy

There are a number of issues to consider when running automatic sitewide Moodle backups:

- **Backup content**: Make sure that everything included in the archives is needed, and anything not required is excluded. For instance, do you have to back up the entire logfile every night?

- **Backup size**: The size of the backup files can be potentially huge (multiple gigabytes). Ensure that you only keep the number of backups that are required and your setup can cope with.

- **Backup timing**: The backup operation is a CPU- and hard disk-intensive operation. Make sure to schedule it when the load on the site is relatively low. If you run multiple sites on the same server, it is a good idea to time-stagger the backups or create a script that makes use of the CLI, as mentioned earlier.

- **Backup frequency**: Do you need daily backups or are weekly backups sufficient? Are there periods (such as weekends) when you can switch off the backup facility altogether?

- **Backup location**: By default, all backup files are saved to the respective courses, which means the backups are held on the same server as Moodle itself. If you have to recover multiple courses, you have to locate each archive separately, which is potentially a very time-consuming exercise.

  You might want to consider copying all files to a single directory, which is then backed up on an external device (tape, external disk, NAS drive, SAN, and so on). An alternative is to temporarily mount a backup device and include its content in the organization-wide backup.

# Drawbacks of site-level backups

Site-level backups are a great way to automate course backups, and to make the life of individual teachers and instructors easier. However, there are a number of drawbacks that should be stressed:

- Course backups are potentially very expensive in terms of time and CPU usage

- It is not uncommon that backups time out, especially on commercially hosted systems that are not dedicated to Moodle

- If teachers and instructors run their own backups, there is a likelihood of duplication of archives, which should be avoided if possible

As the name suggests, you only back up courses, not the entire system. While this is sufficient if you want to recover a simple course or a number of activities, it does not provide a solution to the scenario where the entire system has to be restored. You should not use the course backup facility as your sole backup system. Instead, system-level backups should be used as a supplement, which we will look at next.

# System-level backups

System-level backups cannot be configured or executed from within Moodle. Instead, they will have to be set up on the system (shell) level. If your system is hosted externally, there is a possibility that you will not have access to the system level, which will prevent you from performing this type of backup. Unless the host already runs system-level backups on your behalf, it is time to change to another provider!

There are two types of system backups that are not mutually exclusive:

- **Moodle backups**: These create an archive of Moodle itself, the course content, and user data
- **Snapshots**: These create an image of the system, which is used for disaster recovery purposes, that is, if the system has to be rolled back in its totality

# Moodle backups

Moodle distinguishes between the application software itself and the data that is stored in it. The advantage of this separation becomes apparent when creating backups. A software backup is only required when an update has been installed or customization is taking place, whereas the data has to be backed up more frequently.

## Moodle software

Backing up the Moodle software itself is straightforward. All you have to do is to create a copy of the directory and all its sub-directories where the Moodle software is installed (usually, called `moodle`). Most administrators would create a single archive of the directory for easier handling (in Unix, using the `tar` command with the `-cvf` parameters—`tar -cvf <backupfile>`). This step is usually only required before a system upgrade or when you need to archive your entire system.

## Moodle data

Moodle stores its data in two separate locations:

- **Moodle database**: Most content is stored in the Moodle database. You can either use the export feature of phpMyAdmin (if installed) or use the following `mysqldump` shell command for MySQL to create a single backup file:

```
mysqldump -u <username> -p [-h <databasehost>] -C -Q -e -a
<database>><backup-file>.sql
```

The <username> has to be replaced with the database username, the -p parameter will ask you for a password and the <databasehost> is only required if the database is located on a separate server. <database> is the name of the database and <backup-file> is the name of the archive to be created. It is common practice to use the .sql extension.

To recover the database dump, use the following mysql shell command:

```
mysql -p<database><<backup-file>.sql
```

For more information on mysql and mysqldump, check out the reference sites at www.mysql.com. For other database types, please refer to the respective administration guides.

- **Moodle data directory** ($CFG->dataroot): This is where all course content resides, for instance, assignments, user profiles' pictures, forum posts, and so on. Like the Moodle system, all that has to be done is to create a copy of the directory and all its sub-directories. Most administrators would create a single tarball of the directory for simpler handling (in Unix, using the tar command with the -cvf parameters).

The advantage of this approach is that it is less resource-intensive, can be scripted, and recovery of the full Moodle system is far more straightforward. However, it is impossible to retrieve individual activities without setting up a temporary server, as is possible with course backups.

# Snapshot creation

The creation of snapshots is only briefly mentioned for completeness, as it is not a Moodle administrator role, but a system administrator task. However, you should make sure that such a mechanism is set up in case of any hardware failures.

A snapshot is basically an image of the entire partition on the hard disk that contains the Moodle software itself as well as all the data (database and data directory). The advantage of the snapshot is that the entire system can be rolled back to the point when the image was created. However, any data that has been added or modified since this point in time will be overridden. Snapshots cannot be used to recover a single course or parts thereof, but can only be used for a full replacement of the system.

No matter what combination of backups you choose, frequently verify that the backup procedure is actually working. There is nothing worse than a false sense of security, that is, assuming that all your data is backed up, when it isn't!

# Backup and restore applications

While the prime purpose of backups is the recovery of data in case of loss, there are a number of applications that can be carried out using some of the techniques covered in this chapter. We are going to briefly describe two of them.

## Year-end procedure

Most organizations have some sort of year-end procedure in place. This might be at the end of an academic year, a term, a financial year, or in the case of roll-on/roll-off setups, on a monthly basis. Given the nature and importance of the procedure it is vital that each step is planned well in advance. The key considerations are:

- When do you run the year-end procedure?
- What has to be done?
- Who is involved?
- Where will the archives go?

A list of some typical steps that might or might not apply to your setup is as follows. It gives you an idea of how such a procedure might look and demonstrates the importance of the backup facility:

1. **Archive**: Create backups of all courses and even consider including a system backup. Make sure archives are stored on a separate medium.

2. **Grade export**: Export grades course by course. Print, transfer, and store grades on your student management information system.

3. **Course reset**: Use the reset feature at course level to remove any user data.

4. **Delete users**: Remove or disable the accounts of users who have left the organization.

5. **Next year preparation**: Hide or delete obsolete courses and add new courses. Add new users and assign roles to courses.

# Course templates

There is often a requirement to create a course template, which is used for the creation of multiple courses. This might be in an organization that puts emphasis on the homogeneity of course structure and layout, or an education establishment that wants to simplify the work of its course creators. The steps to achieve this are as follows:

1.  Create a course that will become your course template.
2.  Add all elements (activities, resources, filters, blocks, and so on) to the course, change its settings, and arrange the content as required.
3.  Create a content-only backup of the course.
4.  You can now use the restore mechanism to create as many courses from this template as you wish.
5.  Optionally, you can grant users appropriate rights to the course so they can use the import facility.

# Summary

In this chapter, you have learned the various Moodle backup alternatives. You learned how to create course-level, site-level, and system-level backups as well as data recovery from each type. It is important that your Moodle backup strategy fits in with your organization's overall disaster recovery plan. We have also shown some applications that make use of the backup and restore facilities.

Moodle offers a good range of backup and restore options. However, there are sometimes problems with some of the built-in backup and recovery operations. The common causes for problems are time-outs, memory overload, archives that cannot be read, and third-party add-ons. Be aware that these issues exist and run test recoveries to be on the safe side.

# 14

# Installing Third-party Add-ons

There are a plethora of third-party Moodle software that add new functionality, fix problems, or integrate Moodle with external systems. In this chapter, you will learn the following essentials about installing third-party add-ons:

- **Good, bad, and ugly third-party add-ons**: As externally developed software is not scrutinized by Moodle's quality assurance process, you will have to make your own judgment about the trustworthiness of non-core add-ons. A checklist of criteria is provided to make this decision a bit easier.
- **Popular third-party add-ons**: There are over 800 titles to choose from. For your convenience, we will discuss the most popular ones.
- **Installing third-party add-ons**: We will describe the manual installation process for the popular **Configurable Reports** custom reports builder and the **Book** module, via GIT.
- **Uninstalling third-party add-ons**: Here, we'll show you how to uninstall unwanted add-ons.

Let's start with an overview of third-party software.

## Third-party software—an overview

Moodle comes with a number of core modules that include **Activity modules** (for example, **Quiz** and **Assignment**), **Filters** (**Multimedia plugin** or **Algebra notation**) and **Blocks** (**Calendar**) as well as other components such as **Enrolments** and **Authentication** plugins, course and grade reports, **Repositories** and **Portfolios**, **Question types**, and so on. While the provided functionality sufficiently satisfies the majority of users, there is growing demand for additional software. Also, requirements change over time and new functionality, for instance, support for certain social networking activities, is needed in your Moodle system.

Due to Moodle's open source nature and modularity (that's what the "M" in Moodle stands for, after all), it is relatively straightforward for developers to add new functionality or modify existing features. These can range from minor modifications (patches) or hacks to full blown modules.

You can get access to the **Plugin directory** page via the **Modules and plugins** link in the **Downloads** menu of moodle.org or directly via moodle.org/plugins, which contains all non-core modules and themes.

The **Plugin directory** has recently undergone a major revamp and some add-ons have not been moved to the new repository. During the transition period, you can you can access the legacy version via the displayed "old modules and plugins database" link at moodle.org/plugins.

You have a number of options to navigate through the plugin directory:

- Using the **Search** by keyword
- Using the **Categories** shown on the plugins front page
- Using the **Navigation** in the side block, where you can also register new plugins

Whatever way, you should always end up with a list of add-ons. Once you click on a plugin name, you will be provided with details. An example of a popular block is as follows:

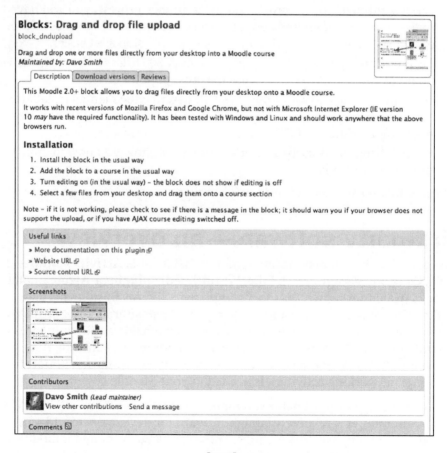

There are currently over 800 third-party Moodle software titles and the number is growing continuously. You will find all kinds of add-ons, from the weird and wonderful to the very powerful.

# Good add-ons and bad add-ons

Every module that is part of core Moodle has gone through a thorough quality assurance process. The potential problem with third-party add-ons is that you don't know anything about the quality of the software.

While it is possible to uninstall modules if they don't suit your purpose, you will have to make sure that you don't put barriers in place for future updates. If an add-on is not maintained, it is unlikely to support any forthcoming versions of Moodle and you will either have to delete the module already in use or you won't be able to upgrade your system. Also, a module might cater to some required functionality but compromise the security of your system.

There are a number of criteria that indicate whether an add-on is trustworthy or not:

- **Popularity**: Moodle keeps statistics about downloads from Moodle, which you can find at `download.moodle.org/stats.php`. In the **Plugins** section, you will see all plugins that have been downloaded in the previous 60 days. While this is no guarantee, the more popular a module, the more likely it is to be of high standard.

- **Ratings**: Each add-on page allows users to rate the software. Both the quality and quantity of the ratings are relevant. Anything over 70 percent usually indicates a good add-on.

- **Level of active support**: Some of the most valuable third-party add-ons have vanished because they are unsupported. Your best bet is if the add-on is supported by a major stakeholder in Moodle such as the Open University or a Moodle Partner. The maintainer should have been active in the community for the past 60 days.

- **Forum posts and comments**: Users are encouraged to post comments, problems, and praise about each module. Read through the posts to get an idea about what other users have experienced. Be suspicious about modules that are not talked about at all. Also, check if there are any reviews in the **Reviews** tab.

- **Documentation**: Each add-on should have a dedicated page in the Moodle Docs. It is usually not a good sign if the page does not exist or is only a wiki stub. Also, it is good practice that a change log is kept for the developed software.

- **Standalone**: It is imperative that third-party add-ons do not modify any core code (known as patches, supplied in the form of DIFF files). This is important as the changes will be overridden with every Moodle update and the modifications will have to be reapplied.

- **Supported versions**: Support for the current versions and one or more previous versions of Moodle is a sign that the software is being actively maintained. You can see any existing versions in the **Download versions** tab.

- **Backup and restore support**: If applicable, the add-on should be supported by the course backup and restore facility. Otherwise, what good is an activity if it is not included in your archives?

- **Code**: If you can read PHP code, have a look at the actual source code of the add-on. Try to find answers to the following questions:
  - Is the code well structured and can it be easily followed?
  - Is the source code well commented?
  - Does the module follow the Moodle coding guidelines (docs. moodle.org/en/Coding)?

- **Official approval**: Moodle has recently tightened the process of accepting third-party plugins to its database. While this process does not guarantee functionality, security, or integrity of the add-on, it evaluates the code at a high level. Once this stage has been passed, it will be accepted in the plugins database. Add-ons stored elsewhere; for example, on the developer's home page, should only be trusted if they come from a well-known source.

- **Developer**: Some developers are known to produce very well-written Moodle add-ons. Programmers affiliated with a Moodle Partner are usually a good bet, as are core developers, Moodle documenters, and particularly helpful Moodlers.

# Popular add-ons

The following is a list of some popular third-party Moodle add-ons (in alphabetic order), available through the **Plugins directory** on moodle.org/plugins, as well as a brief description for each plugin:

- **Accessibility**: This block allows students to change the font size and background color of your Moodle site. It also includes a toolbar that supports text-to-speech functionality.

- **Book**: This activity allows users to create multi-page resources in a book-like format. See how to install this module from a GIT repository in the *Installing the Book module via GIT* section.

- **Certificate**: This fully-customizable activity generates PDF certificates for students once they have fulfilled certain conditions.

- **Checklist**: This Moodle package, comprising an activity module and a block, allows teachers to create a checklist for their students to work through. The teacher can monitor all the students' progress as they tick off each of the items in the list. Items can be indented and marked as optional. Students are presented with a progress bar and they can add their own private items to the list.

- **Collapsed Topics**: This course format lets users expand and collapse individual topics, tackling the issue of the infamous scroll of death.

- **Configurable reports**: This is a powerful report generator that lets you create various custom reports, including filters, groupings, and visual representation. We have covered its functionality in *Chapter 10, Moodle Reporting* and will discuss the installation of this module later on in the chapter.

- **Drag and drop file upload**: This block lets your users drag files from your desktop and drop them onto a Moodle course.

- **Google Oauth2**: This authentication plugin lets users authenticate via their Google login.

- **Jmol**: This filter displays 3D chemical and biological molecular files directly, using the Java-based open source Jmol molecule viewer (`www.jmol.org`).

- **phpMyAdmin**: This module is a repackaged version of phpMyAdmin. Once installed, you will see a new **phpMyAdmin** item in the **Server** menu in the **Site administration** section. This is useful for creating database backup dumps.

- **Progress Bar**: This block is a time-management tool for students that visually shows what activities and resources a student is supposed to interact with, in a course.

- **UploadPDF**: This assignment type allows teachers to annotate submitted PDF files with comments and line annotations.

Keep monitoring the list of recently-released plugins on `moodle.org/plugins` or via the provided RSS feed. There are always great new add-ons being launched, which might be useful for your site. The preceding list doesn't include popular plugins that haven't been updated yet from Moodle 1.9.

# Installing third-party add-ons

A good piece of advice is to avoid experimenting with new add-ons on a production site. Most organizations set up a shadow site of their live server, to be used as a sandbox. Once the installation has been successful, the procedure is re-applied on the production site.

Additionally, it is recommended that you make a complete site backup before installing any third-party software. That way you can roll back in case of a disaster.

To install third-party add-ons, take the followings steps:

1. Download the add-on.
2. Put Moodle in maintenance mode (**Server | Maintenance mode**).
3. Unzip files (either locally or on the server).
4. Copy files in appropriate location(s) — see provided README file for details.
5. Open the Moodle **Notifications** page to run the installer.
6. Test the add-on.
7. Take Moodle out of maintenance mode.

Most add-ons are structured in a very similar way and are installed in the `$CFG->dirroot/local` directory. However, some modules either don't follow this standardized approach or require other steps, especially when the module communicates with other software systems. Each plugin should contain a file (usually called README) with the installation instructions. It is important that you read these first before installing a module.

## Installing the Configurable Reports plugin

For the purpose of demonstrating the installation of a third-party add-on, we have chosen the **Configurable Reports** module for a number of reasons. It satisfies all the criteria outlined earlier, is a very useful activity, is packaged in the standard format, and, due to its popularity, is likely to be in the core of Moodle in the future.

After locating the add-on in the plugins repository, download the latest version of the software (this screenshot is taken from the old **Modules and plugins** database):

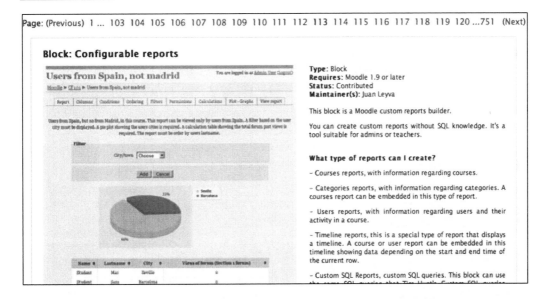

Next, put Moodle in maintenance mode (**Server | Maintenance mode**). While it is possible to add most modules while Moodle is in use, it is not recommended to do so as this can lead to some unforeseen problems.

The module follows the standardized structure of add-ons; that is, it includes the same directory hierarchy as Moodle. It is best to copy the ZIP file to the `$CFG->dirroot/blocks` directory and unpack the file via `unzip configurable_reports.zip`. You might have to change the user and group to the same as the folders in those directories.

Now, go to your **Notifications** page in the **Site administration** section. The module behind this page will recognize that a new module has to be installed and will kick off the installer. You will see a new entry in the **Blocks** table called **blocks/configurable_reports** with the status **Non-standard (about to be installed)**. Once you confirm this via the **Upgrade** button, a number of database tables with fields are created and populated with values. The overall success of the installation will be displayed.

That's it! All you have to do now is to make sure the module works properly in Moodle. In case of the **Configurable Reports** module, go to **Plugins | Blocks | Manage blocks** and you will see an entry for the newly-installed add-on.

It is important that you check that the block is working as intended (see the following screenshot). In case of the **Configurable Report** add-on, you can find detailed information in the Moodle Docs at docs.moodle.org/en/blocks/configurable_reports. We also have a dedicated *Report generation* section in *Chapter 10, Moodle Reporting*.

| Blocks | | | | | |
|---|---|---|---|---|---|
| Name | Instances | Version | Hide/Show | Delete | Settings |
| Activities | 0 | 2007101509 | 👁 | Delete | |
| Admin bookmarks | 1 | 2007101509 | 👁 | Delete | |
| Blog menu | 2 | 2009071700 | 👁 | Delete | |
| Recent blog entries | 1 | 2009070900 | 👁 | Delete | |
| Blog tags | 0 | 2007101509 | 👁 | Delete | |
| Calendar | 3 | 2007101509 | 👁 | Delete | |
| Upcoming events | 4 | 2007101509 | 👁 | Delete | |
| Comments | 5 | 2009072000 | 👁 | Delete | |
| Community finder | 1 | 2010042701 | 👁 | Delete | |
| Course completion status | 1 | 2009072800 | 👁 | Delete | |
| Configurable Reports | 1 | 2007101509 | 👁 | Delete | |
| Course list | 3 | 2007101509 | 👁 | Delete | Settings |

 Finally, don't forget to disable Moodle's maintenance mode and let your users know that new functionality is available!

# Installing the Book module via GIT

An alternative way to install and update plugins is via GIT. Developers are encouraged to maintain their personal GIT repository, which might contain multiple Moodle extensions. We are going to use the popular **Book module** as an example to demonstrate how to install a contributed extension from its GIT repository.

When you browse to the plugin page of the **Book** module you will see a link to **Browse source code** (old **Modules and plugins** database) or **Source control URL** (new plugin directory). Both will direct you to the **github** entry of the module. Github is the de facto standard site for managing GIT repositories:

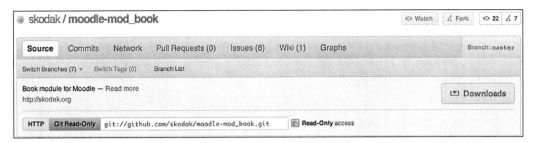

To install the module, you must execute the following steps:

1. Change to the `$CFG->dirroot/mod` directory (this is where all the modules are stored).

2. Execute the following `git` command:

   **git clone git://github.com/skodak/moodle-mod_book.git book**

   This creates a new sub-directory book and makes a local copy of the **Book** code repository. The path is the same as the one you can see in the preceding screenshot.

3. Go to the **Notifications** page in your Moodle system and run through the upgrade screens. The module **mod_book** will be added and the newly-available admin settings will be shown. Once these have been saved, the module will be available in **Plugins | Activity modules | Manage activities**.

The preceding installation steps are sufficient for a one-off installation. However, if you wish to keep the module up-to-date over time, you will have to create a local branch of the module that is synchronized with the remote branch on the GithHub. You will find detailed instructions of how to do this at `docs.moodle.org/20/en/Git_for_Administrators`.

# Installing other add-ons

We demonstrated how to install the **Configurable Reports** activity, which follows the typical installation process. We further cover the installation of the **Book** module via Git. Other add-ons have to be copied to their corresponding locations, for example, filters are located in the filter directory. As mentioned before, the locations should be described in the README file. Any anomalies, such as the copying of the `lang` files, will also be explained in the instructions.

Add-ons that usually require more installation and configuration effort are the ones that integrate with other software systems, both open source and commercial. For example, the WIRIS plugin for mathematical formulae and the Turnitin plugin for plagiarism detection. Again, the instructions provided in the README file or a dedicated page on Moodle Docs will shed light upon the installation and configuration process.

# Uninstalling third-party add-ons

If you decide to uninstall a third-party add-on and the module is listed in the **Activities**, **Blocks**, or **Filters** section in the **Plugins** menu, you must use the provided **Delete** option.

 Deleting an add-on will also delete all user data associated with the module, irreversibly!

The delete operation will remove all data associated with the module and display a message, as shown in the following screenshot, to confirm the success. To complete the deletion and prevent the module from re-installing itself the next time you go to the **Notifications** page, you will have to delete the directory from your server:

You will also have to remove the installed files from `$CFG->dirroot/local` or any other location where the files have been stored. If you don't perform this step, the add-on will be re-installed next time you go to the **Notifications** page. Other types of add-ons that cannot be deleted from within Moodle; for example, the **Assignment** type, will also have to be removed manually.

# Summary

In this chapter, you have learned the essentials about installing third-party Moodle add-ons.

You hopefully got a flavor of the breadth and depth of additional functionality that is available for your VLE. It not only demonstrates the extensibility and popularity of Moodle but also shows a significant benefit of open source software, namely, the ability to programmatically enhance a program to a user's requirements.

Other forms of extending the reach of Moodle are to integrate it with other systems and to network it with other Moodle instances. We will cover these two approaches in the two remaining chapters.

# 15
# Moodle Integration via Web Services

We have already seen that Moodle is a highly modular environment, which guarantees extensibility and adaptability. We have also mentioned that Moodle can be connected to other Moodle instances or Mahara, which we will cover in *Chapter 16, Moodle Networking*. Now, we are looking at the integration of Moodle with external systems via web services.

After providing a brief overview of web services and giving some application examples, you will learn about the following administrative topics:

- **Moodle and web services**: We will provide information about the basics concepts of Moodle web services

- **External systems controlling Moodle**: You will learn to set up the Moodle web service for another application to control Moodle

- **Users controlling Moodle**: You will learn to set up the Moodle web service for a user as client

- **Mobile Moodle**: We will talk through the setting up of Moodle so it can be used with the official mobile Moodle application

We will not cover any programming aspects of web services, as this is not an administrative task. You will find some good documentation for users and developers at docs.moodle.org/en/Web_Services.

# Web services—an overview

It has always been possible to extend Moodle via code (PHP and Javascript). Due to Moodle's open source code base, there has been no limit to the amount of code a developer is able to modify or extend. For you as an administrator, this is not a satisfactory situation, as you have no control over what parts of Moodle are being changed and, equally important, what data is being accessed.

Moodle 2 has a number of APIs that provide an abstract layer to certain functionalities. Examples of these APIs are Portfolio API, Repository API, and File API. These are great for programmers as they reduce the amount of code that has to be (re-)written. In addition to these interfaces, Moodle 2 also introduced web services.

[  Web services enable other systems to perform operations inside Moodle. ]

Why would we want web services? Well, there are three main scenarios we can think of. They are as follows:

- Other systems in your organization; for instance, the HR system, has to trigger certain actions in your VLE. Once a student has been added to the system, an account has to be created in Moodle and enrolment in a number of courses has to take place. Web services simplify this process greatly.

- Mobile applications are gaining enormous popularity with more powerful devices running iOS or Android. Any Moodle application, such as the official one by moodle.org, should be using web services to communicate with your Moodle instance. We will deal with this further down.

- The Community Hub feature requires web services. This will be covered in *Chapter 16, Moodle Networking*.

Why do you, as an administrator, have to care about web services when they have been designed for developers? Well, that's the other big advantage of web services. You, as the administrator, have the ability to control which system is allowed to talk to your Moodle system and which service these systems are allowed to use. That way, you control who has access to your system and limit what they can do.

# Web services in Moodle

First of all, you will have to activate web services, which takes place in **Advanced features | Enable web services**. Next, you will have to enable the **Web services authentication** plugin (**Plugins | Authentication | Manage authentication**). Once this has been done, go to **Plugins | Web services | Overview**, which acts as a dashboard for setting up Moodle web services:

| One system controlling Moodle with a token | | |
|---|---|---|
| The following steps help you to set up the Moodle web service for a system to control Moodle. These steps also help to set up the recommended token (security keys) authentication method. | | |
| Step | Status | Description |
| 1. Enable web services | Yes | Web services must be enabled in Advanced features. |
| 2. Enable protocols | None | At least one protocol should be enabled. For security reasons, only protocols that are to be used should be enabled. |
| 3. Create a specific user | | A web services user is required to... |

| Users as clients with token | | |
|---|---|---|
| The following steps help you to set up the Moodle web service for users as clients. These steps also help to set up the recommended token (security keys) authentication method. In this use case, the user will generate his token from the security keys page via My profile settings. | | |
| Step | Status | Description |
| 1. Enable web services | Yes | Web services must be enabled in Advanced features. |
| 2. Enable protocols | soap amf rest xmlrpc | At least one protocol should be enabled. For security reasons, only protocols that are to be used should be enabled. |
| 3. Select a service | | A service is a set of web service functions. You will allow users to access to a new service. On the Add service page check 'Enable' and uncheck 'Authorised users' options. Select 'No required capability'. |

Enabling web services comes with a potential security risk as you are granting access to Moodle to outside users and systems. The mantra should always be to open up as little services and functions as possible.

Moodle supports two ways of connecting to external entities via web services:

- External systems controlling Moodle
- Users controlling Moodle

Two checklists are shown, one for each approach. As you can see in the following screenshot, the first two steps are identical. We have already enabled web services and also have to enable protocols. Moodle supports four web services protocols: SOAP, REST, XML-RPC, and AMF. We are not going to provide any details about them; for more information check out docs.moodle.org/en/ Development:Creating_a_web_service_client. At least one protocol has to be enabled—which one depends entirely on the external application and the protocols supported. Clicking on the **Enabled protocols** link in the **Overview** screen will guide you to the **Manage protocols** screen under **Plugins | Web services**. Enable a protocol by toggling the show/hide icon in the **Enable** column.

| Active web service protocols | | | | |
|---|---|---|---|---|
| Protocol | Version | Enable | Uninstall | Settings |
| AMF protocol | 2009101900 | ✌ | Uninstall | |
| REST protocol | 2009100800 | ✌ | Uninstall | |
| SOAP protocol | 2009101900 | 👁 | Uninstall | |
| XML-RPC protocol | 2009101900 | ✌ | Uninstall | |

For security reasons, only protocols that are in use should be enabled.

| Web services documentation enablewsdocumentation | ☐ Default: No |
|---|---|
| | Enable auto-generation of web services documentation. A user can access to his own documentation on his security keys page More details. It displays the documentation for the enabled protocols only. |

 Depending on the protocol chosen, you might have to install the respective PHP extension; for example, php5-soap.

It is expected that more web service protocols will be added in the future, in particular a Java and .Net compatible WSDL. Now that we have enabled web services and at least one protocol, let us cover setting up the two web service access types we have already mentioned.

# Enabling web services for external systems

An external system is any application that accesses Moodle and its data in one way or the other. There are eight steps that have to be performed to complete the setup, which follow the workflow described on the web services **Overview** screen:

1. **Create a specific user**: Each application should have a separate user account. That way you can control the capabilities each external system is going to use.

2. **Check user capability**: Depending on the protocol selected above, you have to allow the respective permissions for the user. You achieve this by creating a new role with any of the four capabilities **webservice/amf:use**, **webservice/rest:use**, **webservice/soap:use**, or **webservice/xmlrpc:use**. This role has to be assigned to the web services user in the **System** context.

3. **Select a service**: A service is like a defined interface that an external application can connect to. It is a set of functions, which are covered next. Selecting a service takes place in **Plugins | Web services | External services**. You will have to click on the **Add** link to add a **Custom service**.

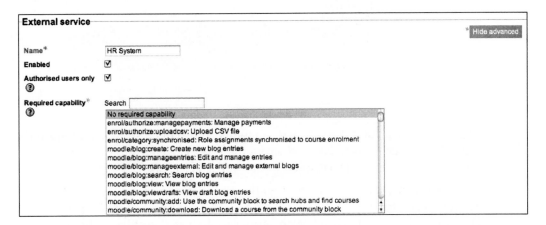

Each external service should have a name and should be enabled. A service has to be accessed via a token (see step 6). The **Authorised users only** setting restricts this access to selected users. If it remains unchecked, all users with the token permission can access the service. You can further restrict access by specifying capabilities that users must have. Once you have saved the service, click on the shown **Add functions** link.

4. **Add functions**: Moodle provides a number of functions that can be accessed via web services. This number will increase in upcoming versions, for example, to support mobile devices. Each function corresponds to a capability in Moodle roles. The function(s) selected depend(s) on what tasks the external system has to perform and should be set up in liaison with the developer in charge.

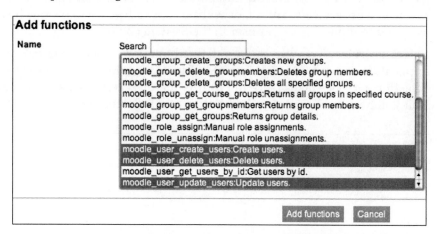

Once you have added the selected functions, you will be shown the required capabilities a user has to have to access the service. Make sure these have been allowed in the role assigned to the web services user.

5. **Select a specific user**: If you checked the **Authorised users only** checkbox when you created the service earlier, you will have to select these user(s). This takes place in **Plugins | Web services | External services** where you see a list of all set up services. Click on the **Authorised users** link, which will guide you to the familiar user selection screen. Select the web services user you created in step 1.

Once you have selected a user, Moodle will check if the account has the appropriate settings in order to access the selected functions. If any of the settings are missing, they will be displayed underneath the **Select authorised user** screen in the **Change settings for the authorised users** section. Clicking on a username will also allow you to restrict access to an IP address (**IP restriction** parameter) and to set an expiry date (**Valid until** parameter):

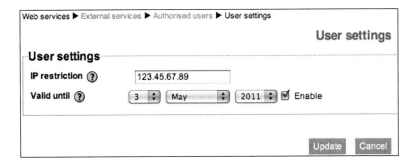

6. **Create a token for a user**: Web services use tokens for security. These are created for each user and can be added in **Plugins | Web services | Manage tokens**. Select a user (or multiple users). Select the service to be accessed from the **Service** drop-down menu. You can optionally specify an IP address (or range) and an expiry date via the **IP restriction** and the **Valid until** parameters, respectively.

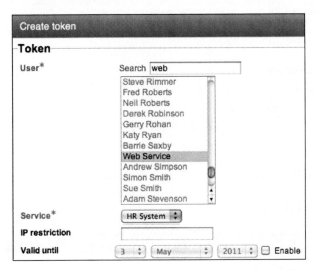

Users will be able to access and reset their web services token in **My profile settings | Security keys** if they have the **moodle/webservice:createtoken** capability.

7. **Enable developer documentation**: Moodle is able to generate documentation for developers for the selected functions in the format of the selected protocol. This is done when you set up the protocols (**Plugins | Web services | Manage protocols**) where you have to check the **Web services documentation** checkbox. Developers will be able to see the documentation as part of their security keys.

8. **Test the service**: Once a web service is set up, functions have been selected, and users have been assigned, it is imperative that you test the service to make sure that it works and, more importantly, that only functionality has been opened up that is required by the external system. This is done in **Development | Web service test client** (select **AMF test client** if you use AMF).

Be careful with executing functions via the test client as they perform them as they are executed for real!

First, you have to select the authentication method from the **Authentication method** drop-down menu (**simple** for username and password, **token** for a security key), the **Protocol**, and the **Function** to test.

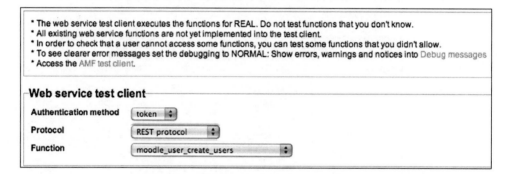

The screen that follows depends on what authentication method has been selected and which function has been chosen. Here, we used the **token** as the and **moodle_user_create_users**:

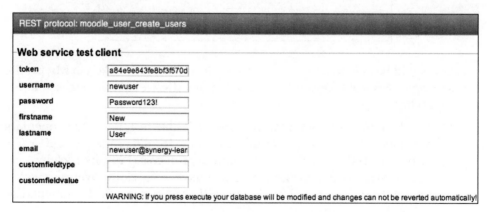

Once you have filled in the required values and executed the command (read the warning), you will see a return value in XML format. To receive a more meaningful message, change the **Debug messages** setting in **Development | Debugging** to DEVELOPER: extra Moodle debug messages for developers. If the result shows a line containing the DEBUGINFO element, an error has occurred. Otherwise, you should check that the function executed actually performed what it was supposed to (in our case, creating a user called **newuser**).

```
URL: http://moodle2.ab.local/webservice/rest/simpleserver.php?wsusername=webservices&wspassword=packt

'<?xml version="1.0" encoding="UTF-8" ?>
<EXCEPTION class="invalid_parameter_exception">
<MESSAGE>Invalid parameter value detected, execution can not continue.</MESSAGE>
<DEBUGINFO>Username already exists: newuser</DEBUGINFO>
</EXCEPTION>
```

# Enabling web services for users

It is sometimes necessary that users have to access web services directly instead of applications, for example, a developer who needs to execute test runs against the system. The process is a sub-set of steps already covered in the previous section, and follows the **Users as clients with token section** on the web services **Overview** screen:

1. **Select a service**.
2. **Add functions**.
3. **Check users capability**: In addition to the protocol use capabilities, the users have to have **moodle/webservice:createtoken** allowed.
4. **Test the service**.

# The Moodle mobile web service

We have already mentioned mobile Moodle a number of times in this chapter. Now, let us have a look at what it is all about and how you enable the powerful service on your Moodle system.

 Moodle 2.1 or greater is required to support the Moodle mobile web service.

Moodle have released a free application for the iPhone that allows users to interact with a Moodle system. At the time of writing (application version 1.0.2), some basic features are supported, such as uploading of pictures and videos, voice recording as well as some messaging functionality, and participants' information. Additional tools will be added in the very near future. An Android version, that is expected to have similar functionality, is in the planning.

The process of enabling the Moodle application to interact with your Moodle site has been greatly simplified. Once the mobile web service has been enabled under **Plugins | Web services | External services**, a built-in service will be activated (see also docs.moodle.org/en/Enable_mobile_web_services). That way there is no requirement for the administrator to set up any functions or capabilities, as these have already been predefined:

### External services

Enable mobile web service    ☑ Default: No
enablemobilewebservice

Enable mobile service for the official Moodle app or other app requesting it. For more information, read the Moodle documentation

It is recommended to enable HTTPS with a valid certificate. The Moodle app will always try to use a secured connection first.

### Information

A service is a set of functions. A service can be accessed by all users or just specified users.

### Built-in services

| External service | Plugin | Functions | Users | Edit |
| --- | --- | --- | --- | --- |
| Hub directory | local_hub | Functions | Authorised users | Edit |
| Moodle mobile web service | moodle | Functions | All users | Edit |
| Public site | local_hub | Functions | Authorised users | Edit |
| Registered site | local_hub | Functions | Authorised users | Edit |

Moodle highly recommends that you run your system over secure HTTP when enabling the mobile web service. We covered the set up of HTTPS in *Chapter 11, Moodle Security and Privacy*.

When you click on the **Functions** link, you will be shown a list of all functions that are used by the mobile web service. However, you cannot modify this list in any way. Additional functions will be added in the near future in sync with newer versions of the mobile applications.

You also have the option to edit the Moodle mobile web service via the **Edit** link. Again, apart from the **Enabled** option, which is the same as the one in the previous screenshot, all values are predefined and cannot be modified:

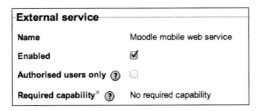

To check that the Moodle mobile web service is working correctly, go and get your snazzy iPhone, download the My Moodle application from iTunes (`itunes.apple.com/gb/app/my-moodle/id461289000`), and enter the site URL, username, and password. If successful, you will see the landing page of your application:

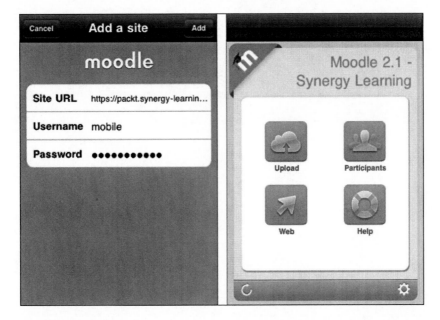

# Summary

In this chapter, you have learned what web services are and how they can be utilized from within Moodle. We covered the two main administrative tasks, namely setting up web services for external applications and enabling web services for users. We also talked through the enabling process of the Moodle mobile web service.

Keep an eye on the roadmap for web services as some great new features are in the pipeline (`docs.moodle.org/dev/Web_services_Roadmap`), for example, web services for offline grading will be added soon.

In the chapter to follow we will cover another option for Moodle to communicate with other systems, namely via Moodle networking.

# 16
# Moodle Networking

Moodle provides a unique functionality that lets you network multiple Moodle sites. This is useful in a number of contexts; for example, when you want to share resources with other VLEs, partner with another organization, or have a multi-campus setup where each site has its own Moodle setup.

After providing an overview of Moodle networking, you will learn about the following topics:

- **Networking prerequisites and security**: You will learn which networking components are required and how security is guaranteed.

- **Peer-to-peer networks**: You will learn how to link two Moodle sites.

- **Moodle hubs**: You will learn how to connect multiple Moodle sites to a central MNet hub.

- **Mahara integration**: You will learn how to set up Moodle with Mahara, a popular open source e-portfolio system that makes use of the networking functionality.

- **Moodle Community Hub (MOOCH)**: You will learn how to connect to a MOOCH and how to set up your own hub. MOOCH doesn't use MNet per se, but it offers related functionality, which is why it is dealt with in this chapter.

The Moodle Docs contain a very well written wiki on Moodle networking and this chapter follows the document in part. You can find this document at docs.moodle.org/en/Moodle_Network.

# Networking overview

Virtual Learning Environments are usually standalone systems. But learning, in addition to doing, is primarily about communication and collaboration (social constructionist theory). Moodle networking overcomes this limitation and provides a powerful facility to establish logical links among multiple Moodle sites. The following two topologies are supported:

- **Peer-to-Peer**: This layout connects two Moodle systems directly. This topology is favorable if you have two partnering organizations or one site that offers courses in which students from another site wish to enrol. This topology is shown in the following diagram:

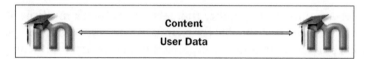

- **Moodle hub**: A hub is a Moodle server (also known as MNet hub) that is configured to accept connections from other Moodle servers, and to provide a set of services to users of these other servers. This topology is favorable if you have a portal that is used for sharing learning resources or courses, and is shown in the following diagram:

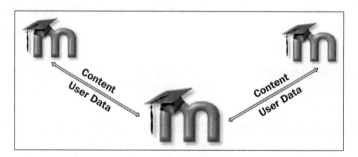

Moodle networking supports **single sign-on** (**SSO**) mechanism, which provides a seamless integration of multiple Moodle systems. Security is guaranteed by fully encrypting authentication and content exchanges.

For more information on Moodle networking and the MNet functionality, visit `docs.moodle.org/en/MNet`.

MNet, which has been designed for Moodle to Moodle pairing, will be replaced with OAuth (for authentication) and web services (for communication and data exchange) in Moodle 2.3 or 2.4.

The two topologies are not mutually exclusive and can be mixed in the same network. An example of a large-scale Moodle network is shown in the following diagram (courtesy of Wrexham County Borough Council), where all participating Moodle instances connect to a hub and some schools have established peer-to-peer connections:

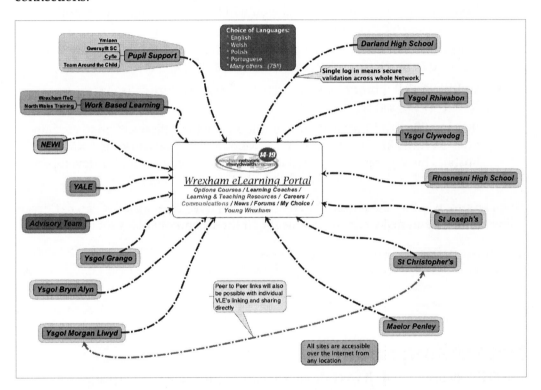

After covering some networking prerequisites and security issues, you will learn how to set up peer-to-peer networks and an MNet hub.

# Networking prerequisites and security

Moodle networking requires a number of additional components, that deal with secure communication and safe data exchange, to be installed on your servers.

## Required PHP extensions

The following elements have to be installed on all Moodle servers that are participating in the network:

- **curl**: A PHP library of calls that are specifically designed to safely fetch data from remote sites. If not installed, you will have to recompile PHP and add `--with curl` when running `configure` script.

- **openssl**: Another PHP library that provides encryption functionality without the need to purchase an SSL certificate (`--with openssl`).

- **xmlrpc**: A PHP library that supports remote procedure calls via XML (`--with xmlrpc`).

  It is possible to add trusted hosts to Moodle, which allows them to execute calls via XML-RPC to any part of the Moodle API (**Networking | XML-RPC hosts**). This is potentially very dangerous and is only meant for developers. In this book, we will not be dealing with this functionality.

To make sure whether the required PHP extensions have been installed, go to **Server | Environment** and make sure the status for all three components is set to **OK**.

| php_extension | curl | ⓘ must be installed and enabled | OK |
| php_extension | openssl | ⓘ should be installed and enabled for best results | OK |
| php_extension | tokenizer | ⓘ should be installed and enabled for best results | OK |
| php_extension | xmlrpc | ⓘ should be installed and enabled for best results | OK |

## Networking security

The PHP extensions, which were discussed earlier, guarantee the secure communication and safe transmission of data between participating sites. Unlike other secure web systems, neither HTTPS nor the purchase of an SSL certificate is required.

To activate Moodle networking go to **Advanced features** and turn on the **Networking** parameter. This step has to be performed on all participating servers in the Moodle network.

Once networking has been enabled, Moodle generates a public/private key pair. Later, when you connect to another Moodle site (which also has a set of keys), the public key is exchanged and you will have to confirm that your site trusts this public key. When the two sites exchange data, the sender will sign each request using their private key and encrypt the message with the public key of the receiver. The receiver, holder of the sender's public key and its own private key, will be able to decrypt the message and execute the request. That's the theory; now, back to the real world!

Go to **Networking | Settings**, where you will see the public key that has been created by OpenSSL. The key has an expiry date that is 28 days from creation, after which a new key is created (so called key rotation). The key can be renewed manually by using the key deletion option on the same screen.

 The key expiry duration cannot be changed via a Moodle parameter, but via a configuration setting (see *Appendix, Configuration Settings*). Add $CFG->mnetkeylifetime = 365 to config.php in order to increase the expiry period to a full year.

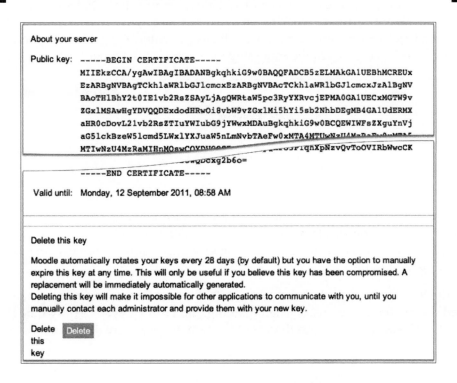

Now that Moodle networking has been enabled and the public key has been generated, it is time to get the servers talking to each other.

# Peer-to-peer networks

First, we will deal with peer-to-peer networks where two Moodle servers are connected. For demonstration purposes, we have set up two Moodle sites (two peers), one is located at `http://packt1.synergy-learning.com` and the other at `http://packt2.synergy-learning.com`. The two sites do not have to be in the same domain or the same organization. For example, two universities or two high schools might want to offer a collaborative course. They both have their own Moodle system in their own domain and they both control who gets access to which part of their site.

If your two sites are hosted in the same domain and you are accessing both sites from the same web browser simultaneously, change the cookie prefix of one site (**Server | Session handling**) to avoid any conflicts.

# Adding a peer

Go to **Networking | Manage peers** and add a new remote host that you want to connect to. We are currently working on `packt1.synergy-learning.com` and to establish a link to the remote server, we will have to enter **http:// packt2.synergy-learning.com**. Then perform the same step vice-versa on the other host:

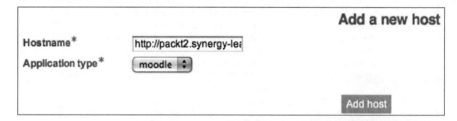

The drop-down menu offers an additional host type—**mahara**. Mahara is an open source e-portfolio system that can be integrated via the Moodle networking mechanism. We will cover the integration later in this chapter. For now, let's leave this setting at **moodle**.

Once the host has been added, the name of the **Site**, its **Hostname**, an optionally **Forced theme** that will be used when roaming, the **Public key**, its expiry date (**Valid until**), the **IP address**, and **Cert details** of the remote server are displayed (as shown in the following screenshot):

| Site | Packt2 |
|---|---|
| Hostname | http://packt2.synergy-lea |
| Force theme | Do not force ‡ |
| Public key | ----BEGIN CERTIFICATE---- |

MIIEfjCCA+egAwIBAgIBADANBgkqhkiG9w0BAQQFADCB4DELMAL~~
EDAOBgNVBAgTB0JIbGZhc3O~~~~~~~~~~~~~~~~~polryGHUyxNEb+Q7igLFDr
~~~~~~~~~~~~~gg: AMBUGA1UdDgQWBBTLF0ABV3HKTBEoponf57uB2trSxDCC

| Valid until | This key expired on Friday, 1 July 2011, 08:21 AM |
|---|---|
| Last connect time | 13:44:48 04/06/2011 |
| IP address | 89.185.150.19 |
| Cert details | |

```
                        C: GB
            ST: Belfast
             L: Belfast
             O: moodle2
            OU: Moodle
            CN: http://packt2.synergy-learning.com
 subjectAltName: http://packt2.synergy-learning.com
   emailAddress:            @synergy-learning.com
```

After you have saved the changes, you will see three additional tabs at the top of the screen that describe details of the peer connection. You can always come back to this screen by selecting the host in **Networking | Peers**.

 Deleted peers are kept on the system and can be re-activated when you attempt to add a new host with the same address.

# Peer services

The SSO supported by Moodle avoids the need to login when roaming to a remote site. The **Services** tab contains four areas. We will currently only focus on the last two which deal with SSO. The enrolment and portfolio services will be dealt with later on.

There are two SSO services that represent a two-way process and both services have to be set up on both Moodle sites by the respective administrators.

Peer services can be published and subscribed. It is important to note that publication and subscription is fully controlled by the local administrator. The administrator of the other site will never be able to modify any of the settings on your site.

Publish the **SSO (Identity Provider)** service to allow your users to roam to the other site without having to re-log in there. Subscribe to this service to allow authenticated users from the other site to access your site without having to re-log in.

Publish the **SSO (Service Provider)** service to allow authenticated users from the other site to access your site without having to re-log in. Subscribe to this service to allow your users to roam to the other site without having to re-login there.

Take the example of the two collaborating universities, which we mentioned earlier. University A would publish the identity provider and University B would subscribe to it. Students from University A are now able to access the restricted areas at University B's site without having to re-log in.

| Service | Local users | Remote users |
|---|---|---|
| Publish Identity Provider | Allow roaming | |
| Subscribe Service Provider | Allow roaming | |
| Subscribe Identity Provider | | Grant access |
| Publish Service Provider | | Grant access |

Each service has a reciprocal dependency on the other server as shown in the preceding table. For example, the subscribed **SSO (Service Provider)** on the local site requires the **SSO (Service Provider)** to be published on the other site. To allow roaming in both directions, all four boxes on both peers in your Moodle network have to be checked by the respective administrator.

# Peer logs

Moodle records detail logging information about each action that takes place in its system. Each record or hit contains data about:

- Who did (user)
- What (action)
- When (date and time)
- Where (IP address)

The monitoring and tracking works in exactly the same way as discussed in *Chapter 10, Moodle Reporting*. The only difference is that the remote sites can be selected from the first drop-down menu of the available filters:

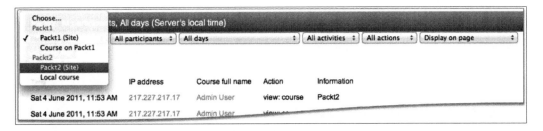

# Profile fields

When a user from one site roams to another site for the first time, a local user account is created and certain profile fields will be populated by fetching the data from the remote site. The default fields can be overridden by selecting any of the shown profile fields in the provided list. This setting exists for **Fields to import** (users who roam from another site to the local site) and **Fields to export** (vice versa) as shown in the following screenshot:

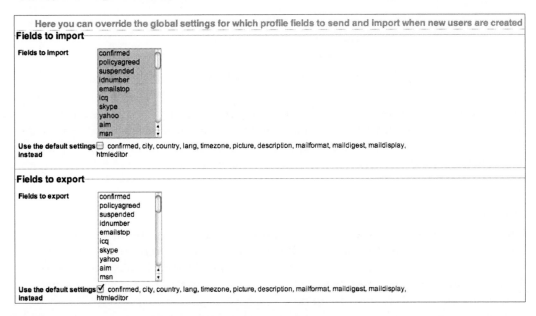

The default fields can be changed in **Networking | Profile fields**. Fields that are included on your import list, but excluded on the remote site's export list, will be ignored.

Bear in mind that no password will be stored on the remote server. As the authentication mechanism will be set to **MNet authentication**, Moodle will check the credentials every time a user logs in. We will deal with authentication in the section that follows.

# Network authentication

To initiate roaming, you will have to enable the Moodle network authentication plugin on both sites. Go to **Plugins | Authentication | Manage authentication** and enable the **MNet authentication** plugin. Every time a new user from a remote site logs in to this site, a user record is created automatically.

| MNet authentication |
| --- |
| Users are authenticated according to the web of trust defined in your Moodle Network settings. |

| | | |
| --- | --- | --- |
| RPC negotiation timeout: | 30 | The timeout in seconds for authentication over the XMLRPC transport. |
| These host's users can roam in to your site: | | |
| Packt2: | http://packt2.synergy-learning.com | |
| Your users can roam out to these hosts: | | |
| Packt2: | http://packt2.synergy-learning.com | |

In the settings screen, as shown in the preceding screenshot, you will see a list of host's users who are allowed to roam in to your site and local users who are allowed to roam out. Only change the **RPC negotiation timeout** parameter if users experience sporadic timeout problems roaming from one site to another.

# Allowing roaming

Only users assigned to a role with the **moodle/site:mnetlogintoremote** capability are allowed to roam to other sites. By default, this **Roam to a remote application via MNet** capability is turned off and has to be allowed for each role. Go to **Users | Permissions | Define roles** or revisit *Chapter 6, Managing Permissions: Roles and Capabilities*, for details on how to do this.

To turn on roaming for all users logged in to your site, allow the **moodle/site:mnetlogintoremote** capability in the **Authenticated user** role. Unless all users are allowed to roam, it is worth considering creating a separate roaming role. Alternatively, if you wish to grant (or deny) access to individual users from a remote host, go to **Networking | SSO access control**. You will have to specify a **Username**, a **Remote host** (the **All hosts** option is only relevant for the community hub mode, which is discussed later) and the **Access level** (**Allow** or **Deny**).

The newly added user name does not have to exist in either Moodle site! In the list of users, the remote hub ID is displayed and not its name. This is the internal ID, similar to a user ID, group ID, or role ID.

# Network servers block

Moodle provides a **Network servers** block, which has to be added to the front page. The block cannot be configured and is only displayed if the role of the logged in user has the **moodle/site:mnetlogintoremote** capability, mentioned earlier, set to **Allow**:

The block acts as a launch pad to access remote sites. Here, in addition to our **Packt2** peer, we have already set up a link to a Mahara instance too. Once you click on the remote server, you will be re-directed to the selected site where you can enrol on remote courses. Your first peer-to-peer network is set up!

Moodle displays a different logged in message in the header. Instead of **You are logged in as <user> (Logout)**, the message reads **You are logged in as <user> from <peer> (Logout)**. This is similar when you masquerade as another user. When you click on your name, you access the profile of the newly created user on the remote server, which cannot be changed. The message **Remote Moodle user - profile fetched from <peer>** is displayed.

You will also see that the information in the **My courses** section includes all remote courses (in our case, only one called **Course on Packt1**).

If you want to deny access of a remote user; for example, because of misconduct, go to **Users | Accounts | Browse list of users** and you will see that an additional column has been added to the list of users. Remote users cannot be edited locally, only the site they have logged in from is displayed. In the right hand column, you select **Deny access** to revoke access to the site. To reverse the operation, select **Allow access**:

| First name / Surname | Email address | City/town | Country | Last access | | |
|---|---|---|---|---|---|---|
| Admin User | alex.buchner@synergy-learning.com | Belfast | United Kingdom | 18 mins 33 secs | Packt2 | Allow (Deny access) |
| Roamer User | roam@null.com | Roam | Romania | Never | Edit | Delete |
| Roamer User | roam@synergy-learning.com | Heidelberg | Germany | 11 mins 48 secs | Packt2 | Deny (Allow access) |

# Network enrolment

This last step is optional and is required only if you wish to grant an administrator in one Moodle system the permission to enroll local users in remote courses, and the other way round. This is useful if you run a shared course that is located on your server, but learners from the remote site should be participants. To minimize the administrative effort at your end, you must grant the remote administrator the right to take on this task, which is limited to courses you have specified.

First of all, on the local site, that is the one that grants the rights to the remote site, go to **Plugins | Enrolments | Manage enrol plugins** and enable the **MNet remote enrolments** plugin. This allows the local server to receive enrolments from its remote counterpart.

Now, go to **Networking | Peers**, click on the remote host and click on the **Services** tab. Publish and subscribe to the **Remote enrolment service**. This grants remote administrators the right to enrol students on your site and allows the local students to enrol in courses on the remote site, respectively. This step has to be repeated on the peer.

Both Moodle sites have now been configured to allow communication between the two servers and courses are set up to enrol remote students. Make sure that you activate the **MNet enrolment** method inside your course (see *Chapter 4, Course Management*, for details).

When you go to **Networking | Remote enrolments client**, you will see a list of remote hosts where local users are enrolled. When you click on the host, courses offered for remote enrolment are displayed. You can then edit the enrolments in the same way you would manage users in a local course.

# Moodle hubs

A Moodle or MNet hub is similar to a peer-to-peer network, with the only difference that it accepts connections from multiple Moodle and Mahara servers. While this could be set up manually using a number of peer-to-peer connections, the hub mode automatically accepts any hosts that try to connect to it. Potentially, this is a big time and maintenance saver, but at the cost of opening up your site to other Moodle instances.

A public learning portal that contains resources to be shared across a number of sites is typically implemented using the hub mode. Each Moodle instance that wishes access to the portal, has to be configured to connect to the hub.

Once networking has been turned on, choose the Moodle site that will act as a hub and go to **Networking | Manage peers** to click on the **Turn it on** button to register all hosts. Effectively, a hub is a regular Moodle site that operates in a special mode.

The **All hosts** site is treated like a peer, with the exception that the **Review host details** tab is empty and the **Logs** tab is hidden. All the other settings are identical to the peer-to-peer parameters. You might decide that traffic (that is, authentication and enrolment) should only go one-way, that is from the different Moodle sites to the hub. You can control this by the SSO **Publish** and SSO **Subscribe** options under the **Services** tab:

|  | SSO (IP) | SSO (SP) | Enrolment |
| --- | --- | --- | --- |
| Moodle hub | Subscribe | Publish | Publish |
| Connecting site | Publish | Publish | Subscribe |
|  | Subscribe | Subscribe |  |

# Integrating Mahara

According to its web site (`www.mahara.org`), Mahara is an open source e-portfolio, weblog, resume builder and social networking system, connecting users and creating online learner communities. Mahara is designed to provide users with the tools to demonstrate their life-long learning, skills, and development over time to selected audiences. It has recently become very popular in vocational and academic settings.

# Mahoodle

Moodle and Mahara (nicknamed Mahoodle) can be easily integrated via the Moodle Network functions. A very good set up guide can be downloaded from `docs.moodle.org/en/Mahoodle`. We will only cover the basic networking-related settings required to establish a link between the two systems. More details can be found in the Mahara documentation or the dedicated Packt title, *Mahara 1.4 Cookbook* (`www.packtpub.com/mahara-1-4-cookbook-for-training-education/book`).

It is assumed that Moodle networking (authentication, role permissions, and so on) has been configured as explained in the previous section. It is further assumed that a Mahara 1.3 or greater site has been set up and networking components have been installed.

Due to the fact that both Mahara and Moodle use the SSO mechanism of the networking feature you can configure Moodle so that logged-in Moodle users can navigate to the Mahara site and, without the need to login, start using the e-portfolio system. If users don't have an account on Mahara, their user data will be imported from Moodle and used to populate their Mahara account.

# Mahara networking

After logging into Mahara as administrator, go to **Site Administration | Configure Site | Networking** and set the **Enable networking** and **Auto-register all hosts** parameters to **Yes**. Once this has been confirmed, the screen will look very similar to its counterpart in Moodle, which is not surprising as both modules have been programmed by the same development team:

## Networking

Mahara's networking features allow it to communicate with Mahara or Moodle sites running on the same or another machine. If networking is enabled, you can use it to configure single-sign-on for users who log in at either Moodle or Mahara.

| | |
|---|---|
| **WWW Root** | http://mahara14.ab.local/ |
| | This is the URL at which your users access this Mahara installation, and the URL the SSL keys are generated for |
| **Public key** | -----BEGIN CERTIFICATE----- |
| | -----END CERTIFICATE----- |
| | This public key is automatically generated, and rotated every 365 days |
| **SHA1 Fingerprint** | 97:78:A6:3D:87:A2:5B:7C:20:0B:31:33:14:8D:5C:2B:0B:5A:56:EE |
| **MD5 Fingerprint** | BB:34:2A:85:19:F8:F3:2F:88:8B:BD:FF:EE:1C:A6:9C |
| **Public key expires** | 18 May 2012, 9:51 AM |
| **Enable networking** | No |
| | Allow your Mahara server to communicate with servers running Moodle and other applications |
| **Auto-register all hosts** | No |
| | Create an institution record for any host that connects to you, and allow its users to log on to Mahara |
| | Save changes |

Now that Mahara Networking has been enabled, go to **Admin Home | Institutions**, add a new institution, and enter its name and display name. At this stage you can leave all other entries, including the hidden locked fields, at their defaults.

Once you have submitted the values, you will be directed to a similar looking screen where you have to select **XMLRPC – Authenticate by SSO from an external application** and add it to the list of supported authentication plugins. This will open a new window (shown in the following screenshot), where you will have to enter the XML RPC options:

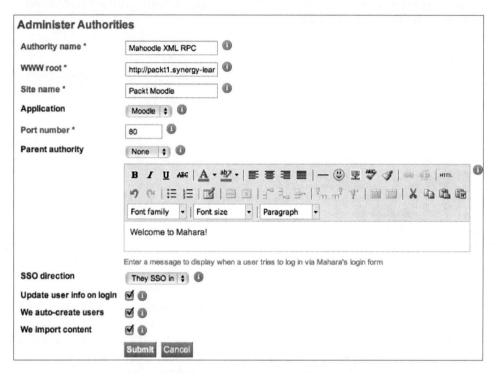

The previous screenshot is the equivalent of the **Peers** and **Services** settings in Moodle.

| Setting | Description |
|---|---|
| **Authority name** | Descriptor of the service. |
| **WWW root** | URL of your Moodle system. |
| **Site name** | Description of Moodle system. |
| **Application** | Moodle or Mahara. |
| **Port number** | Standard port is 80. Only change if you use HTTPS a special port. |
| **Parent authority** | Select another entry if you allow multi-authentication. |
| **SSO direction** | **They SSO in** (allowing roaming from Moodle to Mahara) and **We SSO out** (vice versa) are the available options. |

| Setting | Description |
|---|---|
| **Update user info on login** | Synchronize user data at every login, otherwise only on account creation. |
| **We auto-create users** | A user record is created when a remote user authenticates for the first time. |
| **We import content** | Support for Mahara portfolio plugin (see *Mahara portfolio* section). |

# Adding Mahara to Moodle

Now go back to your Moodle system and add a new host in **Networking | Manage peers**, but this time change the **Application type** from **moodle** to **mahara**.

The host details will be displayed and you will have to save them. Then you will have to configure the SSO Identity and Service providers as you did earlier.

Once this has been done successfully, you will see that the Mahara site has been added to the **Network servers** block on your front page (see the block shown earlier). And that is it! Now, your users can smoothly move forward and backward between Moodle and Mahara without the need to re-login or multiple browser windows.

# Mahara portfolio

We covered Moodle portfolios in great detail in *Chapter 8, Moodle Plugins*. All available portfolio plugins at **Plugins | Manage portfolios** work out of the box, except the one that allows the exporting of content to Mahara. It is shown as **Disabled** by default until the **Portfolio services** have been enabled in the **Services** tab of the Mahara peer (to **Publish** and **Subscribe** both). Once this has been successful, you can enable the **Mahara portfolio** plugin and will be confronted with the settings as in the following screenshot:

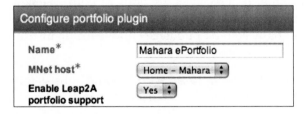

The **Name** field is the entry that will appear when exporting content. Select the **MNet host**, in case you have connected to more than one Mahara site. By default, all content is transferred as files and stored in a dedicated **Incoming** directory in Mahara. If you use Mahara 1.3 or higher, you can set the **Leap2A portfolio support** parameter to **Yes**, enables context-sentitive tranfer of the content. For example, when a user exports a forum entry in Leap2A format, Mahara will import it as a journal entry instead of a file.

 Make sure that the **We import content** setting has been selected in the XMLRPC authentication plugin in Mahara.

Some related functionality that might be of interest is a set of plugins catering for portfolio assignment submission, which comprises of two Moodle add-ons (https://wiki.mahara.org/index.php/System_Administrator's_Guide/ Moodle//Mahara_Integration/View_Submission):

- Local-Mahara (Moodle plugin): This add-on provides you with the functionality to get a list of a user's views on Mahara from within Moodle and submit a Mahara assessment view to Moodle instead of a Mahara group.
- Mahara portfolio assignment (Moodle assignment type): This add-on allows students to select and submit a Mahara view from within Moodle.

There are also plans for a Mahara repository plugin for Moodle, so keep an eye on the Moodle announcements.

# Moodle Community Hub (MOOCH)

According to Moodle Docs, a community hub is a directory of courses for public use or for private communities. It effectively facilitates the creation of a course portal, where each site can either be a receiver, a sender, or both. The new concept is still in its infancy, but it is expected to potentially change the way Moodle courses are advertised and potentially sold by publishers and learning institutions or shared by the community.

Community hubs are not to be confused with Moodle hubs as they both are very distinct concepts. Moodle hubs are for connecting two or more Moodle sites allowing students to participate in courses outside their institution. Community hubs are like yellow pages where courses are searched, advertised, and shared. An optional payment module is planned for the future, opening up the facility for commercial course provision.

Users can enroll and import courses from MOOCH via the **Community finder** block. We are not dealing with this, as it is not an administration task. You can find more information about the community hub itself on `docs.moodle.org/en/Community_hubs`.

Instead, we will be looking at the option of creating your own private community hub; for example, for a network of schools or a number of customers. Parts of this section are following the documentation at `docs.moodle.org/en/Hub_administration`.

A community hub is a standard Moodle site that is run in hub mode. While it is possible to use an existing Moodle site as a hub at the same time, it is not recommended to do so, as the front page is being replaced with a search facility, as shown in the following screenshot:

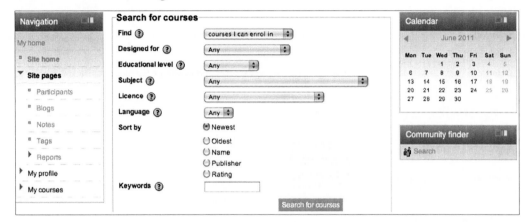

To create a hub server, you will have to go through the following steps:

1. Install a fresh copy of Moodle (see *Chapter 1, Moodle Installation* for instructions).

2. Install the Moodle hub server plugin from the **Moodle Plugins Directory** on `moodle.org` or directly from `github.com/moodlehq/moodle-local_hub` in your `/local` directory (see *Chapter 14, Installing Third-party Add-ons.*).

   Once this has been successful, you should see a new sub-menu called **Hub** in the **Site administration** section:

3. Enable **Web services** and enable the **XML-RPC protocol** in **Plugins | Web services | Manage protocols** (see *Chapter 15, Moodle Integration via Web Services* for details on web services)

4. Configure ReCAPTCHA in **Plugins | Authentication | Manage authentication** (see *Chapter 5, User Management*)

5. Set up SMTP in **Plugins | Message outputs | Email** (see *Communication* section in *Chapter 9, Moodle Configuration*)

6. Once you have managed all these steps, go to **Hub | Settings** to provide the following self-explanatory settings of your hub:

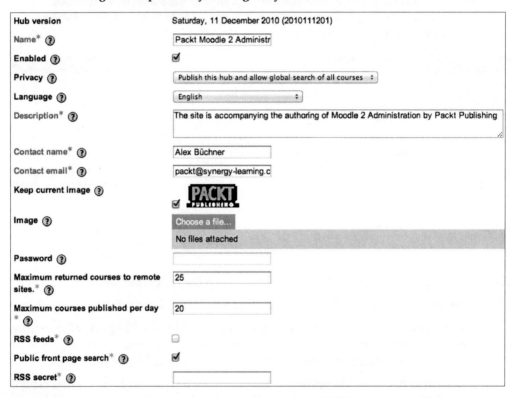

The next step is for other sites to register to your hub. This takes place in **Registration | Register with a specific hub**. Enter the **Private hub URL** and a **Password** if specified. The information to be provided is identical to when you initially register your site with `moodle.org` (see *Chapter 1, Moodle Installation* for details). Once you have submitted the details and successfully entered the ReCAPTCHA, your site is registered with the hub. This means that users of this site can publish and share courses with users of other sites who are also registered with the hub. The external Moodle site and your hub are not connected nor do users become authenticated with your system. It only allows for exchange and collaborative work on courses published on the hub.

You can see all sites that are registered on your hub at **Hub | Manage sites**:

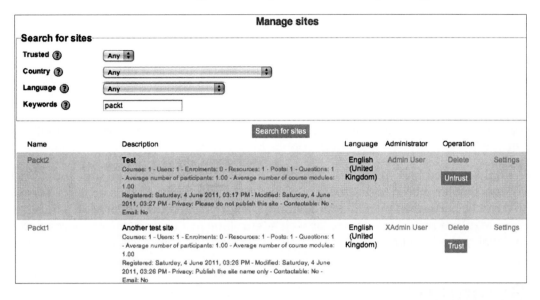

Once you trust a site, it can access your hub via the **Community finder** block.

As soon as courses have been submitted to your hub (via the **Publish** link in the **Course administration** section), you can manage them via **Hub | Manage courses**:

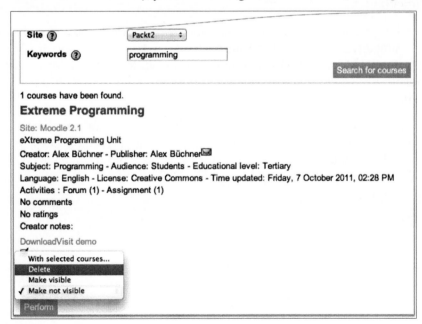

You have the ability to delete courses and change whether they are visible to other users. You can also download or visit the courses, depending on how it has been configured by the external party.

 The hub server creates a number of roles, users, and web services that must not be modified or deleted!

You can also register your hub with `moodle.org` (**Hub | Hub server registration**). Once approved, it will appear in the public list on MOOCH.

We only covered how to set up a community hub and how to manage sites and courses that have been registered and published, respectively. Details on tasks that can be performed by non-administrators, such as searching a course on a hub, download and restoring a course, as well as enrolling in a remote course are covered in detail in the Moodle Docs at `docs.moodle.org/en/Community_hubs`.

# Summary

In this chapter, you have learned how to network disparate Moodle systems. After providing an overview of Moodle networking, we covered some prerequisites and security issues. We then dealt with peer-to-peer networks, MNet hubs, and Mahara integration.

The networking facility that is available in Moodle introduces a new dimension to virtual learning environments. Disparate systems can be connected logically and roaming from one Moodle site to another can be facilitated. This opens up entirely new opportunities whether it is among entities within your organization or with external sites.

The covered Moodle Community Hub will allow the creation of communities of practice, provide a facility to enable enrolment in courses on remote sites, and offer a vehicle for publishers to sell content. It is still early days, but it can be expected that this novel concept will become highly popular with educators, once it has reached a certain momentum.

# Configuration Settings

The objective of the *Configuration Settings* reference is to provide you with a list of parameters that can be modified in `config.php` and to understand the impact that each of the values will have.

We will first look at `config.php` and what types of parameters are supported by Moodle. After providing this overview, we will look at the following two types of configurations settings:

- **Administration Settings**: These are settings that are available via the **Site administration** menu, but can be locked with values specified in `config.php`.

- **System Settings**: We will distinguish between default and supplementary configuration values. The former have been created by the installer and are required for Moodle to function. The latter are parameters that change various behaviors of Moodle.

## Configuration reference—an overview

The configuration file `config.php` contains a number of settings and variables that heavily influence how Moodle operates. It is located in the main directory of your Moodle system (`$CFG->dirroot`) and can be edited with any text editor.

 Be careful when modifying `config.php`! Moodle depends heavily on its content and any faults can cause the software to malfunction.

It is recommended that you create a backup of the `config.php` file before modifying it, so you can roll back to it in case of problems. Also, make sure that the file permissions are set properly as the file contains the database username and password. In a Linux environment, the `owner` and the `group` should be set to `root`, and the `permissions` should be set to `644`.

```php
<?php  // Moodle configuration file

unset($CFG);
global $CFG;
$CFG = new stdClass();

$CFG->dbtype    = 'mysqli';
$CFG->dblibrary = 'native';
$CFG->dbhost    = 'localhost';
$CFG->dbname    = 'moodle2';
$CFG->dbuser    = 'moodle2';
$CFG->dbpass    = 'moodle2';
$CFG->prefix    = 'mdl_';
$CFG->dboptions = array (
  'dbpersist' => 0,
  'dbsocket' => 0,
);

$CFG->wwwroot   = 'http://moodle2.ab.local';
$CFG->dataroot  = '/var/www/moodledata2';
$CFG->admin     = 'admin';
//$CFG->debug    = 5;
$CFG->directorypermissions = 0777;
```

The values in the `config.php` file that we are interested in are the ones that start with a dollar symbol. Each parameter has the following information format:

`$<object>-><parameter> = <value>;`

`<object>` is the part of Moodle in which the parameter is used (`$CFG` or `$THEME`). Third-party modules or custom distributions might have introduced their own objects; for example, `$TOTARA`. We will focus on `$CFG` objects as these are most relevant to administrators.

`<parameter>` is the name of the configuration setting. Each setting has a unique identifier.

`<value>` is the type of values the parameter accepts. This depends on the type of the setting. The following table provides the information for each of the key types:

| Type | Moodle field | Values |
|------|--------------|--------|
| Binary | Checkbox | `True` or `1` and `False` or `0`. |
| Numeric | Number field | The number itself. |
| String | Text field | Text has to be surrounded by single quotes. |
| Password | Password field | Passwords have to be surrounded by single quotes. |
| List | Drop-down menu | Each value is represented by a number or a string. Unfortunately, there is no consistency for the allocation. For example, while the `debug` parameter accepts the values `0`, `5`, `15`, `6143` and `38911`, the `sitemailcharset` parameter accepts `0`, `EUC-JP` and `GB18030`! The easiest way to find out what values are valid is to change the values in Moodle and check the **config changes** report (**Reports | Config changes**). Alternatively, you can check the `mdl_config` table in the database. |
| Array | Multi-select menu | The same applies as for the List type. Values are separated by commas. Again, check the **config changes** report to be on the safe side. |

Each parameter has to be terminated by a semicolon. To comment out a parameter, precede it with two forward slashes.

Before we deal with the different types of settings, let's have a look at the number of tools that might be useful. As there is no list of available settings, you will have to generate your own. To do so, execute the following shell command in your `$CFG->dirroot`:

```
grep -r -h -o '\$CFG->[a-z][[:alnum:]_]*' . | sort-u
```

This will generate a list of all available `$CFG` variables in alphabetical order.

If you are experimenting with configuration variables, you might consider installing the **Admin setting presets** block, which lets users with the site configuration capability to export the site settings to `.xml` presets, import other sites `.xml` presets, load (totally or partially) presets settings, and rollback the applied changes if necessary. You can find more information about the tool at: `docs.moodle.org/en/Admin_presets_block`.

Moodle provides a report that lets you monitor all the changes to any configuration settings via the administration interface. You can find the report at **Reports | Config changes**:

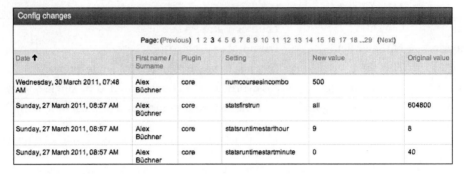

| Config changes | | | | | |
| --- | --- | --- | --- | --- | --- |
| Page: (Previous) 1 2 **3** 4 5 6 7 8 9 10 11 12 13 14 15 16 17 18 ...29 (Next) | | | | | |
| Date ↑ | First name / Surname | Plugin | Setting | New value | Original value |
| Wednesday, 30 March 2011, 07:48 AM | Alex Büchner | core | numcoursesincombo | 500 | |
| Sunday, 27 March 2011, 08:57 AM | Alex Büchner | core | statsfirstrun | all | 604800 |
| Sunday, 27 March 2011, 08:57 AM | Alex Büchner | core | statsruntimestarthour | 9 | 8 |
| Sunday, 27 March 2011, 08:57 AM | Alex Büchner | core | statsruntimestartminute | 0 | 40 |

Another tool that might be useful when dealing with configuration settings across multiple Moodle sites is called Moodle flavours. A **flavour** is a set of Moodle site settings, plugins, and language packs (docs.moodle.org/dev/Moodle_flavours). While its key objective is to package, distribute, and deploy the same settings and add-ons to multiple Moodle sites, it can also be used to back up and restore the configuration settings of your Moodle site. You can download the latest version of the plugin from moodle.org/plugins/view.php?plugin=local_flavours. Once installed (see *Chapter 14, Installing Third-party Add-ons*), you can select the settings to be packaged up in a flavour:

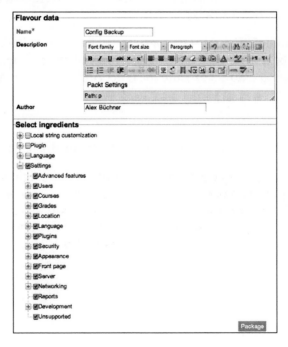

# Configuration reference—administration settings

Each parameter in the **Site administration** menu can be configured via `config.php`. If a value has been set via this method, it is effectively hard-coded and cannot be changed via the Moodle interface; not even by the administrator.

For example, you might want to make sure that an administrator does not, even by accident, turn on HTTPS for logins. Activating this would lock everybody out of the site if no SSL certificate is installed. To do this, enter the following line in `config.php`.

```
$CFG->loginhttps=false;
```

How do you know what parameter is called? Go to the respective setting in Moodle (in this case, **Security | HTTP security**) and you will see the name of the parameter underneath the label.

If the value is specified in `config.php`, Moodle will display **Defined in config.php** besides the parameter, which indicates that the setting cannot be changed by the user. Invalid values are also shown for these hard-coded settings. In the following screenshot, the **Debug messages** value is incorrect while the **Display debug messages** value is correct:

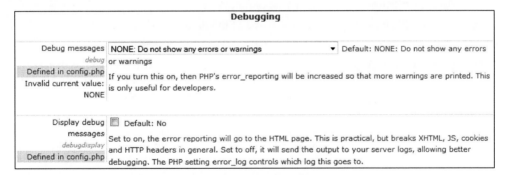

If you wish to force plugin settings, you will have to put them in a special array called `forced_plugin_settings` (see *Optional parameters* section).

# Configuration reference—system settings

This is the actual reference of configuration settings. Explanations have been taken from help pages, forum posts, and comments in source code.

## Default parameters

These are settings that have been created by the installer, derived from `config-dist.php`. Most parameters are compulsory for Moodle to operate, so be careful when changing any of them. The parameters are listed in the following table in the order in which they appear by default in `config.php`:

| Parameter | Description |
|---|---|
| `$CFG->dbtype` (String) | The database system that is used. The four valid values are `mysqli` (MySQL), `pgsql` (PostgreSQL), `mssql` (MS SQL Server), and `oci` (Oracle). |
| `$CFG->dblibrary` (String) | Currently, only `native` is allowed as the entry value. |
| `$CFG->dbhost` (String) | The name of the database host. The valid value is `localhost` or `127.0.0.1` if the database is located on the server as Moodle. If the database is located on another server, the value is any other URL. |
| `$CFG->dbname` (String) | The name of database. |
| `$CFG->dbuser` (String) | The username of the database account. |
| `$CFG->dbpass` (String) | The password of the database account. |
| `$CFG->prefix` (String) | By default, all tables in Moodle are prefixed with `mdl_`. This should only be changed if you run multiple Moodle installations using the same database. |
| `$CFG->dboptions` (Array) | Values that determine database behavior. These include `dbpersist` (whether an existing database connection can be reused to improve performance, potentially decreasing stability), `dbsocket` (when Unix socket is used), and `dbport` (TCP port, if different from default). |
| `$CFG->wwwroot` (String) | This is the full web address (including `http://`) where Moodle has been installed. |
| `$CFG->dataroot` (String) | This is the absolute directory name where Moodle's data dictionary is located. The directory must be readable and writable; but must not be accessible via the web. |

| Parameter | Description |
|---|---|
| `$CFG->admin` (String) | The admin pages in Moodle are located in the `admin` directory. If this has to be changed then specify the new directory here, as some ISPs don't allow its usage. This approach is also potentially advantageous for securing the site from attacks. |
| `$CFG->directorypermissions` (Special) | These are the permissions in Unix format that are applied for directories which Moodle is creating. Default is `0777` (rwx). |
| `$CFG->passwordsaltmain` (String) | Random string added to the md5 password hash. See *Chapter 11, Moodle Security and Privacy* for details. |

# Optional parameters

There are over 350 parameters to be set in `config.php` that are not set by the installer nor can they be modified via the Moodle administrator interface. These optional parameters allow you to modify the behavior of Moodle without the requirement to change any code.

We only cover a representative list of settings ignoring ones that are only relevant to developers and designers. We have also disregarded obsolete and obscure parameters, as well as ones that have a counterpart in the admin settings. Parameters have been listed in alphabetical order and some have been grouped together for simplicity. Available types are Array (A), Binary (B), Numeric (N), List (L), and String (S):

| Name | Type | Description |
|---|---|---|
| `admineditalways` | B | Setting this to `true` enables administrators to edit any post at any time. |
| `amf_introspection` | B | Security setting for AMF web service protocol |
| `apacheloguser` | N | Logging Apache: `0`=off, `1`=user ID, `2`=full name, `3`=username |
| `apachemaxmem` | N | Memory threshold over which Apache children will be reaped after they complete serving the request. |
| `bounceratio` | N | Default is `20`. See `$CFG->handlebounces`. |
| `coursemanager` | A | List of roles that will be treated as if they are a teacher in every course (makes their name clickable on *Course description* page). |

| Name | Type | Description |
|------|------|-------------|
| customfrontpageinclude | S | You can replace the front page with your own version. moodle.org uses this approach. Only the center area will be replaced, not the header, footer, or blocks. |
| customscripts | S | Enabling this will allow custom scripts (to be specified with full path names) to replace existing Moodle scripts. For example, if $CFG->customscripts/course/view.php exists then it will be used instead of $CFG->wwwroot/course/view.php. At present, this will only work for files that include config.php and are called as part of the URL (index.php is implied). Custom scripts should not include config.php.<br><br>Warning: Replacing standard Moodle scripts may pose a security risk and/or may not be compatible with upgrades. However, this is useful when having to patch a particular page without actually overwriting the core code. |
| debugusers | S | Comma-separated list of user IDs that always see debug messages. |
| defaultblocks | A | Default block variables for new courses; for instance, participants, activity_modules, search_forums, admin, course_list, news_items, calendar_upcoming, recent_activity. This setting can be overridden for different course types, such as defaultblocks_social, defaultblocks_weeks, and defaultblocks_topics. |
| dirroot | S | The absolute directory name where Moodle has been installed. |
| disablemycourses | B | This setting will prevent the **My Courses** page being displayed when a student logs in. The site front page will always show the same (logged-out) view. |
| disablestatsprocessing | B | Prevents stats processing and hides the GUI. |

| Name | Type | Description |
|------|------|-------------|
| disableusercreationon restore | B | Completely disables user creation when restoring a course. Enabling this setting results in the restore process stopping when a user attempts to restore a course requiring users to be created. |
| divertallemailsto | S | Divert all outgoing e-mails to this address to test and debug e-mailing features. |
| emailconnectionerrorsto | S | E-mail database connection errors to someone. If Moodle cannot connect to the database, then e-mail this address with a notice. |
| enablegroupings | B | You can turn on/off grouping functionality. |
| filedir | S | You can specify an alternative to `dataroot`. |
| filelifetime | N | Seconds for files to remain in caches (default is `86400` = 24 hours). Decrease this if you are worried about students being served outdated versions of uploaded files. |
| filepermissions | | Same as `directorypermissions` in the default parameters, but for created files. |
| forced_plugin_settings | A | Plugin settings have to be specified as an array of arrays:<br><br>`array('plugin1' => array('param1' => 'value1', ('param2' => 'value2', ...), ('plugin2' => array('param1' => 'value1', ('param2' => 'value2', ...), ...);` |
| forcefirstname forcelastname | S | To anonymize usernames for all students. If set, then all non-teachers will always see this for every person. |
| gradeoverhundredprocentmax | N | If set to `unlimitedgrades`, you can specify a maximum value (1 = 100 percent, `default` = 10). |
| handlebounces | B | This is for handling e-mail bounces. Used in conjunction with `minbounces` and `bounceratio`. |
| htmleditor | B | If set to `false`, only the Moodle text editor will be shown. |
| httpswwwroot | S | `wwwroot` for SSL pages. |

| Name | Type | Description |
|---|---|---|
| includeuserpasswordsin backup | B | Allows user passwords to be included in backup files. Use only if you can guarantee that all your backup files remain private as password hashes can be unencrypted. |
| keeptempdirectorieson backup | B | Keep the temporary directories used by backup and restore them without being deleted at the end of the process. |
| langcacheroot | S | Location where aggregated strings are kept for caching. |
| langlocalroot | S | Alternative directory to $CFG->dataroot/lang. |
| langmenucachefile | S | Location where a list of available languages is cached. |
| logsql | B | Log every database query to a table called adodb_logsql. Be careful, as the table grows very quickly! |
| maildomain | S | Your e-mail domain. |
| mailprefix | S | mdl+ is the separator for Exim and Postfix, mdl- is the separator for qmail. |
| minbounces | N | Default is 10. See $CFG->handlebounces. |
| mnetkeylifetime | N | Number of days after which the networking key is expiring. See *Chapter 16, Moodle Networking* for details. |
| mycoursesperpage | N | Maximum number of courses to display in any list of a user's own courses (0 = one course). |
| noemailever | B | When working with production data on test servers, no e-mails or other messages should ever be sent to real users. |
| opensslcnf | S | Location of the openssl.cnf file. |
| preferlinegraphs | B | This setting will make some graphs (for instance, user logs) using lines instead of bars. |
| reverseproxy | B | Enable when setting up advanced reverse proxy load balancing configurations and port forwarding. |
| showcrondebugging | B | Add debug information to cron output. |
| showcronsql | B | Show executed SQL queries during cron execution. |

| Name | Type | Description |
|---|---|---|
| skiplangupgrade | B | Disables automatic language updates and lets translators (language pack maintainers) to keep their moodledata/lang/* to update manually. |
| sslproxy | B | Enables when using external SSL appliance for performance reasons. |
| tagsort | S | Sort tags in tag cloud by specified field, default = name. |
| themedir | S | Adds extra theme directories outside of $CFG->dirroot. |
| themeorder | A | Priority of themes from highest to lowest. Default is array('course', 'category', 'session', 'user', 'site'). |
| themerev | B | Prevents theme caching. |
| tracksessionip | B | Moodle will track the IP of the current user to make sure that it hasn't changed during a session. This will prevent the possibility of sessions being hijacked via XSS, but it may break things for users using proxies that change all the time, like AOL. |
| trashdir | S | Alternative location for $CFG->dirroot/trashdir. |
| undeletableblocktypes | A | The blocks in this list are protected from deletion; for example, **Navigation**, **Settings**, and so on. |
| unicodedb | B | This setting will put Moodle in unicode mode. Please note that your database must support it. Do not enable this if your database in not converted to UTF-8! |
| upgraderunning | B | Pretends Moodle update is running. |
| upgradeshowsql | B | Shows executed SQL queries during upgrades. |
| usepaypalsandbox | B | For testing PayPal using the PayPal developer sandbox. |

# Index

PostgreSQL 14, 286
Post Office Protocol version 3. (POP3) 139
predefined roles, Moodle 143, 144
preferlinegraphs parameter 376
Prezi 274
private files, internal repository plugins 206
profile categories 106
profile fields 100, 106-109
profile fields, for General category
  authentication method 101
  e-mail information 102
  forum information 102
  language 103
  location 103
  password information 101
  timezone 103
  username 101
profile fields, for Interests category 104
profile fields, for Optional category
  about 105
  contact details 105
  department 105
  ID number 105
  institution 105
  messenger information 105
  web page 105
profile fields, for User picture category
  picture description 104
Profile page 184, 185
profile spam 273
Progress Bar block 327
public learning portal 357

## Q

question behaviours plugin 216
Question creator role 164
question directory, system files 45
Question instances report 260
question types plugin 216

## R

RADIUS 139
RAIDed disks 13
rating directory, system files 45
readme.txt file 199
ReCAPTCHA 364

ReCAPTCHA keys 267
recent files, internal repository plugins 206
Register with Moodle.org (MOOCH) button 264
Remote Authentication Dial In User Service. See RADIUS
report 244
report generation, Moodle
  about 254
  configurable reports 254, 255
  Totara 255, 257
reporting
  overview 243, 244
reporting facilities, Moodle
  about 243-246
  course report 249, 250
  error reports 248
  export of logs 248, 249
  live logs 247
  user report 250, 251
reporting generation, Moodle 243
repositories. See Moodle repositories
Repositories link 55
Repository API 334
repository caching 291
repository directory, system files 45
repository, moodledata directory 46
repository plugin name parameter 205
REST 336
reverseproxy parameter 376
risks 159
role definitions 156-159
roles
  about 57, 63, 64, 143, 296
  Administrator 144
  assigning, to users 146-148
  Authenticated user 144
  Authenticated user on frontpage 144
  best practices 171
  capabilities 155-159
  Course creator 144
  creating 163
  duplicating 163
  examples 143, 164
  Guest 144
  Manager 144
  modifying 159, 160

## Thank you for buying
# Moodle 2 Administration

## About Packt Publishing

Packt, pronounced 'packed', published its first book "*Mastering phpMyAdmin for Effective MySQL Management*" in April 2004 and subsequently continued to specialize in publishing highly focused books on specific technologies and solutions.

Our books and publications share the experiences of your fellow IT professionals in adapting and customizing today's systems, applications, and frameworks. Our solution based books give you the knowledge and power to customize the software and technologies you're using to get the job done. Packt books are more specific and less general than the IT books you have seen in the past. Our unique business model allows us to bring you more focused information, giving you more of what you need to know, and less of what you don't.

Packt is a modern, yet unique publishing company, which focuses on producing quality, cutting-edge books for communities of developers, administrators, and newbies alike. For more information, please visit our website: www.packtpub.com.

## About Packt Open Source

In 2010, Packt launched two new brands, Packt Open Source and Packt Enterprise, in order to continue its focus on specialization. This book is part of the Packt Open Source brand, home to books published on software built around Open Source licences, and offering information to anybody from advanced developers to budding web designers. The Open Source brand also runs Packt's Open Source Royalty Scheme, by which Packt gives a royalty to each Open Source project about whose software a book is sold.

## Writing for Packt

We welcome all inquiries from people who are interested in authoring. Book proposals should be sent to author@packtpub.com. If your book idea is still at an early stage and you would like to discuss it first before writing a formal book proposal, contact us; one of our commissioning editors will get in touch with you.

We're not just looking for published authors; if you have strong technical skills but no writing experience, our experienced editors can help you develop a writing career, or simply get some additional reward for your expertise.

## Moodle Security

ISBN: 978-1-84951-264-0          Paperback: 204 pages

Learn how to install and configure Moodle in the most secure way possible

1.  Follow the practical examples to close up any potential security holes, one by one

2.  Choose which parts of your site you want to make public and who you are going to allow to access them

3.  Protect against web robots that send harmful spam mails and scan your site's information

## Moodle 1.9 Testing and Assessment

ISBN: 978-1-84951-234-3          Paperback: 392 pages

Develop and evaluate quizzes and tests using Moodle modules

1.  Create and evaluate interesting and interactive tests using a variety of Moodle modules

2.  Create simple vocabulary or flash card tests and complex tests by setting up a Lesson module

3.  Motivate your students to excel through feedback and by keeping their grades online

4.  A well-structured practical guide packed with illustrative examples and screenshots

Please check **www.PacktPub.com** for information on our titles

## Moodle as a Curriculum and Information Management System

ISBN: 978-1-849513-22-7        Paperback: 308 pages

Use Moodle to manage and organize your administrative duties, monitor attendance records, manage student enrolment, record exam results, and much more

1. Transform your Moodle site into a system that will allow you to manage information such as monitoring attendance records, managing the number of students enrolled for a particular course, and inter-department communication

2. Create courses for all subjects in no time with the Bulk Course Creation tool

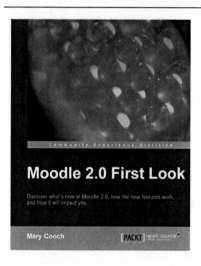

## Moodle 2.0 First Look

ISBN: 978-1-849511-94-0        Paperback: 272 pages

Discover what's new in Moodle 2.0, how the new features work, and how it will impact you

1. Get an insight into the new features of Moodle 2.0

2. Discover the benefits of brand new additions such as Comments and Conditional Activities

3. Master the changes in administration with Moodle 2.0

Please check **www.PacktPub.com** for information on our titles

Lightning Source UK Ltd.
Milton Keynes UK
UKOW011019070112

184895UK00001B/17/P